ELOCUTION:

THE

SOURCES AND ELEMENTS

OF

ITS POWER.

A TEXT-BOOK FOR SCHOOLS AND COLLEGES, AND A BOOK FOR
EVERY PUBLIC SPEAKER, AND STUDENT OF
THE ENGLISH LANGUAGE.

By J. H. McILVAINE,

Professor of Belles Lettres in Princeton College.

NEW YORK:
SCRIBNER, ARMSTRONG & CO.,
1876.

Entered according to Act of Congress, in the year 1870, by
CHARLES SCRIBNER AND COMPANY,
in the clerk's office of the District Court of the United States for the Southern
District of New York.

JOHN F. TROW & SON,
PRINTERS AND BOOKBINDERS,
205–213 *East 12th St.*,
NEW YORK.

PREFACE.

The author of this work has been engaged in the practice of public speaking, almost without interruption, for thirty years; during the last ten of which, he has also been a systematic student and teacher of the art of elocution. When he accepted the chair of Belles Lettres in Princeton College, in 1860, he received a special request from the Board of Trustees to work up this much neglected department of education, although it was not properly included in the duties of his professorship; and with this object in view, they gave him a laborious and faithful assistant in Prof. S. G Peabody. The notes and criticisms, which gradually accumulated upon his hands in successive courses of instruction and training, are here offered to the public in a systematic form, now that his work in the College is drawing to a close.

The attention of teachers and students of this art, is requested, in appreciation of the following points. 1. Nearly one half of the work consists in the exhibition of the intellectual, moral, esthetical and physical sources of power in delivery, which, it is believed, have never before been treated of as included in the art of elocution. 2. The second part contains several chapters on Phonology, in which, especially under the heads of articulation, accent and pronunciation, new views are advanced, which it is hoped may have an interest for phonologists, students of the English language, and all who desire to pronounce it correctly, independently of the relation of these chapters to the principal object of the work. 3. The whole matter of the work has been carefully analyzed or generalized under principal and subordinate heads, in order to facilitate the comprehension of particulars, and to aid the memory in recitation. This last point the author regards as of such importance, that he has allowed the beauty of a perfectly plain page to be sacrificed to the utility of black letter and italics, for the purpose of distinguishing these principal and subordinate heads.

It will be evident to all who may look into this work, that it has cost a great deal of labor; so much, indeed, that the author pities himself when he thinks of it, and cannot but fear that it might have been more usefully employed. Yet he cannot flatter himself that the work does not contain many errors and defects. Such as it is, however, it is offered to the public, not without the hope that the views presented may continue to be useful to many who are engaged in the study or practice of this beautiful and most useful of all arts.

PRINCETON, Feb. 26, 1870.

CONTENTS.

INTRODUCTION.

CHAP.		PAGE
I.	The Importance of a Good Delivery	1
II.	Utility of the Study of Elocution	15

PART I.

I.	Preliminary Observations, and Fundamental Principles	45
II.	Power in Thought	50
III.	Feeling	58
IV.	Earnestness	83
V.	The Mental State of Direct Address to the Audience	93
VI.	Attention and Sympathy	103
VII.	Mastery of the Subject-matter in Extempore Discourse	116
VIII.	Facility of Remembering in Memoriter Delivery	129
IX.	Familiarity with the Manuscript	138
X.	Vitality, Favorable Moods, and Physical Regimen	153
XI.	Self-control	165

CONTENTS.

PART II.

CHAP.	PAGE
I.—Method of Treatment	177
II.—The Vocal Organism in Relation to Vocal Culture	181
III.—Articulation	199
IV.—Accentuation	227
V.—Pronunciation	239
VI.—The Qualities of the Voice	294
VII.—The Powers of the Voice	308
VIII.—Pitch and Inflection	321
IX.—Time and Pause	346
X.—Force	360
XI.—Emphasis	368
XII.—Gesture	384

INTRODUCTION.

CHAPTER I.

THE IMPORTANCE OF A GOOD DELIVERY.

§ 1. The principal reason for discussing this subject is that the importance of elocution is very imperfectly appreciated, both by educators and public speakers.

It would seem to be obvious of itself that they whose business it is to speak in public, should spare no pains in order to be able to speak well. As a matter of fact, however, we often find it far otherwise. For while good writers are not at all uncommon, good speaking is notoriously a rare accomplishment. The professions which depend most immediately upon speaking, are crowded with failures; and of the many young men of superior talents, and culture, who thus fail, few seem to have any suspicion that the chief, and often the sole cause, is their wretched delivery. And whilst rhetoric is thoroughly taught, elocution has hardly any recognized place in our systems and institutions of liberal education.

Hence it seems plain that this art is very imperfectly appreciated, not only by educators, but also by professional orators themselves. It is in place, therefore, to offer here some considerations which may serve to exhibit the importance of a good delivery.

§ 2. Oral speaking is essential to eloquence, and even to language itself.

1. *That oral speaking is essential to language is proved by the authority of the greatest masters of linguistic science.*

The following quotation is from Wilhelm von Humboldt, who has been called the father of Comparative Philology. "We must exclude everything from the definition of language, but actual speaking. .... The essence of language lies in the living utterance, in that which does not suffer itself to be apprehended in the sundered elements of written words. .... It is only by the spoken word that the speaker breathes his own life into the souls of his hearers. .... Written language is only an imperfect and mummy-like embalming, of which the highest use is that it may serve as a means of reproducing the living utterance." In fact it was the recognition of the truth thus enunciated, which rescued the study of language from that inveterate pedantry by which it had long been paralyzed, and made it that living and progressive science which it has now become.

2. *That oral speaking is essential to eloquence is proved from the etymology of the word, from the fact that the power of a word is inseparable from its sound, and from the fact that the masters of eloquence have always been speakers.*

(1.) The etymology of the word eloquence is the same with that of elocution. Both of these words alike have for their base or root the idea of speaking. Further, they are compounded of *e*, from, and *loquor*, I speak; expressing the notion of speaking *from* something. From what then does true eloquence speak? Doubtless the conception which suggested this composition of the word, was that eloquence speaks from the heart of man. It is from the depths of the rational and moral nature that the articulate human voice streams forth; of which nature, therefore, it constitutes the most perfect, the noblest, that is to say, the eloquent expression. Hence it is only in an inferior sense that unspoken words can be called eloquent.

(2.) The true power of a word is inseparable from its sound. The articulation, tones, inflections, accent and emphasis, as also in the play of the features, and all the motions of the limbs and body, with which a word is spoken, are essential elements of its expressiveness and power. They express modifications and shades of thought, and ever-varying intensity of emotion and passion, which written words do not even suggest. They are, therefore, the flesh and blood, the very life, of which written words are little more than the bony skeleton.

(3.) The models of eloquence have always been speakers. That the greatest masters of eloquence, in all ages of the world, have been orators, requires no proof. It needs only to run over their names. But why should this be so, if oral speaking were not essential to the blossom and golden fruit of true eloquence?

§ 3. **Delivery is to discourse what performance is to music.**

This view of the importance of delivery in discourse, is confirmed by the close analogy that subsists between music and articulate speech. For music is a language of tones addressed to the sensibilities, or emotional nature, whilst speech is a language of tones and articulations addressed to the intellect and the sensibilities; and both these forms of language may be noted in written symbols, and reproduced in vocal utterances. The analogy between them is therefore very close, and we shall find it useful hereafter in many ways. But here what we have to consider is that it holds good to exhibit the importance of delivery in the three following particulars.

1. *Both discourse and music produce their proper effects by means of sound.*

For as the most accomplished musician can comprehend only a little of the sentiment and force of a piece of music, and can derive but a feeble pleasure from barely running his eye over the score; as it is only when he comes to render it with his voice or instrument that its full and proper effect can be produced upon himself or others;—such, in great measure is the difference between the power and effect of discourse as presented to the eye, and that which it produces when addressed to the ear.

2. *Both discourse and music, when poor but well rendered, are better than when good and poorly rendered.*

As a poor piece of music, well performed, produces a better effect than that which is ever so good in itself, but ill-performed, so an inferior discourse, well delivered, will commonly be found to accomplish its object far better than a superior discourse badly delivered.

3. *Both discourse and music, when good but poorly rendered, are powerless, or they defeat their own aims.*

As a good piece of music, badly performed, fails of its proper effect, and either awakens no emotions at all, or a wholly different class from those which are intended, so the best discourse in the world, being spoiled in the delivery, either falls powerless and dead, or exerts an influence to defeat its own aims. Such discourses in the pulpit often put their hearers to sleep, when they are intended to excite to watchfulness and prayer; they are heard with weariness and pain, when they are intended to impart spiritual refreshment and joy; or aiming to awaken pity and love, they call forth only indignation and disgust. In these and other particulars delivery is to discourse what performance is to music.

§ 4. The opinions of the great orators and rhetoricians are strongly in favor of the importance of a good delivery.

The most celebrated orators and rhetoricians, in all ages of the world, have ascribed the very greatest importance to a good delivery. The views of only a few of them can be given here.

1. *Massillon*, court preacher to Louis XIV., and one of the most eloquent men of his time, being asked, which of his sermons he regarded as the best, replied, " The one I remembered best ;" by which he meant, of course, the one he had delivered best.

2. *Quintilian* also teaches us that " it is not of so much importance what our thoughts are, as it is in what manner they are delivered; since those whom we address are moved only as they hear." We need not subscribe to this statement in its utmost force, yet the authority is a very high one.

3. *Cicero*, as standing in the very front rank, both of rhetoricians and orators, is a still higher authority; and he expresses himself yet more strongly, if possible, in the following words : " All the parts of oratory succeed as they are delivered. Delivery, I say, has the sole and supreme power in oratory Without it a speaker of the greatest mental power cannot be held in any esteem ; while with this qualification, one of moderate abilities may surpass those of the greatest talent."

INTRODUCTION. 7

4. *Demosthenes*, the highest of all authorities, expresses himself in the strongest words of all. Both Cicero and Quintilian inform us that he, being asked what was of the first importance in oratory, replied, " Action ; " being asked what was next in importance, replied again, " Action ; " and being asked what was of the third degree of importance, he answered still, " Action." Thus according to Quintilian he continued to give the same answer as often as he was questioned; " so that," in the words of this author, " he may be thought to have esteemed ' action ' not merely the principal, but the only excellence." In order now to appreciate the full force of this, it must be understood that what the Greeks meant by *action*, was precisely that which the Romans, and we after them, call *delivery*.

5. *Æschines*, likewise, the great rival, and barely the inferior of Demosthenes, having read to his class at Rhodes, where he taught eloquence, the Oration on the Crown, which had procured his banishment from Athens, and the class expressing their unbounded admiration — exclaimed, " And what if you had heard him deliver it himself ! " thus, notwithstanding its unrivalled excellence as a rhetorical composition, ascribing its irresistible power to the delivery.

Such have been the views upon this point of all the great rhetoricians and orators, with hardly an exception, whose opinions have been left on record; and it would seem that, with such an array of authority against them, those who undervalue the importance of a good delivery are changeable with little less than infatuation.

§ 5. The example of Socrates in that he wrote nothing, but confined himself to oral discourse, shows his appreciation of the power with which thought is clothed by delivery.

It may not be at once apparent how the example of Socrates, who was not an orator in the common acceptation of the word, can be adduced in illustration of the importance of good delivery. But we must remember that he was eminently a talker, and perhaps the greatest master of the art of discourse in Athens, during the flourish and bloom of Athenian eloquence and culture. Also he was the most successful educator, with a single exception, the world has ever seen. He educated a greater number of world-renowned men than ever before or since came forth from the school of any one teacher. His success appears so wonderful to those who have looked into it, that an eminent philosopher of modern times, Condillac, himself a practical educator, hazards the assertion, that "since the time of Socrates the secret of education has been lost." Now that all-moulding influence which this man exerted, had for its sole instrumentality, oral speaking—he wrote nothing. All that we know of the doctrines he inculcated, or of the methods he employed, is derived from the writings of his disciples; among whom such men as Plato and Xenophon could find no better way of commending their philosophical speculations to the world, than by professing to report the conversations of their great master

So deeply was he impressed with the conviction that the great work which he had undertaken could be accomplished by no instrumentality except oral speaking, that he deliberately rejected every other. For when asked why he did not write out his teachings in a permanent form, he is said to have replied: "I would rather write upon the hearts of living men, than upon the skins of dead sheep." The significance of such words from such a man can hardly be overestimated.

§ 6. **The example of the Lord Jesus Christ, in that he also wrote nothing, shows a similar appreciation of the superior power of oral discourse.**

A similar but stronger argument may be drawn from the example of a greater than Socrates, our Lord Jesus Christ. He, being the incarnate Word of God, was the only perfect master of human eloquence that ever lived—*never man spake like this man.* He also was an educator, who sought to impress himself upon his disciples, and to mould them into his own likeness; and his success was such that they all became celebrated throughout the world, and their influence upon its history has been immeasurably greater than that of any other men the world has ever seen. He also wrote nothing—he confined himself to the sole instrument of oral speech. Now when we consider how desirable it seems to us that he should have written out in precise form, and in minute detail, those divine truths by the faith of which the world was to be regenerated and purified, instead of leaving them to be reported from his lips by those who heard him, we cannot fail to see that it must have been with deliberate design that he confined himself to oral speech. He also evidently would write his doctrines upon the hearts of living men, rather than upon the skins of dead sheep.

From this striking agreement between the two greatest men (if it be lawful so to speak) and most successful educators the world has ever known, and whose vitalizing influence upon human nature has been so much deeper and wider and more permanent than that of any others, it may perhaps be inferred that Condillac's lost secret of education is to be found in that all-moulding *personal* influence of the teacher, which can be exerted through no other instrumentality but that of the truth orally delivered. If this were so, it would teach us a lesson of transcendent value with respect to the importance of such a delivery as shall be adequate to express, and to impress upon others, the truth which we have to communicate.

§ 7. The fact that the Lord ordained the oral preaching of the gospel as the means of propagating the Christian religion, confirms the preceding interpretation of his example, and affords another argument for the importance of delivery.

The foregoing interpretation of the example of Christ is confirmed by the fact that he expressly ordained preaching as the great means and instrumentality for the propagation of the gospel — the Christian religion. For this also must have been with deliberate design, in view of adequate reasons. One of these, no doubt, was the great number of persons who were then, and have been in every subsequent age, unable to read. But this could not have been the controlling reason. For if so, the preaching of the gospel would be unnecessary to the learned, and might be superseded, in their case, by the silent perusal of the written Word. It is perfectly certain, however, from experience, that in the case of the learned, the solitary reading of the Scriptures, however important in itself, is no substitute for the oral preaching of the gospel. The great reason, no doubt, was that Jesus, who *knew what was in man*, was intimately acquainted with all those latent sensibilities of the soul, which can be reached and moved by nothing so powerfully as by the voice of the living preacher, by the truth incarnate, as it were, and uttering itself in an oral form. With divine wisdom he adapted the means of our spiritual renovation to the principles of human nature.

For when the Word is thus preached by the voice of a living man to a congregation of living men, it produces an effect upon their souls which is altogether peculiar. When, *e. g.* a Whitefield utters the words, *O wretched man that I am, who shall deliver me from the body of this death!* they have an intensity and power unknown to the silent and solitary reader in his closet. Accordingly, as we know, some of the greatest successes of the gospel were achieved before the New Testament was committed to writing, by the voice of the living preacher alone.

This fact that the Lord, for such reasons, ordained the oral preaching of the gospel as the great means of salvation, is perhaps the very strongest argument that could be given for such a delivery as shall be adequate to the truth. For the reasons in view of which we are required to preach the gospel, evidently require that we should preach it as well as possible; that is, in such oral forms as shall not disguise, nor obscure, nor pervert, but which shall be, in some measure at least, adequate to the expression of its great, world-regenerating ideas.

§ 8. Bad delivery is a main cause of inefficiency in the pulpit.

It is a complaint far more general than clergymen themselves are commonly aware, that their ministrations are not clothed with that power which the cause they advocate demands, but are, in fact, characterized by an unnatural feebleness. Some there are who ascribe this to a lack of ability in the ministry; others to a moral cause, namely, that the preachers themselves have little heartfelt experience of the truth which they seek to impress upon their congregations. But these, although the most obvious suggestions, cannot always be the true reasons. For not unfrequently able and godly men are extremely feeble in the pulpit; whilst others wield a far greater power, who yet are not distinguished from their brethren either by talents or piety. It is more rational, as well as more charitable, to account for the fact by that wretched elocution which is so common in the pulpit; and which, if it were not for the sacredness of its themes, and the solemnities of Divine worship, would not be tolerated by any audience in the world. For it has been well observed by one of the most accomplished pulpit orators of our time, that "one reason why preaching is so much less effective than we should antecedently expect it to be, is that there is less of it than we ordinarily suppose. .... Much of that which passes for preaching does not deserve the name. It may be called a poor kind of singing, a tedious method of drawling, a soporific way of reading; but it is not such living utterance of thought as enkindles the eye, such gushing forth of emotion as cannot but have the effect of eloquence. .... All the dull, clumsy, turgid, weak, insipid, and in any way affected methods of delivery, are to be subtracted from the sum total of what is denominated preaching; and then, how small the remainder!" There can be no doubt but that the prevalence of such abortive attempts at delivery, is a principal cause of that feebleness in the pulpit which is so much complained of, and of that want of interest in the preaching of the gospel which is manifested by increasing numbers of intelligent, and otherwise well disposed people, and which is one of the most sorrowful facts of our time.

§ 9. Bad delivery is one of the most common causes of the ministerial throat disease.

It would seem then, that he who imagines himself to be preaching the gospel whilst he violates almost every law of oral speech, deceives himself, and commits no little sin—a sin which, like all others, does not fail to punish itself. For those wasting throat diseases, with which clergymen are afflicted more than any other class of public speakers, are often traceable physiologically to bad management of the voice, to the violation of those laws which nature has prescribed to articulate speaking—laws which, like all others established by the God of nature, can never be violated with impunity. This view is confirmed by the fact, to which many can bear witness, that no more effectual remedy for these diseases has been discovered, than a thorough course of sound elocutionary training.

CHAPTER II.

UTILITY OF THE STUDY OF ELOCUTION.

§ 10. The principal objections to this study are, that delivery cannot be taught, that the study of it does harm rather than good, and that in order to be good speakers all we have to do is to speak naturally.

It is a question which has been much disputed both in ancient and modern times, whether a good delivery be a gift of nature, or an accomplishment to be acquired by art. The number and respectability of those who have maintained the former view, and the plausibility of some of their arguments, are such as to challenge our candid attention. The principal objections to this study, and those which have the most weight with intelligent persons, are the following.

1. *Delivery cannot be taught because it is incapable of analysis.*

Those who make this objection assure us that good speaking, or an eloquent delivery, is a result so extremely complex, and one that is due to such a multitude and variety of interworking causes, that it must forever defy the most subtle and powerful analysis, and defeat all attempts to reduce it to the laws upon which it depends: consequently, that it cannot be taught nor learned, and the study of it can do no good, but must prove at best a waste of time and labor.

2. *The study of elocution cannot fail to do harm.*

There are those, however, who oppose this study on the higher ground that it does harm. These objectors tell us that, by directing the attention of the student to the manner abstracted from the matter of discourse, and by putting him under training and practice according to fixed rules, it cramps the natural freedom of speaking, renders the delivery cold, spiritless and artificial, and generates awkwardness, mannerism, affectation, and almost every other vice of elocution. "Probably," says Archbishop Whately, "not a single instance could be found of any one who has attained, by the study of any system of instruction that has hitherto appeared, a really good delivery; but there are many —probably as many as have fully tried the experiment—who by this means have been totally spoiled, who have fallen irrecoverably into an affected style of *spouting*, worse in all respects than their original mode of delivery."

3. *We must ignore all rules, forget that there is any such thing as art, and speak naturally.*

Those who make such objections tell us that this is the one sole precept by the observance of which it is possible to attain to good speaking. In confirmation of this, they point us to the natural grace and propriety of common conversation, and to that with which children express themselves; and they call us to observe how all this is lost, giving place to innumerable vices of elocution, as soon as the speakers, whether children or grown persons, are put under training.

§ 11. **The influence of these objections has been very great, and has led to the general neglect of this study; hence the necesity of refuting them.**

The foregoing objections to the study of elocution are extremely plausible; they are urged by very high authorities in education; and they fall in with our natural indolence. Hence they have exerted, and do still exert a great influence, not only upon the public mind, but also upon educators and speakers themselves. Thus it is that systematic study and methodical training in this art have so generally fallen into neglect and disuse. For, as already observed, it hardly enters as an appreciable element into the prescribed course of a liberal education. The consequences of this, however, would have been far worse than they are, if it had not been for the zeal and labors of professed elocutionists, giving private lessons in our collegiate institutions, but who often have no regular connection with the faculty. The want of elocutionary training is especially noticeable in the education of clergymen, who are instructed to spare no pains in mastering the nicest theological distinctions, until they can split a theological hair into east, west, north, and south parts—an accomplishment which, however valuable for purposes of strife and debate can afford, it would seem, but little aid in proclaiming the great and simple facts and truths of the gospel—whilst yet they devote hardly any time or labor to acquiring a good delivery, without which it is impossible for them to preach with acceptability or power. Hence the absolute necessity that we should here undertake to refute these objections, and to indicate the utility of elocutionary studies and training.

§ 12. Elocution is an art, therefore it can be taught and learned; that by which it is distinguished from other arts, does not make it an exception; it is the art of speaking, the first elements of of which we learn in childhood by imitation.

1. *Elocution is an art because it conforms to the definition of art.*

The most general definition of art, is knowledge applied to production. Elocution conforms to this definition; for it applies the knowledge of vocal sounds to the production of oral discourse. Now it belongs to the very nature of an art that it does not come of itself, but it must be taught and learned. Hence it is never expected that any one should attain proficiency in any other art, such as music or painting, war or surgery, ship-building or shoe-making, without having studied and learned it. Nor can any valid reason be assigned for making this art the sole exception.

2. *The fact that it is an art which all must exercise does not make it an exception.*

Speaking is distinguished from some other arts by the fact that it is one which all persons must exercise or practice, after some fashion, in all the affairs of life; and hence all are endowed, in a higher or lower degree, with the organs and faculty of speech. But this does not make it an exception; for herein it agrees with other arts, the art of thinking, *e. g.* which it is conceded may be taught, and must be learned. Every objection from this source against improvement of the organs and faculty of speech by training and culture, is therefore equally valid against the training and cultivation of the organs and faculty of thought.

3. *The art of speaking is essentially an imitative art, the rudiments of which are actually taught and learned in childhood.*

It would seem to be impossible to deny that the art of speaking can be taught and learned when we consider the significance of the above statement. For elocution is nothing else but the art of speaking or talking, and our first studies and training in it commence in childhood. The child learns to form his first articulate sounds, and every step of his subsequent progress is taken, by means of the closest observation and imitation of that which he hears from the lips of his mother or nurse; and he continues to be an infant, that is, he remains dumb, if he does not hear others speak. By repeated efforts to imitate the sounds he hears, with many failures, he slowly gains a partial control of the organs of speech, until he learns to express himself as they do who are his models and instructors, copying all their faults as accurately as their excellences. There is indeed a certain characteristic grace in all the utterances of childhood, which will require hereafter to be explained. But the point to be emphasized here, is that all these are properly and essentially *elocutionary* studies and exercises, by which the child takes his first steps, and makes his first progress, in the art of speaking. Why should these exercises, or this progress, be arrested when he becomes a boy, or young man? Under better instruction and better models than have been afforded by his mother or nurse, or other children with whom he has associated, why should he not correct the faults he has learned from them, and continue to make progress until he attains to the highest excellence in speaking? For the process is the same; and that is no sound instruction or training in elocution, which does not aim to develop in the student the same habits of close observation and vocal imitation by which he learned to speak at first, and without which he would have remained forever dumb.

§ 13. The phenomena of delivery admit of adequate analysis— presumed from its analogy to other arts, and proved from the fact that they have been successfully analyzed—a complete analysis not necessary.

1. *It may be presumed that the phenomena of delivery admit of analysis from the analogy of elocution to other arts.*

The phenomena of the most eloquent delivery are hardly more complicated than those of poetry, music, painting or sculpture; yet this objection is not urged against instruction and training in these arts. The music of a full orchestra, *e. g.* is a wonderfully complicated result; yet it admits of a perfect analysis, and even of exact notation, by the aid of which it can be communicated through instruction, and reproduced in precisely the same form, and with similar effects, at pleasure. Why should it not be equally possible to analyze the phenomena of delivery, and thereby to discover, so as accurately to describe and note what that is which makes one man's speaking so much better than another's, so that it may be recognized at sight, and reproduced at pleasure?

2. *These phenomena have been successfully analyzed.*

But we are not left to depend solely on the foregoing analogy. For that it is possible thus to analyze, describe, and classify the excellences as well as the faults of elocution; to explain the different varieties and shades of expression which give effect not only to common discourse, but also to the most impassioned eloquence—that it is possible to reduce the qualities of good speaking to the principles and laws upon which they depend, and to deduce from these laws a body of rules for the purpose of instruction, training and practice in the art, precisely as in the case of musical notation and exercise— this work has been actually accomplished in great part by an American author, Dr. James Rush, in his profound and original treatise on the human voice; in which we have already a truly philosophical foundation for the whole art of elocution.

3. *A complete analysis is unnecessary.*

But if it were true that such a minute and extended analysis as is required in music were impossible in elocution, it would not follow that this art cannot be taught nor learned. For such an analysis is not even desirable, except perhaps for the teacher, in whose hands even it is liable to very grave abuse. A too minute analysis, and a great multiplication of rules, as we shall see hereafter, is a very serious error in teaching elocution—an error which is the principal source of those vices of delivery which are justly chargeable to study and training in this art. All that can be made profitable to the practical student is a sound and broad analysis of the *Sources of power* in delivery—which has never before been attempted in any work on elocution—together with an exhibition of the principal *Elements of power*, that is, of the leading excellences to be cultivated, in contrast with the most common and glaring faults to be corrected. The attempt to go beyond this into very minute details, which is a general characteristic of previous works on this subject, cannot fail to be attended with many bad results.

§ 14. **The inherent difficulties of this art, arising from the numerous mental operations which must be carried on simultaneously, and many of them as sub-processes, are such that they cannot be overcome without study and practice.**

They who tell us that in order to speak well all we have to do is to speak naturally, do indeed characterize by this expression the highest possible attainment in elocution ; but they ignore all the facts of experience by assuming that to speak naturally is just the easiest thing in the world They might as well inform us that in order to become great painters, or musicians, we have nothing to do but to paint naturally, or sing naturally, or play on the violin naturally. This precept, so flippantly given, leaves out of view all the difficulties of the art ; some of which are the following.

1. *The number and variety of the mental operations which must be carried on simultaneously in all good speaking, are very great.*

(1.) Those of invention and style, or of memory, or of reading. For according as we speak extempore, or memoriter, or from manuscript, we have either the processes of invention and style, with all the vast multitude of subordinate operations which these imply ; or those of remembering what we have committed to memory ; or those of taking in from the manuscript through the eye, the thoughts which we have to deliver to others.

(2.) We have to keep steadily in view the object which we aim to accomplish in the minds of the audience.

(3.) We must have a perception and feeling of the meaning of each word in itself, and in all its grammatical relations and connections, at the very moment of speaking it.

(4.) We must ourselves be affected with the sentiment. For it is indispensable to success in oratory that our own hearts should be deeply and keenly affected with all the emotions and passions which we seek to enkindle in the hearts of others.

(5.) We must hold the audience in our mental grasp, in the full and strong consciousness that we are speaking directly to their minds.

All these mental operations, which will require to be fully unfolded hereafter in their relations to delivery, together with a multitude of others, must be carried on simultaneously in all good speaking. Now it is simply preposterous to assume that this can be done by any one, without his ever having learned to do it.

2. *Many of these and other mental operations have to be carried on almost unconsciously, and suppressed entirely from the oral expression.*

This is the great difficulty which must be overcome in order to speak well, compared with which all others are as nothing. In order to understand it we must glance here at what will require to be more fully developed hereafter, namely, that all speaking, whether good or bad, expresses the leading or predominant operations of the speaker's mind: and if those operations predominate which properly belong to the giving out or expression of thought, the speaking can hardly fail to be good: but if those which do not properly belong to such expression are predominant, the speaking will express these, and cannot but prove an utter failure. The following examples will illustrate this statement.

Utility of the Study of Elocution. 25

(1.) The operations of memory must be suppressed. In speaking from memory, the whole intellectual process of remembering what is to be delivered must be kept from manifesting itself; no sign of it can be allowed to appear in the vocal expression. Hence this laborious operation, together with all the anxieties attending it, must never become prominent in the consciousness of the speaker; it must be carried on strictly as a sub-process: otherwise it will confuse those other mental operations which properly belong to the expression of thought, and either mar or destroy the effect of the delivery.

(2.) The operations of invention and style must be suppressed. In speaking extempore, all these laborious operations have to be carried on, for the most part, unconsciously; otherwise the speaking will express them, and little else.

(3.) The operations of reading must be suppressed. The case is similar in speaking from manuscript. All the mental operations of taking in the sense through the eye, which are in fact the reverse of those which belong to giving it out, must be carried on unconsciously; for when they become the leading operations, the speaking expresses them, and thus becomes the reverse of true expression.

Here now we have the great difficulty to be overcome. It is that of carrying on all such mental operations strictly as sub-processes, and for the most part unconsciously, in order that they may not appear in the speaking; together with that of keeping all the mental faculties intently engaged in those operations which properly belong to the expression of thought, and to the work of impressing it upon others. This is the grand obstacle to excellence in speaking, which, if there were no others, would make instruction, training and practice indispensable to success.

§ 15. The objection from the grace and propriety of children is refuted by the considerations, that children do not speak well in the sense required by this objection, that they do not have to grapple with the difficulties of the art, and that the grace which they do manifest passes away with the simplicity of childhood.

Nothing has tended more to disguise and conceal the preceding difficulties, and to cherish the idle notion that it is the easiest thing in the world to speak well, than the reference so frequently made to the natural grace and propriety with which children express themselves. Hence it has been rashly inferred, in the face of all experience, that they would continue to do so if they were left to themselves, and that all the awkwardness, mannerism, affectation, and other faults, which they manifest as soon as they are put under methodical training, are due to this cause. We are now prepared to appreciate the force of this objection.

1. *Children do not speak well in the sense which this objection requires.*

There is, indeed, a natural grace and beauty in almost everything which children say and do; but this appears, and is almost or quite as charming, in their defects and errors, as it is when they act and speak correctly. Children speak as they hear; and, as we have seen, they copy the faults of their models as accurately as they do their excellences Few of them are so fortunate as to have perfect models in their nurses, or mothers, or other children with whom they associate. Hence they commonly articulate feebly and indistinctly. They make mistakes in pronunciation and emphasis. They err in intonation and inflection, and in a thousand other particulars. These defects and errors in children's speaking are commonly such that if they were manifested in a public speaker, he could hardly be understood, and certainly would not be listened to. But because they are the mistakes of children, whom we do not expect to speak otherwise, and are accompanied by a certain infantine simplicity and grace, they either pass unnoticed, or perhaps are regarded as beauties.

2. *Children do not have to grapple with the real difficulties of the art.*

This explains in part the fact, in so far as it is one, that children do speak with a certain propriety and grace. For they do not have to express any of those subtle, extended and involved processes of thought, which belong to public speaking; nor do they encounter those difficulties of predominant and sub-processes, which have been described (§14—1, 2). This is equally true of grown persons in common conversation. In neither case do the speakers have to carry on as sub-processes, so that they shall not appear in the expression, any laborious operations of invention and style, or of remembering, or of taking in the sense of a manuscript. Hence it is comparatively easy for them to speak without those peculiar faults which are so common in oratory. But as soon as any of these difficulties are encountered, whether in the exercises of the class-room, or in the actual attempt of untrained or inexperienced persons to address a public assembly, all these faults immediately appear; nor can they in most cases be corrected otherwise than by systematic instruction and practice.

3. *The grace of childhood in speaking as in other things naturally passes away.*

The principal reason why children are graceful in speaking, is one which shows us that this grace cannot continue; that it is naturally evanescent. For it is the same thing that makes them graceful and charming in everything else, namely, their simplicity, or innocence, that 'sparkle of the purity of man's first estate.' Their self-consciousness and evil passions are yet undeveloped, and their life is one of almost pure spontaneity. 'The commandment has not yet come to them, and they are still alive without the law; but the commandment will come to them, and they will die under it.' The development of their self-consciousness and corrupt nature is inevitable; and as this takes place it naturally manifests itself in constraint, awkwardness, mannerism, affectation, and other faults, not only in speaking, but also and equally in every other department of their life and conduct. They lose their simplicity, and the grace of it, in everything else, as well as in speaking. In order to prevent as much as possible these sad consequences of the common fall, to correct these natural departures from rectitude and propriety, we put them under instruction in manners and morals, just as we do in speaking. Left to themselves, what would become of their morals, or manners? As little can we expect from them in speaking, apart from that instruction and training which are as indispensable in the one case as in the other.

§ 16. **The objection drawn from natural eloquence is refuted by the considerations, that men without education have excelled in other arts, that in everything nature or genius holds the first place, that the so-called natural orators have risen to excellence by self-culture, and that the possession of superior endowments is the strongest reason for cultivating them.**

1. *Men without education have excelled in other vocations.*

The preceding views do not require us to deny the obvious fact that some men, without much previous study or preparation, have attained to great excellence as public speakers. For this fact is no argument against the utility of the study of elocution. Taken as such it proves too much. For in every other sphere of life, or vocation, persons are found who, without the advantages of a regular education, and with little special training or practice, excel others who have been most highly educated, and most carefully prepared for their special professions or pursuits. If this objection had any force, it would be equally valid against all education, and against all study and methodical training for the professions, and other avocations and pursuits.

2. *In everything nature or genius holds the first place—poeta nascitur.*

This principle is freely conceded, and it is one which is especially applicable to the liberal arts. For this is the true understanding of the above Latin proverb, which is of much wider import and application than is indicated by its form. It is in fact a highly condensed expression, involving that figure of speech in which a part is put for the whole. For here *poet* stands for *artist*. It signifies, therefore, that in order to attain to excellence in any liberal art, it is necessary to be born with a certain genius or aptitude for it. This applies of course to elocution. Hence the possession of such extraordinary endowments would be a sufficient explanation of that great power in delivery which has been attained by some persons without much previous study or preparation. For great genius is a great thing. It gives its possessor many advantages over other men, and enables him, with comparatively little effort or labor, to achieve more than they can by the utmost diligence, and most strenuous toil of a life-time. Such men may perhaps dispense with rules and regular training; for it is the high prerogative of genius to be a law to itself, and to give laws to other less gifted souls. But all this surely is no argument against instruction and training, even in such cases, much less in that of those who are less bountifully endowed.

3. *The so-called natural orators have risen to excellence by laborious self-culture—orator fit.*

We have in this proverb the same figure of speech as before; for here *orator* also stands for *artist*. Hence the words signify that the artist becomes truly such, that is, he attains to the highest excellence, only through much study and culture. This holds equally good in the case of the so-called natural orators, who, as we know from their biographies, have always found much private study, and laborious self-culture, indispensable to compensate for the deficiencies of their early education. Of this we have many illustrious examples. Thus Patrick Henry, one of the most eloquent of uneducated orators, whilst yet a country shop-keeper, is known to have made, for several years, the art of speaking his daily and systematic study and practice. Henry Clay also, whilst yet a youth employed upon a farm, laboriously cultivated his great natural gifts by committing to memory the finest passages of eloquence, and speaking them in the open air to imaginary audiences. To this practice he owed, in part, no doubt, that great strength, and matchless sweetness of voice, with which he charmed, for so many years, the Senate of the United States. Other distinguished examples might easily be given; and a similar explanation, probably, of almost all the cases in which excellence in speaking has appeared to be the result of the uncultivated gifts of nature.

4. *The possession of superior endowments or aptitudes for any pursuit, is the strongest reason for cultivating them.*

It is, indeed, surprising that intelligent men can be found, who are bold enough to advocate the notion that we ought to rely upon the gifts of nature alone for excellence in the art of speaking, whilst in every other pursuit of life the principle here stated is universally conceded. When, *e. g.* a youth manifests a strong natural bent, or genius, or aptitude for engineering or machinery, medicine or law, this is never accepted as a reason why he should rely upon his superior natural endowment; but it is always regarded as a strong reason why he should be put to the study and practice of that pursuit for which nature has best adapted his faculties. By this means we expect him to attain to excellence, and never without it. The argument surely ought to be equally valid where there is a superior genius for public speaking.

§ 17. The vices of elocution often ascribed to study and training, are seldom legitimately due to this cause, but mostly to the inherent difficulties of the art, to false systems of instruction, to the pedantry of the student, to inadequate training, and are corrected by thorough training.

1. *The cases in which the study of elocution has a bad effect are comparatively rare.*

It may be conceded that there are some cases in which this study seems to have a permanently damaging effect upon the delivery; but these are believed to be comparatively rare, and that it is their rarity which makes them so conspicuous as to give any plausibility to the objections which are drawn from this source. For whatever Archbishop Whately may have found to be true in England, with respect to the numbers who were "utterly spoiled," it is perfectly certain that in this country, as a general thing, our poorest speakers are those who have neglected, and our best speakers are those who have most laboriously availed themselves of the advantages of study, training and practice in this art. The truth is that the faults which are often ascribed to this, are mostly due to other causes, the principal of which require to be here enumerated and explained.

2. *These vices are due chiefly to the inherent difficulties of the art.*

Some of these difficulties have been already exhibited (§14—1, 2). They are first encountered when the student is put under training; and hence it is erroneously inferred that the faults which then manifest themselves, are due to the training itself. But what proves that this is not so, is that these faults are sure to appear, all the same, in every unpracticed attempt to speak in public. Let any one who has never tried it undertake to address a public assembly, and he will soon discover how easy a thing it is to "speak naturally" and without these faults—faults which are really due to the inherent difficulties of the art. In order to correct them we have to resort to the same means which are found to be indispensable in all other arts, namely, instruction, training and practice.

3. *They are partly due to false systems of instruction.*

In elocution, as in all other arts, false systems and wrong methods of instruction could not fail to come into vogue, nor to work more or less mischief. Accordingly, in many of the books which treat of this subject, and which are now before the public, there is that very serious error which has been already indicated (§ 13—3), and which consists in a wearisome minuteness of detail, and multiplication of rules, to such an extent that it is hardly possible they should be remembered, much less that they should become inwrought into the mind of the student, so that the observance of them should not even be a matter of consciousness. A single professor of commanding ability and high position, is known to have exerted in his day a wide-spread deleterious influence by means of such a depraved system, which he elaborated and taught. He certainly did 'spoil' a considerable number of very promising young men. The peculiar manner of his pupils made it easy to recognize them wherever they were heard. But all this, it must be remembered, is no less true of the other arts, and even of science and morals, than it is of elocution; and if it were not, it could be no argument against sound instruction, and right methods of training and practice.

4. *These faults are sometimes due to the incorrigible pendantry of the student.*

Some men are born poets, others are born pedants. Now pedantry consists in doing everything according to rule, irrespective of those innumerable circumstances which modify the application of rules. The genuine pedant can never forget his rules, even for a moment, nor act from the dictates of common sense, nor from the inspirations of genius. When such a man comes to the study of elocution, the rules of the art take full possession of his mind, to the exclusion of the object of speaking, the matter of discourse, and all those mental operations which properly belong to the expression of thought; for which he might have had some place in his mind if he had never heard of the rules or precepts of the art. To such a person the systematic study of this, or of any other liberal art, can do little good. His genius, if such it can be called, is wholly mechanical; and the less he knows of such matters the better it will be for him. But all this again is evidently no argument against the study, by generous young men, of this liberal and beautiful art of public speaking.

5. *These faults are due in fine to inadequate training.*

For such training not only leaves the natural faults of speaking uncorrected, but it often aggravates them. This result is necessarily incident to the incipient stages of the training period. But this also is equally applicable to all other arts and pursuits. For whatever we are not accustomed to do embarrasses us when we begin it. If we have already made some irregular progress in the exercise of any art, systematic study and training, however indispensable to the perfect mastery of it, will, at first, retard our progress. Thus, if a child has learned to read in some imperfect way, without dividing the words into syllables, such a division will, at first, greatly embarrass him. Syllabication, though confessedly useful to learners, will puzzle rather than aid those who have learned to read without it. In like manner, a person who has learned to "sing by ear," when he first begins to "sing by note," will not for awhile be able to sing as well as before. For whilst the precepts and rules of any art are new to the mind, and it requires a self-conscious effort to put them in practice, of course there can be no freedom nor power. But this is no more than to say that whilst a child is learning to read, it cannot read well—surely it would be very wonderful if it could.

6. *Thorough training corrects these faults—ars est celare artem.*

This is true in elocution, as in all other arts Freedom and power, the highest blossoms and ripe fruit of art, are not attained until the prescribed rules, methods and processes are rendered perfectly familiar, inwrought, so to speak, into the very structure of the mind, so that the observance of them is no longer a matter of consciousness or constraint Thus art becomes a second nature; or rather it enables nature to manifest herself with her original freedom, purity and power. For evermore it is the true aim and last attainment of art, to bring us back to nature, from which we have wandered far away through ignorance and sin. Artificialness is the characteristic of defective art. Thus a person of good natural ear and voice, who sings without art, but with a certain grace and simplicity, and gives to the listeners a certain degree of pleasure, but who, when placed under instruction and training, begins to manifest awkwardness and constraint, comes forth at last, when the work of art is perfected, with the freedom and power of a Jenny Lind, to charm and bless the world. The tendency of systematic and thorough study and training is to the production of similar results in the wider and nobler sphere of eloquence.

§ 18. **Elocution has great educating power because it is a liberal art, and because it brings the student into the closest communion with great minds.**

A positive argument of great force for the utility of this study, is derived from its educating or developing power. This is certainly as great as that of any other branch of a liberal education. Indeed, for the development of personal power, elocution has the advantage, in certain respects, over most other studies. This statement, although contrary to the opinion of most educators, will be confirmed by those who have had any experience in teaching elocution, and who cannot fail to have often observed a remarkable and rapid development in generous young men, when they apply themselves to its exercises. This seems to be due to the two following among other causes.

1. *As a liberal art, it calls forth a nobler exercise of the faculties than mere science.*

Almost everything in the common curriculum of a liberal education, except the arts of rhetoric and elocution, belongs to science. Now science terminates in mere knowing, whilst art applies knowledge to the production of what did not before exist; that is to say, science is simply determinative, whilst art is creative. Art therefore is the crown of science, implying a nobler exercise of the faculties; for as *faith without works is dead*, so also is knowledge. Hence the exercise of a liberal art cannot fail to exert a stronger influence in the development of personal power, than any mere intellectual pursuit.

2. *It brings the student into the closest communion with great minds.*

In this study the student is required to store his memory with the finest passages of eloquence and poetry; the influence of which in the culture of the esthetic, moral, and other faculties, is necessarily very great. But in order to render such passages with their proper effect, he must study to enter into their sentiments, to catch the spirit of their authors. By the strenuous exercise of his imagination, intellect and sensibilities, he must learn to place himself in their circumstances, to possess himself of their thoughts, to appreciate the force of their arguments, and to fill himself with the magnanimity and sublimity and pathos of their sentiments;—in a word, he must learn to think as they thought, and feel as they felt, at the very moment when they charmed or fired the hearts of great national assemblies, or poured forth those imperishable strains which forever enchant the world. This is a fundamental principle in all sound elocutionary instruction and training. The student can do nothing in this art, except in the degree in which he learns to do this. In this way he comes into the most intimate communion with the great minds of the world; he is 'made to drink into their spirit,' he nourishes himself with their power, and grows strong with their strength. There is no other study or exercise which produces the same effect in an equal degree. Even in the translation of the finest passages of the ancient classics, the student cannot so fully enter into the spirit of his author. For if, in rendering a strain of eloquence from Demosthenes or Cicero, he should come to feel as the orator felt whilst delivering it, he would be prompted to speak it as the orator spoke it, instead of merely reading it; and the least approach to such a delivery in the translations of the class room, would assuredly bring down the house!

§ 19. **The final argument for the utility of this study is derived from the example and authority of the great masters of eloquence.**

If all other arguments for the utility of the study of elocution should fail, the example and authority of the great masters and teachers of eloquence ought alone to be conclusive.

1. *In modern times* we know that the most eloquent speakers have commonly been the most diligent in the study and practice of this art (§ 16—3).

2. *The ancient teachers* carried their pupils through such a protracted and laborious course of exercises in elocution as appears to us at this day almost incredible (§ 97—3).

3. *Demosthenes* was a proverb for the rigor of his elocutionary exercises. In order to strengthen his naturally feeble voice and articulation, he accustomed himself to declaim with pebbles in his mouth, whilst walking rapidly up hill, and on the sea-shore to sound of the breaking waves. Thus he developed that clearness of articulation, and strength of voice, which enabled him to subdue into silence and awe those tumultuous assemblies of the Athenian democracy, where the noise and confusion were often like that " on the lip of the many-sounding sea."

4. *Cicero* tells us that after he had commenced to speak in public, he found his voice and delivery so inadequate that he gave up his profession for a time, left Rome, and spent several years abroad in the study of elocution, under the greatest masters

of the art in Greece and Asia Minor. He returned to Rome and resumed his profession, with a voice which became proverbial for its sweetness, compass and power, and with a delivery which charmed that most eloquent age in the history of the world. Now such examples are an authority for which no counterpoise is possible. For these men must be presumed to have known what they were about—whether study and training in the art of which they were the greatest masters, were profitable or not.

5. *Conclusion of the argument in the words of Quintilian and Cicero.*

Hence we may fitly conclude this whole argument in the modest words of the great Quintilian: " Let those who think it is enough to be born, in order to become great orators, enjoy their opinion; but let them be indulgent at the same time to the pains I take [to form the orator], who believe that there can be no consummate excellence except where nature is aided by art;" or in the yet more forcible words of Cicero: " To say that there is no art in the greatest things, when not even the least can be done without art, appears to be the part of those who speak inconsiderately, and who err in the gravest matters."

PART I.

THE SOURCES OF POWER IN DELIVERY.

I.—Power in the Thought.

II.—Feeling.

III.—Earnestness.

IV.—Consciousness of Direct Address to the Audience.

V.—Attention and Sympathy.

VI.—Mastery of the Subject.

VII.—Facility of Remembering.

VIII.—Familiarity with the Manuscript.

IX.—Vitality, Favorable Moods and Physical Regimen.

X.—Self-Control.

PART I.

CHAPTER I.

PRELIMINARY OBSERVATIONS AND FUNDAMENTAL PRINCIPLES.

§ 21. *The object for which the sources of power are here included in the art of elocution, is to counteract the tendency to an artificial style of speaking, otherwise incident to the study, and to stimulate, quicken and develop the faculty of oral discourse.*

The works on this art which are now before the public, confine themselves mostly or exclusively to the treatment of the Elements of power in delivery. The tendency of this, to a certain extent, has been to divorce the study, training and exercises which Elocution prescribes, from the sentiments which it is intended to express; in other words, to sunder that organic and vital union, which subsists between delivery and those intellectual, moral and esthetic states and workings of the speaker's mind, from which it derives its inspiration and its power. The result of this has been such an artificial style of speaking as to render colorable, though by no means to justify, the objections against this art which have been already discussed (§ 10). In order to counteract this tendency, to obviate these objections, and to stimulate, quicken and develop the faculty of oral speaking, as well as for the sake of systematic completeness in the treatment of the subject, it is now proposed to consider, in some detail, the principal Sources of power in delivery. From this exhibition it is hoped that their fundamental importance will be made to appear, together with the grave deficiencies of every system in which they are omitted, or which fails to treat them in their vital relations to elocutionary power.

§ 21. The most fundamental principle of the art of delivery is that speaking normally consists of the expression of the leading, or dominant states of the speaker's mind, to communicate which to the audience is all that he can legitimately aim or hope to do.

This principle is essential alike to the understanding of the subject, and to success in all the training, exercises and practice of the art. It has, indeed, the appearance of being very far from the truth; yet, in the sense in which it is here intended, with no reference, of course, to voluntary efforts at the disguise or concealment of one's sentiments, which efforts, however, are hardly ever more than partially successful, it is unquestionable.

1. *The connection between thought and language is so vital that it is almost impossible to divorce them.*

Such is the vital connection between the mental states, on the one hand, and the organs of speech, tones, and all the vocal utterances, on the other, that it is next to impossible, whatever be the lexicographical meaning of the words we employ, to speak otherwise than as we really feel. For all the outward signs, both of voice and gesture, which go to constitute delivery, take their form and character from the mental operations, both intellectual and emotional, with which the speaker, at the moment of speaking, is immediately and chiefly occupied. It is only those operations which are secondary and subordinate that can be suppressed from the expression. Those which predominate in, and govern the consciousness, it is well nigh impossible to suppress. These lie so near, and are so immediately the causes of the oral and visible signs by and through which we express ourselves, that almost of necessity they come forth, and manifest themselves in their true character.

2. *Examples.*

In illustration and confirmation of this principle it may suffice to adduce the following examples.

(1.) The mental recognition of the emphatic meaning of a word, prompts to giving it vocal emphasis. A speaker who thinks of the meaning, and feels the power of an emphatic word, at the very moment of speaking it, can hardly fail to emphasize it aright; and if he does not think of its meaning, nor feel its power, he certainly will not emphasize it at all.

(2.) Doubt or uncertainty expresses itself in rising inflections. He whose mental state is characterized by either of these words, will spontaneously express it by a raised pitch, and upward inflections, on his most significant words; whilst the feeling of certainty or confidence will affirm and manifest itself by downward or falling inflections.

(3.) Earnestness will make the impression of earnestness. Whoever is in downright blood earnest, will be sure to express it, and to impress it upon his audience; whereas he who only affects it, may rant and rave, and "tear a passion to tatters," but he will not succeed in expressing what he does not feel, but only feigns.

§ 22. **The leading mental states or operations in all good speaking are the following: that of holding firmly in the mental grasp the object which the speaker aims to accomplish in the minds of the audience; the desire to accomplish it; the consciousness of speaking directly to the audience for this purpose; and the feeling of the power of the thoughts and emotions which he aims to express.**

The development and application of the principle laid down above (§ 21), would require us to investigate and determine what these leading states or operations of mind are, the expression of which constitutes good delivery; in other words, which belong essentially to the giving out or expression of thought, and to impressing it upon other minds. These, in their most general forms, we should find to be as here enumerated, corresponding in part to the Sources of power in delivery. They govern the consciousness of the speaker, and consequently give character and form both to the oral and visible signs by which he expresses himself. In fact when these mental states predominate in his consciousness they express themselves, and the expression of them is the highest excellence of speaking.

§ 23. All other mental operations which accompany speaking, are properly sub-processes, and require to be suppressed.

These are the exercise of memory, the work of invention, arrangement and style, or reading from the manuscript, the study of the audience, the exercise of self-control, the feelings of timidity, anxiety and fear, and similar exercises of the mind. These, in all good delivery, are carried on or operate, for the most part, unconsciously, and are suppressed from the expression. For whenever they are allowed to become predominant in the consciousness, they displace or confuse those which properly belong to the expression of thought, give character and form to all the signs employed, and produce all the vices of elocution. The delivery, in fact, consists of the expression of these properly sub-processes, but which have now become the leading or governing states of the speaker's mind.

§ 24. The great problem of delivery is, how shall the speaker think and feel, at the moment of speaking, just what he wishes to express?

From the preceding views it is plain that the great problem which elocution is required to solve, but which has hitherto been excluded from the art, is really a mental one, as here stated. The solution of this problem is the precise aim of the following discussion of the Sources of power in delivery.

CHAPTER II.

POWER IN THE THOUGHT.

§ 25. The tendency of power in the thought is to inspire the delivery with power.

As in order to speak at all, it is necessary to have something to say, so in order to speak well, it is necessary to have something to say which is worthy of being spoken. This statement, however, requires to be qualified. For it is obvious that the delivery may be much better than the matter of discourse; just as a good discourse may be utterly spoiled in the delivery. If this were not so, there could be no place for Elocution, as a distinct art from Rhetoric. All that is here meant is that the strong tendency of power in the thought is to inspire the delivery with power, and that the best possible elocution is otherwise unattainable. In proof of this, it might be sufficient to adduce the fact, well known to all teachers and students of this art, that, for purposes of practical training and exercise, we find a very great advantage in the selection of the most eloquent passages from the orators and poets. But it is desirable to unfold and confirm this principle by other considerations.

§ 26. There is a natural congruity between the thought and the expression of it.

This natural agreement, congruity, or consistency between the character of the thought to be expressed, and the expression which appropriately belongs to it, is essential to the possibility of oral speech. There is such a congruity also between the thought and its rhetorical form, the unspoken words, or diction; but it is much more striking between the thought and its vocalization, or delivery by the voice. Hence animated thoughts agree with an animated delivery; feeble and spiritless thoughts agree with a feeble and spiritless delivery; and a truly powerful delivery is inconsistent with thoughts which have no power in themselves. But inconsistencies and incongruities are difficult to be realized in one and the same act, such as that of public speaking; whilst things which agree and are consistent with each other are comparatively easy to be realized. Hence good elocution, when we have good thoughts to express, is comparatively an easy thing; but it is extremely difficult when our thoughts are poor and barren and feeble. This congruity, also, between good thoughts and good speaking, materially aids the effect of both upon the audience.

§ 27. Thought exerts a powerful influence to determine its own forms of expression.

1. *Thought and expression mutually influence each other, but the influence of thought is predominant.*

There is a vital connection between thought and expression, both in its rhetorical and oral forms. But especially does the thought to be expressed, and the articulated and oral expression of it, constitute one organic whole; the different members of which exert a moulding influence reciprocally upon each other. But the influence of thought upon expression is predominant, that of expression upon thought, subordinate. For we do not speak until we have some thought to express, which guides us in the selection and oral formation of the words which it requires. Thought is the spirit and life of which expression is the organized body; and it is ever the peculiar form of life which determines the character of the organism in and through which it shall be manifested. Human life does not and cannot manifest itself in a brute form.

2. *Examples.*

The following examples may serve to exhibit this vital connection between thought and expression, and the manner in which that which is symbolized determines the symbolization.

(1.) Dull, sluggish and confused thoughts naturally tend to express themselves in heavy, sluggish and confused elocution; whilst elevated, impassioned and powerful thoughts prompt and inspire an elevated, impassioned and powerful delivery.

(2.) Clear and articulate thinking naturally expresses itself in clear and articulate speaking; whilst blurred and inarticulate thinking can hardly express itself otherwise than in blurred and indistinct articulation. In fact, the character of the thinking, in this respect, exerts a marked influence upon the physical organs of speech, upon their size, shape and physiological conditions. For a more full elucidation of this point, see under the head of articulation, § 122—1.

§ 28. Power in the thought gives that rational confidence to the speaker which is essential to power in delivery.

1. *In order to deliver a discourse with power, the speaker must believe that there is power in it.*

The importance to the speaker of a rational confidence in himself, and in what he has to say, is such that it might well be treated as an independent and original source of power. Whoever has compared his own delivery when inspired with such confidence, with what it becomes when he is conscious of having none but feeble thoughts to express, will be at no loss to appreciate the truth and force of this statement. Clergymen have abundant experience of it, in the fact that they find it almost impossible to preach old sermons with anything like the freshness and power of a first delivery. This is especially the case when the preacher himself has made any considerable mental progress in the meantime, unless the discourse has been carefully worked over, and brought up, in matter and form, to his advanced stage of development and culture.

(1.) Such confidence purifies and elevates the delivery, and communicates itself to the audience.

For when the speaker fully believes that his thought is good, and ought to have weight with the audience, this conviction releases him from the anxiety and torment of fear lest he should fail, or make a fool of himself, and thus tends to purify his elocution from the vices with which the expression of these feelings must otherwise load and enfeeble it. Unaffected therefore by this cause of embarrassment and distraction, he is free to throw all his faculties and energies into the proper work of delivery; and he is inspired with courage and hope, which naturally impart fullness and depth to his tones, breadth and significance to his inflections, clearness to his articulation, propriety and force to his emphasis, and dignity and grace to his gestures and manner. This confidence also enables him to expect, and by expecting to engage the attention and sympathy of his audience, by which his elocution is still further elevated and purified. Besides this, his own appreciation of what he has to say tends to communicate itself to them by all the secret channels of sympathy, so that they are insensibly led to receive it with a like appreciation. But all this is power in delivery.

(2.) The want of such confidence has the opposite influence. It renders it almost impossible for the audience to feel any confidence in what is said, even though it be composed of the most eloquent sentiments that oratory or poetry ever produced. For if the speaker himself does not think it worthy of being spoken, how can he deliver it so as to impress them with the feeling that it is worthy of being heard? In spite of himself, in every tone and inflection of his voice, in his articulation, emphasis and gesture, he cannot fail to reveal, express, and impress upon the audience, his own leading state of mind, which in this case is that of condemnation of what he is delivering; and thus he leads them to condemn it. Add to this the torment of anxiety and fear, or rather the conviction that he is making a fool of himself; the consequent withdrawing of his faculties from the proper work of delivery; and all the vices of elocution which the inevitable expression of such a state of mind implies, render it simply impossible to speak with any power. His conscious feebleness of thought makes him feeble in delivery.

2. *In order to feel such confidence the speaker must have a discourse which is worthy of it.*

This is the surest way, although the statement must not be understood to imply that none but speakers of superior powers of thought can attain to excellence in this art; nor that it will always succeed in producing the necessary confidence. For there are two classes of persons to whom the rule in its utmost rigor does not apply.

(1.) Those who are incapable of severe criticism upon their discourses may feel confidence in them, though unworthy of it. A speaker of inferior literary or rhetorical ability may feel great confidence in an inferior discourse, and consequently may deliver it so that it will produce an effect upon the audience far beyond its real merits. In such persons the critical faculties are not commonly developed beyond those which are employed in the actual production of their discourses; hence, although they are not able to originate thoughts of any great power, yet, because they are also incapable of any high degree of self-criticism, they often feel a good degree of confidence in what they have to say, and consequently are enabled to deliver it with good effect. But even in such cases; it is indispensable that the thought should be as good as the speaker can make it; that he himself should not be capable of criticising it too severely; otherwise, however poor it may be, it cannot fail to be still further marred in the delivery.

(2.) Those whose critical faculties are developed in excess will hardly feel confidence, however excellent their discourses. The peculiarity of such persons is that their critical faculties are developed so far in advance of those upon which execution or production depends, that they are disgusted with everything they do; and the more they labor upon their own thoughts, the more they are discouraged. They are over educated, having had too much theoretical instruction or study, and too little practice; so that their energy in production has become enfeebled or paralyzed. They are found in every sphere of art and of life. Of this class the character of Hamlet is an illustrious type, in which

> The native hue of resolution
> Is sicklied o'er with the pale cast of thought.

(3.) The rule is of general application to all of well-balanced minds.

With most of us, however, and with all of anything like evenly balanced minds and culture, it will be found that the only sure way to nourish and maintain a steady confidence in the matter of our discourses, such as is indispensable to the successful delivery of them, is to make them as perfect as possible. In this way only is it possible to secure the highest degree of power in delivery. Without this no speaker, however gifted or accomplished in extempore discourse, ought ever to deliver himself on any serious occasion, except from absolute necessity. The reasons for this which Elocution alone supplies, to say nothing of Rhetoric, are altogether insuperable.

CHAPTER III.

FEELING.

§ 29. The emotions and passions of the soul are the true inspiration of eloquence.

> Si vis me flere, dolendum est
> Primum ipse tibi.

THERE is no more fruitful source of power in delivery than the emotions and passions of the soul. These are the true inspiration of eloquence itself, as also of poetry, music, painting, sculpture, and all the esthetic arts. This fundamental principle has been expressed, once for all time, in the well known lines of Horace, of which the following is a very inadequate translation.

> Responsively the human features laugh
> To those that laugh, and weep to those that weep.
> Would'st make me weep? Then thou thyself must grieve,
> Telephus, or Peleus; thy words of woe
> Then touch my soul: but if thy mandates fail
> In aught becoming thy true character,
> I laugh, or sleep. Sad features speak sad thoughts;
> The frown, of wrath; sweet smiles, of sport and joy;
> A serious face bespeaks a serious mind.
> For nature forms us *first* within to feel
> The changeful lot of life—thrills with delight,
> Impels to anger, weighs us down with grief,

FEELING.

And chokes us with keen anguish—*then* declares,
With voice conformed, her great interpreter,
The changing passions of the fervid soul.

**§ 30. The passions have their own peculiar language of mys-
tical signs.**

In the preceding quotation from one of the greatest masters of art, we have set forth, not only the indispensable necessity of feeling in order to power in elocution, but also the great reason for this necessity; namely, because the passions have their own peculiar language of mystical signs.

1. *These signs consist of all the different qualities of voice, changes of pitch, inflection, articulation, time, force, and emphasis, together with all the infinitely various expressions of the countenance, and all the positions and motions of the body.*

In fact, each several passion, mode of feeling, and state of mind, has its own peculiar dialect, so to speak, of this symbolical language. For these signs, whether addressed to the ear or the eye, are very different, not only for the different passions, but also for their ever-varying degrees of intensity, and for all their modifications and blendings with each other; and they vary still further in persons of different temperaments, culture and circumstances. This language, therefore, constitutes a most copious, significant and expressive part of delivery. For it is by means of it that the emotions and passions of the soul communicate themselves from one person to another, along with the intellectual operations, indeed, but often independently, and without the intervention of thought.

2. *Examples.*

The following examples, somewhat modified, are taken from an anonymous work of the last century, referred to by Walker in his Elocution, and following which he has given us between seventy and eighty similar examples of this mystical language of the passions. The signs here imperfectly indicated are only a few out of an almost infinite variety, by which these passions, in their innumerable degrees and modifications and blendings with other feelings, may be manifested.

(1.) The passion of anger expresses itself in some persons by a flush, in others by a livid paleness of the countenance. It wrinkles the forehead, and contracts the eyebrows. It flashes with a fierce light in the eyes, expands the nostrils, gives rigidity to the muscles, clinches the fists, stamps the foot, and violently agitates the whole body. Its words are sometimes rapid, noisy and harsh, with the voice pitched high; sometimes the voice is on the lowest key, the words slow, and the articulation much hardened. Violent and vindictive passion will often force out the breath, imperfectly vocalized, in a sharp hissing sound. The first Napoleon, it is said, when very angry, hissed out his words so as to be nearly unintelligible.

(2.) The passion of sorrow, when not excessive, renders the countenance pale and dejected, with the eyes cast down, and suffused with tears. The arms hang loosely at the sides, the hands are open, the fingers spread, and all the muscles of the body are relaxed. The voice is low and plaintive, the words slow, and frequently interrupted with sobs and sighs. When the passion is violent, it distorts the countenance, as if with pain, wrings the hands, beats the breast, tears the hair, and sometimes throws the body at full length on the ground; often it raises the voice in loud complainings, even to shrieks and screams. Overwhelming sorrow is still and silent: it suppresses the tears and the voice, and renders the countenance dull and heavy, as if all the faculties were stupefied.

(3.) The passion of love, in different degrees of timidity, expresses itself by approaching or shrinking from its object. When in doubt of the reception it shall meet with, its approaches are made with much hesitation, confusion of manner, and sometimes trembling. Blushing and paleness succeed each other in the countenance. The voice is low and soft and tremulous. The articulation is broken and confused, according to the strength of the passion, and the lack of self-control. When declaring itself, or pleading with great importunity, it may easily bring the lover to his knees. The eyes are now either turned away, or fixed upon the object, and the speech is either rapid and voluble, or confused and broken. When secure of its object, it gives a smile to the lips, a serene glow to the countenance which seems to radiate light, a liquid brilliancy to the eyes, and a tenderness of expression and grace to all the motions of the body.

§ 31. **No art can teach this language without the feelings by which it is inspired; yet the study of its signs is legitimate and useful.**

1. *Feeling bears a relation to the knowledge of these signs like that of the ear to sounds, and of the eye to colors.*

The preceding examples—a very few of the signs by which two or three of the most common passions are manifested—may serve to evince, not only that there is such a language, but also that it is copious and complicated beyond any possibility of analysis, and almost of conception. For this reason among others, it can never be taught or learned so that it can be employed with its proper effect, except as it is inspired by the passions themselves of which it is the medium of expression. In a peculiar sense, it is the language of nature, and nature only can teach it. All that we can ever know of it, for practical use, by mere study, is little more than the deaf can know of sounds, or the blind of light and colors.

2. *The study of these signs, however, aids the speaker to express the passions which he actually feels.*

The above statements are not intended to affirm that the knowledge of these signs, in so far as this may be acquired by observation, study and experience, has no legitimate place or use in elocution; or that it cannot aid the speaker in expressing the passions by which he is actually inspired. For it is evident from the preceding examples, that, to a certain extent, these signs are capable of being distinguished, described, classified, and referred to the different emotions and passions of which they are the natural expression. Such a knowledge of them is an important element of that aid in delivery which art affords to nature; and hence it ought not to be neglected by any who aspire to the highest excellence and power. For when the speaker is truly inspired by the feelings which he aims to express, and to excite in the audience, he will be greatly aided by a competent knowledge of this symbolical language. Feeling is thus rendered a more abundant source of power. For as the speaker is himself excited by the tones of his own voice, so this whole language of passion tends to excite in his bosom, and to facilitate in expression, the passions he wishes to communicate. In a word, the knowledge of these signs is of great value in that sphere in which art comes in to aid, but does not subvert or displace nature.

§ **32. Feeling is indispensable in impassioned, argumentative, explanatory, and every species of discourse.**

The actual delivery of thought, taken in the most comprehensive sense of the word, as inclusive of all the emotions and passions, implies that we are first in possession of it ourselves; for a man cannot deliver to others what he does not himself possess. Hence the feeling of the power of the thought, is indispensable to the delivery of it with power, in every species of discourse.

1. *Feeling is most indispensable in impassioned discourse.*

The preceding views with respect to the mystical

language of the passions, have their principal bearing, of course, upon the impassioned discourse of excitation and persuasion. But the indispensable necessity of feeling in this, the highest sphere of eloquence, may be still further evinced. For how, it may asked, is it conceivable that a man who does not love justice, and abhor crime, should speak in defence of the one, or in condemnation of the other, without such feigning as must betray itself, and mock his attempts at power in delivery? Is it possible that any one should give such true and effective and powerful expression to the love of the truth, the right, the beautiful, and the good, as to excite these emotions in the hearts of others, when he does not feel them himself? How can a man so speak as to kindle up in others the love of God, and of their neighbors, when he himself loves neither his neighbor nor his God? All this evidently involves a problem which no art can, or ought even to attempt to solve. For no feigning can ever produce the effect of unfeigned emotion; and without feeling true art itself is impossible.

2. *It is also necessary in argumentative and explanatory discourse.*

Feeling, taken in a somewhat wide sense, is also necessary in both these species of discourse. For it is indispensable that the speaker should be deeply sensible of the meaning and bearing of the thoughts which he has to express, that he should himself feel the force of the arguments which he aims to enforce upon others, in order to deliver them with their proper effect. Both in argument and explanation, he must grasp in his mind the thought as a whole, and in its several parts, and must be sensible of the meaning and force or power of every important word, not only in itself, but also in its various relations and connections, at the very moment of speaking it. It would be difficult to lay too much stress upon this point. For it is here that men of great talents often miserably fail: that is, from the bare fact that they have no feeling of the meaning and power of their words, at the moment they are spoken. Hence their feeble articulation, meaningless or false tones and inflections, misplaced emphasis, and mechanical gestures.

3. *In every species of discourse, the influence of the appropriate feeling is to clothe the delivery with power.*

It is impossible for a person of a dull, heavy, or sluggish soul to speak well. The true orator is a man of keen and deep sensibility; he is all alive, even to his finger nails. It is this which gives him that charming animation or vivacity, which enables him always to command the attention and sympathy of his audience, and which is almost irresistible. It is this which inspires the tones, inflections, articulation, emphasis and gesture, so that it seems to be the feeling itself which speaks, rather than the man. It flashes in the eye, it plays upon the countenance, so that the features seem to talk as expressively as the lips. It pours itself into the audience by the mysterious channels of sympathy, and kindles in their hearts all the passions which glow in the speaker's own bosom.

§ 63. Play actors produce their great effects by genuine feeling.

1. *The successful tragedian is affected as the person whom he personates.*

It may occur as an objection to these views, that play actors produce the very greatest effects by their fictitious representations. But it is a mistake to suppose that they produce them by simulated, of feigned emotions; for the genuineness of stage feeling does not admit of being questioned. The actor, in in order to succeed in his art, must learn the secret of opening the fountains of feeling in his own bosom He must himself be moved as if he were in truth the person whose character he personates; and in his most successful efforts he sometimes loses, for the time, his consciousness of his own proper identity. His emotion becomes so profound and entrancing that his distinct personality seems to be absorbed in the character which he represents. This is the great secret of the tragic art, which has given the great tragedians their almost irresistible power over the emotions and passions of the human soul.

2. *Examples and authorities.*

It would be easy to cite any number of examples and authorities in support of this statement, if it were necessary.

(1.) Walker gives among others the following: "I have often seen Powell, in the character of George Barnwell, so overwhelmed with grief in that pathetic address,

> Be warned, ye youths, who see my sad despair,

as to be incapable of expressing himself in the most impressive manner." (For the necessity of self-control, see Chap. XI.)

(2.) Quintilian tell us: "I have often seen actors, both in tragedy and comedy, when they laid aside their masks, after going through some distressing scene, quit the stage in tears."

(3.) Cicero also to the same effect, particularly where, after having quoted a passage from the Telamon of Pacuvius, he adds: "Even the player who pronounced these words every day, could not deliver them effectively without a feeling of real grief."

3. *In genuine feeling the players not unfrequently shame the preachers.*

For, as it has been often remarked, whilst the former deliver fiction as if it were the truth, the latter not unfrequently utter the most solemn and glorious truth as if it were the merest fiction. Such preachers, if this word be not abused, ought surely to apply to themselves those terrible self-reproaches of Hamlet, which afford us another striking evidence of the genuineness of histrionic feeling.

> O what a rogue and peasant slave am I!
> Is it not monstrous that this player here,
> But in a fiction, in a dream of passion,

> Could force his soul so to his own conceit,
> That from her working all his visage wanned,
> Tears in his eyes, distraction in's aspéct,
> A broken voice, and his whole function suiting
> With forms to his conceit—and all for nothing?
> For Hecuba!
> What's Hecuba to him, or he to Hecuba,
> That he should weep for her? What would he do,
> Had he the motive and the cue for passion
> That I have?
>   Yet I,
> A dull and muddy-mettled rascal, peake,
> Like John-a-dreams, unpregnant of my cause,
> And can say nothing.

§ 34. The speaker should endeavor to excite in himself the feeling which is requisite for speaking, for which there are various and effective means.

It is evident from what has now been determined, that great importance must attach to the question, by what means can we command the requisite feeling on each occasion of speaking? That there are such means has always been understood by the play actors, and the knowledge and diligent use of some of them go far to explain the great power of the tragic art. But a large number of public speakers seem either to be ignorant that there are such aids, or to despise them. It is doubtless one cause of the feebleness of pulpit delivery, that so many clergymen neglect the invaluable helps which art supplies, in exciting their own hearts with the feeling of the truth which they seek to impress upon others. This remark is not intended to apply to all the aids mentioned below, some of which, in-

FEELING. 69

deed, are so general in their nature, and have so much more exalted relations than any which they bear to this subject, that it seems almost improper to bring them within the purview of this art.

§ 35. **The first means of exciting the requisite feeling, is careful meditation on the causes and reasons for feeling which are offered by the occasion, object, and sentiments of the discourse.**

The first and most generally available means, which our art teaches, of exciting in ourselves the requisite feeling, is thorough meditation beforehand upon the causes or reasons for feeling, which are supplied by the occasion and circumstances, the object which we aim to accomplish, and the sentiments we have to deliver. Each of these seems to require a separate consideration.

§ 36. **Meditation of the occasion and circumstances of speaking tends to excite the requisite feeling.**

The circumstances in which we have occasion to speak are often adapted to affect the heart of the speaker with the deepest emotion. This influence may be lost for want of due appreciation. Hence it is necessary for him to grasp these circumstances with his mind, and apply them to his own heart, especially in those aspects in which they have greatest adaptation to touch and excite the sensibilities of the soul. The following cases will explain what is here intended.

1. *The occasion of speaking may be the untimely death of a great man.*

Such a man may be cut off by assassination from the highest official station, and the greatest moral influence, for whose death a whole nation may be filled with grief and indignation, and draped in mourning. If now, in such a case as this, any want of emotion were conceivable, what an overwhelming array of circumstances may the speaker cause to pass before his mind to excite it! How can even a brief meditation of these fail to awaken the deepest emotion!

2. *The speaker may be called to speak in the national legislature upon a great subject.*

As a member of the Senate or House of Representatives of the United States, he may have to speak in the hearing of thirty or forty millions of freemen, his fellow citizens, and of the whole civilized world, upon a question of peace or war, or some other measure, which must affect for good or evil the life of the nation, and the welfare of the people, for generations and ages to come. Now, with a due appreciation of the solemnity and responsibility of every word spoken in such circumstances as these, there could be no want surely of that deep and full emotion which inspires delivery with power.

3. *He may be called to offer terms of forgiveness and reconciliation to men for their sins, being clothed with the character and responsibility of an ambassador of God to man.*

In this case the speaker's relations to God, and his relations to his audience, together with their character and circumstances, being grasped with the mind, and duly appreciated, are adapted to excite the most powerful and tender emotions in his own heart. To say nothing of meditation upon these circumstances beforehand, a few moments' consideration after entering the pulpit, of the assembly before him, many of them in deep mourning, their hearts burdened with sorrow; the consideration of their secret griefs, their manifold temptations, their dangers, fears and spiritual wants, and especially their need of spiritual succors and consolations—a few moments' consideration of such circumstances as these will often flood the heart of the Christian minister with such deep emotion, and so fill his eyes with tears, that he must check himself by a strong effort of will, in order to be able to speak at all.

§ 37. **Meditation of the object of speaking tends to excite the requisite feeling.**

The object which the speaker aims to accomplish in the minds of the audience, when thoroughly meditated and held before his own mind, will often be found even more powerful to excite his emotional nature, than the circumstances or occasion of speaking.

1. *The object may be to impress upon the audience the worth of American citizenship.*

In this case the speaker should endeavor to possess his own mind with the feeling of the innumerable blessings, social, civil and religious, which this high privilege confers, and which renders it so exceedingly precious to all who enjoy it, and are able to appreciate it. Also he should consider the long and bloody struggles, the faith, constancy and self-sacrifice, by which our nationality was established, and by which it has been maintained and preserved. Such considerations will commonly enter into the topics of his discourse, but in order that his own feelings may be duly affected by them, he ought thoroughly to meditate upon them in special application to his own case, until he feels for himself something of the worth and preciousness of his own American citizenship.

2. *Or it may be to win souls to Christ.*

In this case he should meditate much upon the worth of a single soul, and its almost infinite capacities of happiness and misery. He should bethink himself of some of the priceless blessings, both in this life and in that which is to come, which Christ bestows upon all who come unto him; and of the appalling guilt, and everlasting misery, with which men load themselves by rejecting or neglecting the great salvation. Above all, he should thus endeavor to impress his own heart with the all-constraining love which Jesus has manifested by giving his life on the cross, a ransom for our lost souls. And if, after such a meditation, though brief, the speaker can come before his audience, and behold a thousand, or a hundred of such souls, waiting with respectful attention, to hear what he has to say, and still be destitute of feeling, let him dismiss the congregation, and tell them that he was never called to preach the unsearchable riches of Christ to perishing sinners.

§ 38. **Meditation of the sentiments we have to deliver tends to excite the requisite feeling.**

1. *This is the most effectual means.*

The sentiments of a discourse, in order to be appropriate, must spring out of the occasion and the object for which it is delivered. Hence meditation of the sentiments includes, to a certain extent, that of the occasion and object of speaking, and constitutes the most effective means of exciting the requisite feeling. For in order that the thoughts or sentiments of a discourse should produce their proper effect upon the speaker himself, they must be taken up by his mind; his mind must be filled with them; they must be brought into combination with each other until they ferment, as it were, or effervesce, and overflow; and this is effected chiefly by meditation.

2. *This is the principal means of exciting the speaker's feelings in the delivery of the sentiments of others, as also in the exercises of elocutionary training, and in the delivery of play actors.*

The most important lesson which the student has to learn, in delivering the sentiments of others, is to fill his mind with them; to meditate upon them until he has made them thoroughly his own. For until he has learned to do this, and has thereby fired his own heart, he cannot speak; and when he has learned this, he has already ceased to be a tyro, and has begun to be a master in his art. The example of play actors in this respect is worthy of attention. For the amount of study, minute attention, and patient meditation, which they bestow upon their authors, in order to possess themselves of every shade of thought and sentiment, that they may render them to the audience with their true power, is almost incredible. It is this habit of mind, with respect to the study of Shakspeare, of which Garrick gives us a glimpse in the following couplet:

> 'Tis my chief wish, my joy, my only plan,
> To lose no drop of that immortal man.

3. *The same meditation is necessary in the delivery of our own sentiments.*

We are tempted to think that we cannot help feeling the power of our own thoughts, when we come to deliver them, notwithstanding all experience proves the contrary, and shows that we need to possess our minds with them, and to apply them to our own hearts, with as much assiduity and pains taking meditation as if they were the sentiments of others.

(1.) The advocate, *e. g.* is called to defend a client from injustice and oppression. In this case the topics entering into the defence, which are best adapted to excite emotion—such as the state of society which would result if such wrongs should go unpunished, the insult offered to the majesty of the law, and to all good citizens, and the pitiable condition to which the sufferer himself and his family have been reduced—such topics should be profoundly meditated by the speaker, until the sentiments make their due impression upon his own heart, and the fire of feeling is kindled up in his own bosom.

(2.) Or the preacher of the gospel is about to deliver a discourse on the sacrifice of Christ, for the object of awakening trust and love in his audience. Here he ought to meditate beforehand on the faithfulness and love which Christ has manifested by the sacrifice of himself in our place; upon his constancy to our cause in the face of all his temptations to abandon it; and upon the elements of trustworthiness and loveliness which are embodied in his person and character; until he has thoroughly possessed himself of such causes or reasons for emotion, in application to his own case, and until the fountains of trust and love are opened in his own soul. This will enable him to speak so that none will criticise his want of feeling, or his power in delivery.

§ 39. **The second means of exciting the requisite feeling is the cultivation of the sensibilities.**

It has been already observed, as everywhere implied in the discussion of this source of power, that a speaker, in order to be truly eloquent, must be a man of sensibility. Hence the systematic cultivation of the emotional faculties of the soul, must be regarded as an important means of being able to command the requisite feeling for each occasion of speaking.

1. *The emotional nature is capable of such cultivation and development.*

There is, indeed, a great difference between good and able men, in this respect, as in all others, but there are none in whom this class of faculties are not capable of being quickened and purified. The esthetic and moral affections—sensibility to beauty physical, intellectual and moral; sympathy, compassion, hope and joy; the love of truth, duty and justice—these, and all other right affections of the soul, are as capable of culture and development as the intellectual faculties.

2. *The method of cultivating the sensibilities is by exercising them upon their appropriate objects.*

All the sensibilities of the soul should be systematically exercised upon their appropriate objects; the esthetic, in the contemplation and enjoyment of beautiful objects: the moral, upon moral objects. Sympathy and pity, *e. g.* should be exercised in sympathizing with, and in relieving the wants and sufferings of those who are in affliction and calamity; and so of all the others. Without such exercise, the sensibilities of the soul grow feeble, especially as we advance in years, and our power to call forth the requisite feeling, on our various occasions of speaking, declines. This is one reason why some speakers, whilst young and immature, are much more effective than in later life. Instead of gaining, they lose power from decline of their susceptibility of emotion and passion.

FEELING.

§ 40. The third means of exciting the requisite feeling is the cultivation and exercise of the imagination.

1. *The imagination is properly an original source of power in delivery.*

The imagination is characteristically the faculty of art. It is this faculty, above every other, upon which depend the arts of poetry, music, painting, sculpture, architecture, acting, and, hardly in a less degree, that of elocution. In this art it is of such importance that it ought to be treated as an independent and original source of power. For the sake of brevity, however, it is here taken as a principal means of exciting that feeling in the speaker which is indispensable to excellence in delivery.

2. *It is by the exercise of this faculty that the play actor is enabled to feel as the person whom he personates.*

By the imagination only is the player enabled to identify himself with his stage character, and thus come to be affected with all the emotions and passions which belong to that character. It is by the same faculty, moreover, that he forms distinct, vivid, and heart-moving conceptions and images of all those causes, reasons and occasions for emotion, which are supposed to operate in the case, or which would affect his sensibilities if he were in truth the living person whom he represents. Hence he feels as the character whom he personates is supposed to have felt, speaks as he spoke, and acts as he acted. This is in part the explanation of that marvellous power which the great tragedian exercises, in exciting the emotions and passions of the audience and spectators.

3. *A similar exercise of the imagination is required in the training exercises of elocution.*

The teacher of this art will not have failed to observe that the difference between those who are quick, and those who are slow to learn, turns as much upon the degree in which this faculty is possessed or developed, as upon any other cause. For precisely as in the case of the actor, it is by the exercise of the imagination that the student is enabled to bring himself under all those influences which inspired the author of the passage which he attempts to reproduce. Thus he also becomes for the time, as it were, the orator or author whose sentiments he is delivering; and hence is enabled to feel as he felt, and to speak as he spoke, or as the words were intended to be spoken.

4. *The imagination is equally necessary to feeling, in the practice of oratory.*

For it is by this faculty that we form those distinct and vivid conceptions and images of the truth which we have to deliver, and of the scenes and incidents which we have to describe or narrate, by which our own hearts become affected with the very same feelings which we wish to excite in the audience. This it is also which teaches us to lay hold of those individual and special traits, and "touches of nature," which are most powerful to affect our own feelings, and those of the audience. It enables us also to enter into the sympathies of the audience, and to identify ourselves with those whose sorrows we portray, so as to feel the same sorrow ourselves.

5. *This whole view of the influence of the imagination in exciting the speaker's feelings, is confirmed by the highest authorities.*

(1.) Cicero upon this point delivers himself as follows: "There is such force, let me assure you, in those thoughts and sentiments which you apply, handle and discuss in speaking, that there is no occasion for simulation or deceit; for the very nature of the language which is adapted to move the passions of others, moves the orator himself in a greater degree than any who listen to him .... I never yet, I assure you, tried to excite sorrow, or compassion .... when speaking before a court of judicature, but I myself was affected with the very same emotions that I wished to excite in the judges." Elsewhere he gives us this precept, that "we must represent to our imaginations, in the most lively manner possible, all the most striking circumstances of the transaction we describe, or of the passion we wish to excite in ourselves."

(2.) Quintilian also teaches us that in order to feel as we ought, and thus to exercise the power of moving the feelings of the audience, we must form such images and representations of absent objects, that they shall seem to be present, and we shall seem to see them with our eyes.

"A man of lively imagination," he says, "is one who can vividly represent to himself things, voices, actions, with the exactness of reality; and this faculty we may readily acquire if we desire it. When, for example, the mind is unoccupied, and we are indulging in chimerical hopes, and waking dreams, these images beset us so closely that we seem to be not thinking but acting, on a journey or a voyage, in a battle, or haranguing an assembly, or disposing of wealth which we do not possess. Shall we not then turn this lawless power of our minds to advantage? When I make a complaint that a man has been murdered, shall I not bring before my eyes everything that is likely to have happened when the murder was committed? Shall not the assassin suddenly rush forth? Shall not the victim tremble, cry out, supplicate, or flee? Shall I not behold the murderer striking, the murdered falling? Shall not the blood and paleness and expiring gasp of the murdered man present themselves fully to my mental view? .... For thus our feelings will be moved not less strongly than if we were actually present."

§ 41. The fourth and last means of exciting the requisite feeling is the formation of a right moral character.

It has been much disputed, especially by Cicero and Quintilian among the ancients, and by Theremin in modern times, whether, after all, eloquence be not a virtue, rather than an art; that is, whether any but a really good man can speak with the greatest power. The true solution of this question seems to be, that virtue is not in all cases essential to eloquence, but that it is essential to the highest eloquence on moral and religious subjects and occasions.

1. *Virtue is not essential to all forms and degrees of eloquence.*

For it is undeniable that there are subjects and occasions on which men of by no means the best moral character may be, and have been truly eloquent. The power of oratory in the ancient heathen republics is of itself abundant proof of this, which is confirmed, moreover, by many examples in modern times. For some of our great judicial and forensic orators, both in Europe and this country, have been men not of the strictest morality. A similar remark might be made, perhaps with still greater force, of some of the most eminent tragedians.

2. *But virtue is essential to the highest eloquence on moral and religious subjects and occasions.*

The reason of this, in so far as it pertains to elocution, is that none but a man of high moral character can feel, in view of this class of subjects, as the speaker must feel in order to deliver himself with the greatest power. For the aim of such discourses is to do good, to make men wiser and better, to inform and convince them of moral truth, to awaken and quicken their admiration and love of whatsoever is morally admirable and lovely, and to persuade them to act and live in a virtuous and holy manner. The subjects or themes of discourse correspond to these objects or aims; and with both these, doubtless, the character and heart of the speaker must be in full sympathy, that is, he must be a good man, in order to speak with the greatest effect. Here eloquence is a spiritual power. It was this chiefly which made the delivery of Whitefield and Sommerfield so irresistible.

3. *The feeling which is requisite to the preaching of the gospel with power, is to be sought in prayer for the influences of the Holy Spirit.*

This it is, above everything else, which affects our own hearts with the feeling of the truth which we wish to impress upon others, and clothes our preaching with spiritual power. For that Spirit which gives divine efficacy to the preaching of the gospel, dwells in the heart of the preacher. The anointing of the heart makes the lips eloquent. The baptism of the Spirit is the gift of tongues.

CHAPTER IV.

EARNESTNESS.

§ 42. Earnestness is one of the principal sources of eloquence.

EARNESTNESS is equally essential to eloquence both in its rhetorical, and in its oral or elocutionary forms. It cannot always, indeed, make a man eloquent, for he may lack other qualifications; but no man can be truly eloquent without it. In its relation to rhetoric it has often been treated of, though commonly in a somewhat vague manner; but in order to appreciate its importance in elocution it is necessary to form a precise conception of its nature and mode of operation.

§ 43. Earnestness in speaking is a distinct conception of the object aimed at in the minds of the audience, and a strong desire to accomplish it.

It will be seen from this definition that earnestness is in part a feeling, and therefore included, to that extent, in the preceding chapter. There are however many reasons why it is indispensable to treat it separately, as an independent and original source of power in delivery. Among these are the following.

1. Because of the general nature, and distinguished importance of the feeling which enters into it, and which, perhaps, is more essential to good speaking than any other.

2. Because it includes also an intellectual operation, namely, that of the distinct conception of the object which the speaker aims to accomplish in the minds of his audience.

3. Because both this conception of the object, and the desire to accomplish it, are among those leading states of mind which ought always to govern the consciousness of the speaker, and the expression of which constitutes good delivery.

4. Because each of these elements of earnestness has its own separate relations to power in elocution, in consequence of which each requires a distinct exhibition in these relations.

§ 44. The distinct conception of the object to be accomplished in the minds of the audience by speaking, is one of the governing intellectual operations in all good delivery.

1. *The object of speaking is either explanation, conviction, excitation, or persuasion.*

Rhetoric teaches us that the object of speaking must always be conceived of under some one of these four general forms. In all speaking, we aim either to inform or instruct the audience, by explaining to their faculties of understanding some fact or truth; or to convince their judgments by proving some truth, or disproving some error; or to excite their sensibilities; or to persuade them to some action, purpose, or course of life. Most frequently, however, the object of speaking appears under the last of these forms, with the first three as means of accomplishing it. Whatever the object be, it is necessary to form a distinct conception of it before we commence to speak, and to hold it firmly in the grasp of the mind from the beginning to the end of the discourse.

2. *In all good delivery this conception governs the subordinate intellectual operations, as the conception of right or justice in the mind of an honest man, governs the other operations in driving a bargain.*

This conception of the object of speaking need not, indeed, be always an immediate object of consciousness; the speaker need not be always actually thinking about it; but it must at all times underlie and support the other intellectual operations, as the conception of honesty should underlie the operations of a business transaction. It must preside over them all, and give them direction, as in the case of the traveller, the conception of the place to which he is going presides over, and gives direction to all his steps. It constitutes the light, or medium of vision, through which all subordinate objects are made manifest to the speaker's mind. For in all good delivery the speaker does not even think of what he is saying, as having any character, form, or meaning for its own sake, but simply as adapted to effect the object at which he aims in the minds of the audience.

2. *This conception enables the speaker to suppress the sub-processes.*

This conception of the object, being thus held in the grasp of the mind, throws all those intellectual operations which are secondary and subordinate, into the background, and enables the speaker to suppress them, so that they shall not manifest themselves in the delivery (§§ 22—23.) Thus it subordinates all the processes of memory, and of reading, and of invention and style; in this last case, whatever pertains to the extempore working out of the matter and form of the discourse. Hence these sub-processes have no effect in marring or enfeebling the delivery.

§ 45. The desire to accomplish the object is one of the governing exercises of the sensibility, quickening and regulating the whole mental action.

1. *The influence of this desire is analogous to that of the conception of the object, and it extends beyond this analogy.*

For it bears a relation to the other exercises of the sensibility, similar to that which the conception of the object bears to the other intellectual processes. This relation does not therefore require to be again developed, because the analogy holds good throughout, even to the fact that the desire need not be at all times immediately prominent in the consciousness, although in good speakers it is always in full and controlling activity. But its influence extends beyond this analogy, in that it is not limited to the other operations of the sensibility, but it affects also no less powerfully the intellectual faculties, and their operations.

2. *It stimulates and quickens all the mental faculties to their utmost capacity of energy and activity.*

This desire to accomplish the object, when full and strong, stimulates the intellect, so that it becomes capable of more rapid and effective thinking than it is at other times. Its influence is equally great upon all those feelings whose function it is to co-operate in giving power to delivery. When, *e. g.* a man's life, or reputation, or any other object most dear to him, depends upon his convincing a court of his innocence, the strength of his desire to accomplish this object can hardly fail to energize all his faculties, both intellectual and emotional, to their utmost capacities.

3. *It regulates the other feelings, the uncontrolled activity of which might otherwise mar the delivery.*

Self-control will require to be treated hereafter as an original source of power; here, therefore, it will be sufficient to indicate the general relation of this desire to the regulation of the emotional activity. In the case above supposed, then, of a man pleading for his life, the desire to save it would prompt and enable him to keep all his other feelings under severe restraint, lest they should manifest themselves in such a way as to mar his delivery, and defeat his object. In all other cases it is indispensable that this desire to accomplish the object of speaking, should never cease to exert its influence and control of the other feelings. For if any other be allowed to get the better of this, and to manifest itself without control, it may easily produce an effect upon the audience directly the opposite of that which is desired. Sorrow, *e. g.* manifesting itself in copious tears, may choke the utterance, and become extremely offensive, producing all the effects of drivelling. Unrestrained passion of any kind may lead to indistinctness of articulation, vociferation, and a thousand other faults, any one of which would go far to defeat the object of speaking. Even when the desire to effect the object may seem to give way for a moment to an outgushing of pity or grief, or to a blast of indignation or scorn, it is still necessary that it should not really cease to control the other emotions and passions.

§ 46. Earnestness purges the delivery from the expression of irrelevant thoughts and feelings, and gives to the signs employed their characteristic excellence.

From the consideration of these two elements which enter into earnestness in speaking, and of their relations to the other mental operations and exercises, we shall be the better able to appreciate the influence of this source of power upon the delivery.

1. *It purges the delivery from the expression of irrelevant thoughts and feelings.*

This at least is always its tendency. For wher

the intellect of the speaker is fully occupied with the thought of his object, and his heart with the desire of accomplishing it, this leaves no place for any thoughts about himself, his tones, inflections, articulation, emphasis, or gesture, nor for any conceits or anxieties about his manner; consequently it purges, or tends to purge, his delivery from the vices of awkwardness, mannerism and affectation, in which such thoughts and feelings never fail to express themselves. His mind, being freed from such distracting and enfeebling occupations, naturally throws all its faculties and powers into the proper work of delivery. It may be said, therefore, that nothing purifies the mind and whole manner of the speaker, like being in dead earnest.

2. *It gives to the Signs employed, whether oral or visible, their characteristic exce'lence.*

This again is its tendency. It gives simplicity and directness to the whole manner, and adapts it to effect the object in view. It clothes the gestures with propriety and force. It imparts seriousness and gravity to the features, depth and power of expression to the eye. It gives fullness, strength and depth to the voice, and a certain characteristic quality, which makes it seem to come not so much from the throat or lungs, as from the depths of the heart—a quality which is sure to reach the hearts of the audience. Also it brings to bear upon the audience a steady and sustained mental pressure, imparting a *sostenuto* character to the whole delivery, which is never intermitted even in the longest pauses, and which is one of the most telling traits of a strong delivery. In fine, it is the earnestness of the speaker, which, in the words of our greatest American orator, comes "beaming from the eye, speaking on the tongue, informing every feature, and urging the whole man onward, right onward to his object."

§ 47. **Particular occasions may inspire earnestness; but in order to secure it in speaking upon great social, moral, and religious subjects, it is necessary to be an earnest man.**

It can hardly be considered as belonging to elocution to treat of the means by which earnestness may be acquired; and in so far as this might be proper, it has been anticipated in the preceding discussions of the means by which we may secure the requisite feeling for each occasion of speaking. Yet it may be well to allude to one or two points here, in order further to aid the student in availing himself of this source of power in delivery.

1. *There are particular occasions which will inspire any man with earnestness.*

Thus the advocate will naturally be in earnest in defending his client when his professional reputation depends upon his success, or when the case will pay well, or when he desires to defeat and humble a professional rival. The politician also may be very earnest in speaking in order to secure the election of a favorite candidate, by whom he hopes to be promoted to office, or from other merely selfish and partisan motives. In general, it is easy to be in earnest in the pursuit of any object in which we feel ourselves to be deeply and personally interested.

2. *But in order to be in earnest in speaking upon great social, moral and religious subjects, it is necessary to be an earnest man.*

(1.) In the pulpit especially, where we address frequently the same audience, upon great moral and religious truths, all motives of a selfish or worldly character will commonly fail to impart earnestness to the delivery. Here it is indispensable that the whole moral nature of the speaker should be habitually filled and inspired, not occasionally and in a factitious manner excited, by the desire to accomplish the object for which he speaks. Here nothing can supply, even for elocutionary purposes, the want of a living faith, and a personal interest, in the solemn and glorious truth we have to declare, or the want of a deep and heart-piercing conviction that the salvation of those to whom we speak depends upon their believing it, or the want of an habitual and all-constraining desire that they should believe and be saved. This was the source of the eloquence of the prophets and apostles, as it has been of all other great and powerful preachers of the gospel.

(2.) In like manner, all the other great human interests, if we would promote them by speaking, must lie at all times very near our hearts. They must be the objects for which we not only speak, but constantly live. We must take serious views of serious things; habitually exclude all low and grovelling and unworthy thoughts, and fill our souls with pure, lofty and magnanimous sentiments; sentiments which are superior to all selfish considerations; sentiments above the fear of death, because they belong to that in us which is immortal. In a word, we must be able to draw our inspiration from the deep fountains of patriotism and philanthropy, from the love of our country and our kind, from liberty, justice, truth and God. It is this which inspires delivery with power.

3. *Ingenuous youth are naturally attracted to the study of eloquence.*

Hence that beautiful enthusiasm, which is so characteristic of ingenuous youth, naturally attracts them to these studies, and prompts them to eloquence; whilst that levity and mockery in presence of the high aims and solemn responsibilities of life, in which the foolish only indulge, are no less fatal to their hopes of eloquence than of every other excellence.

CHAPTER V.

THE MENTAL STATE OF DIRECT ADDRESS TO THE AUDIENCE.

§ 48. **The perfection of oratory is the perfection of talking to people.**

Oratory is oral discourse addressed immediately and directly to the minds of people who constitute an audience. Hence it may be said that the beginning, middle and end of oratorical excellence is nothing else but the perfection of talking to people. The mutual relations between the mind of the speaker and those of the audience, are attention and sympathy on their part, and on his, that of speaking directly to them. Both of these relations are among the most fruitful sources of power in delivery. The full and steady consciousness in the mind of the speaker, of direct address to the minds of the audience before him, is the third, and in many respects one of the most important of the four leading mental operations the expression of which constitutes good delivery (§ 22.) In fact, it inspires elocution with so many and such great excellences, whilst the want of it, which is extremely prevalent, occasions so many and such damaging faults, that it may properly be called the first law of oratory.

§ 49. **While speaking directly to the audience the speaker is engaged in his proper work, and consequently he *is* enabled to do it well.**

Speaking directly to the people before him is the orator's proper work in delivery—his whole business for the time. Hence it requires his undivided attention—the exercise of all his faculties and powers. Whilst, therefore, he is thus engaged in his proper work, whilst it constitutes the dominant operation of his mind and consciousness, he is giving his attention to what he is about, he is minding his present business. The natural consequence of this is that he does his work well, just as in any other case in which a person gives himself up to the work which he has in hand. Conversely, when the speaker loses his consciousness of direct address to the people before him, his state of mind is that of forgetting what he is about; he is not minding the business he has in hand; he is occupied with something else, inconsistent, and often totally incompatible with the expression of what he has to deliver. Hence it becomes impossible for him to do his work well, just as in every other case in which a person forgets what he is about, and allows his mind to become otherwise occupied.

§ 50. **Speaking directly to the audience brings the speaker into the true vital relations to them, by which he is enabled to grasp them with his mind, and exert a direct mental influence upon them.**

1. *The vital relations of the speaker to his audience are similar to those of the great musical artist.*

These relations are of the utmost importance in delivery, as also in music; and hence they will require to be more fully treated under the head of attention and sympathy as a source of power. In explanation of them, it may be proper to refer to a conversation which occurred between the author and Ole Bull, the Norwegian violinist. Speaking of the effect of his "Mother's Prayer," which the evening before had melted the audience to tears, he said: "Do you know that I do not produce these effects by the mere sounds of my violin? I produce them by the direct action of my mind upon the minds of the audience. I employ the tones of the instrument simply for the purpose of opening the channels through which I myself act upon their hearts." This idea he then proceeded to unfold in a profound, but somewhat mystical discourse upon the mental sources of power in art.

2. *In these relations the speaker grasps his audience with his mind, and exerts that direct mental influence upon them which is the magnetism of eloquence.*

Speaking directly to the audience implies of course a strong consciousness of their presence, and of the thoughts or sentiments as addressed to them. It implies, moreover, that the speaker thinks of them as people, that is, as persons clothed with all the attributes of human beings, in a word, as men and women. He grasps them thus with his mind, and holds them steadily in his mental grasp. This enables him to gain their attention and sympathy, and to bring all his personal power, as a man, to bear upon them, as men and women of like passions with himself. Thus he pours his thoughts and feelings into them through the open, but ever mysterious channels of the sympathetic affections. This direct mental action of the speaker upon the minds of the audience, is one of the great secrets of a powerful delivery; it is the magnetism of eloquence.

3. *The loss of the consciousness of speaking directly to the audience breaks up these vital relations, paralyzes the action of the speaker's mind upon the audience, and renders it subject to the dominant influence of the sub-processes.*

Whenever the mental act of speaking directly to the audience ceases, or ceases to be one of the dominant mental operations, the speaker no longer recognizes the presence of the audience, or it becomes to him something dim, shadowy and ineffectual. He does not grasp them with his mind, nor engage their attention. His thoughts are withdrawn from them, and leave their thoughts to wan der from him, and from all that he pretends, but u terly fails to say to them. The leading operations of his mind become those of invention and style, or those of remembering, or those of taking in the sense of his manuscript; or his mind becomes chiefly occupied with other irrelevant thoughts, perhaps still more incompatible with true expression Hence the delivery, if such it may be called, being of necessity the expression of the mental operations in which he is immediately and chiefly engaged (§ 21), becomes wholly false and powerless.

§ 51. **Speaking directly to the audience moulds, adapts and directs all the signs employed to their true object or aim.**

1. *The signs employed in speaking to others are different from those employed in solitary musing, or when the consciousness of the presence of others is lost.*

The same thoughts and feelings when expressed in the presence of others, and directed to their minds, commonly take somewhat different signs, both oral and visible, from those which are natural when one is speaking to himself. In some cases this difference may appear to be very slight, but it is not therefore insignificant. In others it is evident and palpable; as, *e. g.* in the greater degree of loudness and distinctness which is natural in speaking to a large audience, compared with what would be required in solitary musing. In like manner, it will be found upon careful observation, that the manifestations of love, anger, disgust, and all other feelings, in the presence of others, and as directed to their minds, cannot be confounded with those which these passions sometimes seek in solitude for their own relief, or when the consciousness of the presence of the audience is lost.

2. *The consciousness of speaking directly to the audience gives their true form and character to all the signs.*

Inasmuch as all speaking consists in the expression of the leading operations of the speaker's mind (§ 21), it is evident that the mental action of speaking directly to the audience must always predominate in the consciousness of the speaker, in order that the delivery should take on its true character and form, and should keep true to its object. It is this mental state which gives to all the signs, both of voice and gesture, their last modification and adaptation to the object which they aim to effect. The mind of the speaker, *e. g.*, being directed to his audience, his eye naturally follows his mind—he looks at them ; and not barely as "a sea of faces," without distinction, but he scans their individual countenances, notes their several expressions, and thus becomes conscious of the effect which he is producing upon them. All the gestures are affected in a similar manner. Thus also the voice, as we have seen, naturally becomes sufficiently loud, and the articulation sufficiently hard and firm, to ensure that the speaker shall be heard and understood by the most distant person to whom he is speaking. Similar modifications are produced upon every sound, and every variation of sound, which he utters. In fine, it is this consciousness of the presence of the audience, and of speaking directly to them, for the accomplishment of his object, which gives the last moulding touch to all the signs. It is this which gives point and direction to all those arrows of significant sound and gesture, which every moment are launched, by the force of his thoughts and passions, from the speaker's lips, eyes, countenance, and from all the motions of his hands, arms and body, into the minds and hearts of his audience, and which makes them feel that they are the object of a well-manned battery, playing upon them with no uncertain aim.

§ 52. **The loss of this consciousness of direct address loads the delivery with vices, by rendering it the expression of the sub-processes, by perverting all the signs, and by enfeebling its rhetorical form.**

1. *It renders the speaking the expression of the sub-processes.*

Whenever this consciousness of speaking directly to the audience ceases to be a dominant operation of the speaker's mind, it naturally gives place to some of the sub-processes (§ 23). These now become the leading mental operations, and give shape and form to all the signs; and the expression of these sub-processes constitutes the delivery. If this leading operation be that of recalling, by a labored effort, what the speaker has committed to memory, his speaking becomes, as we shall see more fully hereafter, nothing but a wretched performance upon this mental act of remembering, without any true or vital relation to the communication to others of the thoughts or sentiments of his speech. If it be that of extempore invention, he stands musing before the audience, instead of speaking to them; and if it be that of taking in the sense of his manuscript through the eye, the speaking truly expresses that, and nothing else. In fine, if the leading mental exercise be that of thinking about himself, his tones, inflections, articulations, emphasis, or gestures, or of seeking to know what the people think of him, whether he is succeeding or not, or of anxiety or fear lest he should be making a failure—no matter what it is which now constitutes the leading operation of his mind, it must be this, and nothing else, which he expresses and delivers to the audience.

2. *It deforms and perverts all the signs.*

The mind of the speaker being withdrawn from the audience, his eye again follows his mind. It ceases to take in the people before him; it becomes either vacant, expressing abstraction from the business in hand, or it wanders listlessly over the audience, with a dim and confused glance which takes note of nothing, or it is raised to the ceiling, or confined to the manuscript, or closed. The voice no longer adapts itself to the size of the audience; it is either too low, or too loud; the movement, either too fast or too slow; and those variations required by the sentiment are no longer given. All the sounds and gestures become equally inappropriate, and foreign to the communication and impression of the thoughts and feelings which the words are intended to express.

3. *It vitiates the delivery by enfeebling its rhetorical forms.*

The loss of this consciousness perverts those forms in which the speaker seems to address the audience most directly, into such feeble abstractions as the phrase, "my hearers," in the place of strong personal attributes, such as "my friends," "my neighbors," "my brethren," "my countrymen," "my fellow citizens." For "my hearers," though often heard from the lips of good speakers, is essentially vicious, because it does not spring out of the conception of the audience as composed of persons, with all the passions of human beings, but regards them as abstractions, clothed with the single function of hearing. How wretchedly does it compare with the Ἄνδρες Ἀθηναῖοι, of Pericles and Demosthenes, and with the Ἄνδρες ἀδελφοὶ, of St. Peter and St. Paul! If the speech which Shakspeare puts into the mouth of Brutus, on the death of Cesar, began with "my hearers," instead of "Romans, countrymen, and lovers," not Roscius himself, nor Garrick, nor Kemble could give it any power in delivery.

§ 53. The way to maintain this consciousness of direct address to the audience is to be in earnest.

The only influence which can enable the speaker to maintain in constant activity the consciousness that he is speaking directly to the audience, is the full and clear conception of the object at which he aims, and the strong desire to accomplish it; that is, to be in earnest. But this is itself so fruitful a source of power, that it has already required to be treated separately.

CHAPTER VI.

ATTENTION AND SYMPATHY.

§ 54. Attention and sympathy are so connected with each other as to form one source of power in delivery.

SYMPATHY is here taken in its most comprehensive sense, as inclusive of all the sympathetic relations and influences between the audience and speaker, and between the individuals of whom the audience is composed. The attention of the audience is here joined with sympathy, making one source of power in delivery, for the reason that it is the necessary condition apart from which the sympathetic affections cannot be excited in the interest, or in aid of elocution. Each however has its separate relations to elocutionary power, which must not be overlooked.

§ 55. Eloquence is the joint product of the mental action of the speaker and audience; the orator's sensibility to the states of mind in the audience is very great.

1. *The reciprocal influence of speaker and audience is of great importance, especially where the speaker frequently addresses the same audience.*

This reciprocal influence is productive of some of

the most interesting and important results in elocution. In fact it is such that good delivery, and even eloquence itself, may properly be regarded as a joint product of the mental operations of speaker and audience. It can hardly be over estimated where the speaker is called frequently to address the same, or nearly the same audience, as in the case of the pastor of a Christian congregation.

(1.) The influence of the speaker upon the audience is exemplified in the case of a pastor who is dull and feeble in his delivery. For the tendency of his spiritless harangues is to render the audience habitually inattentive, unsympathizing and insensible. But if the pastor be an animated and interesting speaker, the tendency of his ministrations will be to develop habits of attention and sympathy in his people, to sharpen their minds, and quicken their sensibilities, and to render them more and more appreciative of eloquence.

(2.) The influence of the audience upon the speaker is such that an attentive and sympathizing congregation can hardly fail to develop speaking talents, and powers of eloquence, in their pastor, of which in other circumstances he might never have become conscious, nor given any manifestation; whilst an inattentive, unsympathizing and stupid people will exert a strong influence to dwarf the faculties, and put out the intellectual light of their minister, who might otherwise have attained to no inconsiderable excellence as a pulpit orator.

2. *The sensibility of the true orator to the mental state of the audience is very great.*

In fact the degree of this sensibility is an infallible test of natural genius for public speaking. For he who does not feel the need of the attention and sympathy of his audience, who hardly knows whether he has it or not, and who can speak about as well without it as with it—for there are such speakers—that man is incapable of eloquence, and ought to dismiss all thoughts of becoming an orator. The speaker who has any natural adaptation or genius for this art, seems to reflect, as it were, all the states and changes of mind and feeling which take place in those to whom he is speaking. He seems to know by instinct whether he is heard by the whole audience, whether he has their attention, whether they understand what he is saying, and whether they are favorably or unfavorably affected by it; and he feels as if it were almost impossible for him to proceed in his discourse, until he has succeeded in fixing their attention, and in gaining their sympathy.

3. *In his most favorable moods this sensibility sometimes rises to an almost preternatural height.*

In such mental states the speaker is affected by every breath or current of thought and feeling in the audience. He feels himself to be the object of a separate stream of mental influence from every person in the audience, as if they were all so many galvanic batteries, with all the several wires of communication centring in his own bosom. By such mysterious cords of sympathetic communion, all their states of mind, and changes of feeling, are telegraphed to his mind. When he is in the full tide of successful oratory, sweeping the whole audience along with him, as a river at flood, if then he should happen to say anything which calls forth opposition, or if unexpectedly there should be started some oblique or contrary current in their minds, he becomes aware of it the moment he enters it, even when he may be wholly unable to divine its cause, or what he may have said to excite it. The swimmer passing suddenly from a warm into a cold current of water, cannot be more immediately sensible of the change.

§ 56. **The quickening influence which the audience exerts upon the faculties of the speaker, is one of the most fruitful sources of power in delivery.**

1. *Even opposition in the audience may aid the speaker.*

Such extreme sensibility as that which has just been described, has indeed its disadvantages, but its advantages greatly preponderate. A speaker who lacks confidence may be overcome by an adverse state of mind in the audience, so that he cannot proceed. But its effects upon a strong speaker, who is confident of his powers, is to excite and nerve him to greater efforts to make head against the opposition, and to overcome it. Thus the adverse influence is converted into a stimulus and quickening of all his faculties and powers.

ATTENTION AND SYMPATHY. 107

2. *A favorable sentiment in the audience has a still greater quickening influence.*

When the impression which the speaker makes is altogether favorable, as the audience becomes more and more attentive, and more and more favorably excited, he draws from their states of mind, every moment, new and stronger inspiration, and ever-increasing power. The tension of thought in the audience, and their excited feelings, poured in upon him through the channels of sympathy, intensify the action of his own intellect, flood his heart with emotion, and quicken, purify and elevate every faculty of his mind and body. Sometimes this influence will seem almost to lift him off his feet; he will seem to tread on air. He now speaks in a kind of ecstasy or rapture. However long he may be engaged, he is unconscious of fatigue or effort. All seems to pass in a moment of time. The audience also are unconscious of time, for this is eloquence.

§ 57. The attention and sympathy of the audience enable the speaker to suppress the sub-processes, and to exert all his faculties in the proper work of delivery.

These are the more special benefits which are derived from this source of power; not, however, that it will yield them to every speaker, but such is its tendency.

1. *An attentive and sympathizing audience relieves the speaker from the consciousness of the sub-processes, and enables him to suppress them.*

This arises from the fact just exhibited, that the

influence of such an audience quickens and intensifies that whole mental action which is engaged in the expression and communication of thought. Under this influence, if the speaker uses his manuscript, he is unconscious of being dependent upon it; he does not know that he turns the leaves, nor even that he has it before him. Speaking from memory, he is unconscious of the exercise of this faculty; a flood of light seems to pour itself over the whole discourse in his mind; so that by a single mental act, he comprehends and sees it from beginning to end. Speaking extempore, he is unconscious of labor or effort in invention, arrangement, or verbal expression; his thoughts seem to come by inspiration, to fall of themselves into the most appropriate and lucid order; to choose their own words, and to secure the most effective utterance. Thus released from the consciousness of these and other sub-processes, he instinctively suppresses all manifestation of them; they have no tendency to appear in false intonation, misplaced emphasis, nor in any other of those innumerable vices, with which they are otherwise certain to load and enfeeble the delivery.

2. *The influence of such an audience enables the speaker to exert all his faculties in the proper work of delivery.*

The whole tendency of such attention and sympathy, is to render all the other sources of power available in the highest degree. For it establishes and confirms in the mind of the speaker the consciousness of speaking directly to the people before him; it enables him to grasp and hold fast the object which he aims to accomplish in their minds, and intensifies his desire to accomplish it; it deepens his feeling of the power of the thoughts and sentiments which he expresses; it fills his heart with the emotions which he seeks to excite in the audience; and it gives him confidence by assuring him that he is not making a failure, but is achieving success.

3. *It purifies the signs employed, and renders them forcibly expressive.*

As the effect of the speaking becomes more and more apparent, in the increasing stillness and attention of the audience, this effect returns upon the speaker himself, with a corresponding increase of his power over the signs which he employs. His efforts are intensified that he may not allow the audience to lose a thought, nor the shade of a thought, which he has to deliver. Thus his articulation is purified and strengthened; his voice increases in force, compass and flexibility; it becomes more full and deep and pure; greater breadth and significance are given to his inflections; his eye and countenance become more animated and expressive. The position and motions of his body become more graceful, appropriate and striking; and the gestures made with his arms and hands more free and forcible. A similar effect is produced upon all the sounds he utters, and upon all his **gestures.**

§ 58. The effect of the speaking is greatly increased by the sympathy of the audience with each other.

1. *The sympathy of the audience with each other is one of those influences which make oral superior to written discourse.*

The influence of such sympathy can hardly be overestimated, although the manner in which it produces its effects is very imperfectly understood. Both thought and feeling are thus propagated from mind to mind, and from heart to heart. This fact goes far to explain the superiority of oral over written discourse, that the highest form of eloquence is embodied in oral speaking (§ 2—1, 2), and that the gospel must be proclaimed by the voice of the living preacher (§ 7).

2. *It gives to discourse an effect beyond its inherent merits.*

Counting upon the influence of this sympathetic action of the minds of the audience upon each other, the speaker may expect, and thus become enabled to produce vastly greater results than were otherwise possible. His thoughts and sentiments, when he comes to deliver them, will naturally have a far greater effect upon the audience than could be anticipated from their intrinsic merit. In fact that which in the study appears to be comparatively poor and feeble, is often thus found in delivery to have the effect of eloquence.

3. *The attention of the audience is indispensable to this sympathy.*

In order to such results, it is necessary that the

ATTENTION AND SYMPATHY. 111

attention of the audience should first be gained, and concentrated upon the thoughts and sentiments of the speaker, as they are delivered. This is indispensable to the free play, and greatest effect of the sympathetic action. For even a single person who is inattentive, or whose mind is otherwise occupied, not only fails to contribute his share to the effect, but he presents an obstacle to the propagation and flow of the common feeling, and exerts a positive influence in crossing and confusing the mysterious currents of sympathy and thought.

4. *Concentration of the faculties of all intensifies the result.*

When the attention of the audience has been gained, their sympathies with each other begin to act; and then all their intellectual power, and all their sensibilities are easily excited, by the mutual action of their faculties upon each other. For when the minds of a whole assembly are thus occupied with one and the same thought, as this is expressed by the speaker, that thought is perceived more clearly, and felt more deeply, than it could ever be by any individual alone ; and when a common passion has been excited in a crowded audience, it works more powerfully, and produces unspeakably greater effects, than in any other circumstances.

§ 59. **The means of engaging attention and sympathy are sentiments worthy of attention, a simple, earnest and** respectful manner and tones, the eye fixed upon the audience, pauses and striking figures of speech.

1. *All pains should be taken to engage the attention and sympathy of the audience.*

The importance of this source of power is evident from what has been said; in fact it is such that the speaker should neglect no lawful means to avail himself of it. It would seem that a great many of the eccentricities which appear in some popular orators, both in their style and manner of delivery, are to be understood as mere expedients to awaken and fix attention. Such eccentricities cannot be justified, although they may be pardoned, because there are perfectly legitimate means of securing this indispensable result, which, rightly applied, can hardly fail on any ordinary occasion. They are partly of a rhetorical character, and belong only in part to elocution.

2. *The speaker must have something to say which is worthy of attention, and adapted to awaken sympathy.*

This is the first and most important of such means, one which will go far to secure the end; whilst without this, everything else ought to fail, and in the long run is pretty certain to do so. (See PART I. Chap. II.)

3. *His manner and tones must be simple, earnest and respectful.*

A simple, frank and artless manner, free from pretentiousness and affectation, and one at the same time earnest, respectful and affectionate, has great power to engage attention, and awaken sympathy. These are the principal elements of what is called an *engaging* manner. Nothing is more engaging than childlike simplicity. An affected, pretentious, or pompous manner forewarns the audience that the speaker is a fool. Also the tones of the speaker's voice should express sincere respect for the audience, an affectionate interest in them, and an earnest desire for their attentive and favorable consideration of what he has to say—as if he felt, what he ought always to feel, that it were almost impossible for him to proceed without it.

4. *The speaker's eye should be fixed upon the audience.*

It is indispensable that the speaker should not allow his eye to become fixed upon his manuscript, nor to wander around the walls, or up to the ceiling, nor to express in any way abstraction from the business in hand. He must bring his eye to bear steadily upon the people before him, scanning their countenances individually, and noting every sign of attention, or of the want of it. Where he perceives inattention, or any lack of interest, he should keep looking at the persons in whom it is manifested, and seem to direct his words more particularly to them, until he makes them feel that he is almost calling them by name. This however requires care to avoid giving offence. He must, indeed, be ever on his guard, in such circumstances, against the temptation to manifest annoyance or irritation.

5. *Pauses and striking figures of speech may be introduced.*

When the speaker finds it difficult to fix attention, he may resort to other expedients which, in favorable circumstances, ought not to be necessary. One of these is to pause in his exordium, and remain silent for a moment, until his object is gained. Another is to throw into his discourse a more than common bold and striking rhetorical figure. Either of these expedients will hardly ever fail to secure immediate and fixed attention.

6. *In difficult cases he may exercise authority over the audience, but with special care not to manifest irritation.*

Whenever the audience proves refractory in an extraordinary degree, which will sometimes be the case, the orator must not yield to them, or he is lost. He must try to rise with the difficulty, and by his voice, countenance and manner, exert a certain authority over them, for which his position and relations to them afford him peculiar advantages. But here again he must be on his guard against irritation. For if he show temper, they will not be slow to perceive that they have gained the mastery; and having discovered his weak point, they will not be tender of it. Therefore, with unruffled temper, and perfect good nature, by his eye, countenance, tones and whole manner, he should seem to say, My friends, I am here to speak to you, and I am going to do it; you are here to listen, and you have got to do it—the sooner you begin, the better it will be for us both.

7. *Some such means as the preceding will commonly prove effectual.*

By such means as these, unless there be some extraordinary cause of opposition, the orator can hardly fail to succeed in fixing the attention of his audience, through which he may readily excite their sympathies, and derive all the aids to delivery which flow from this source of power.

CHAPTER VII.

MASTERY OF THE SUBJECT-MATTER IN EXTEMPORE DISCOURSE.

§ 60. Mastery of the subject is a source of power in every species of delivery, but especially in extempore speaking.

It is a fundamental principle, alike applicable to every species of discourse, that we must have some notion of what we are going to say, before we undertake to say it. Speaking, therefore, on any serious occasion, without preparation beforehand, except where it cannot be avoided, is a very foolish thing, which no sensible man will ever allow himself to do, except under dire necessity; nor then does he ever expect to do justice, either to himself or his subject, in rhetoric or elocution. But here this source of power is to be treated in its special relations to extempore speaking, under which expression is included all forms of delivery, except those in which the discourse is fully written out, and spoken either from memory or manuscript. In this case, the more full and complete our mastery of the subject-matter of discourse, the more fruitful as a source of power in elocution does it become.

§ 61. **The necessity of full preparation beforehand is evinced from the number, complexity and difficulty of the sub-processes, which must be carried on simultaneously in strictly impromptu speaking.**

1. *The number and complexity of these processes is almost incredible.*

When called suddenly to address an audience, without any previous preparation, the speaker, whilst rising slowly to his feet, must select his subject, and determine in his own mind the object which he aims to effect. These prerequisites will commonly be suggested by the occasion, and hence will demand but little reflection. At the same time, he must fix upon a topic for his introduction, and construct his first sentence. Whilst delivering this as slowly as possible, in order to gain time, he must forecast, to some extent at least, his next sentence. Thus making his way slowly through his introduction, he must be occupied also in shaping his proposition, analyzing his subject, and arranging by co-ordination and subordination, the principal heads, and secondary topics of his whole discourse; and all this, with strict reference to the object which he aims to accomplish. If he succeed in doing this by the time he comes up to the enunciation of his proposition, he may feel himself comparatively safe for a good speech. During the discussion, whilst delivering each sentence, he must construct the next, and so with the successive paragraphs. At the same time, he must select **his** words, and must keep his mind running on ahead, correcting defects in his analysis, perfecting the arrangement of his topics, and forecasting his peroration. Simultaneously he must be more or less engaged in studying the audience, and in efforts to fix their attention, and enlist their sympathies. Now to carry on all these processes at one and the same time, even if there were nothing else to do, would seem to be well-nigh impossible. Yet such is the prodigious activity of the mind, under the stimulus and excitement of this kind of speaking, that, wherever it is highly successful, they are all, and many more, carried on as sub-processes, for the most part unconsciously, in strict subordination to the principal or leading operations, which properly belong to the delivery or expression of the thoughts and sentiments.

2. *The difficulty of carrying on all these sub-processes as such at the same time, necessitates preparation beforehand, wherever this is possible, in order to relieve the mind.*

The preceding analysis exhibits the toil and labor which a good speaker, in strictly impromptu discourse, instinctively undergoes to possess himself, as much as possible, with the knowledge of what he is to say, before he comes actually to say it. But the difficulty of carrying on, as sub-processes, all these laborious operations of invention, arrangement and style, and many others, and of suppressing all manifestation of them, when the whole burden of them is thrown upon the mind at once, in the very moment of delivery, is very great. In every such case, their strong tendency is to become predominant in the consciousness of the speaker; to overshadow and dwarf all those operations which properly belong to delivery; and consequently to manifest or express themselves in all the vices which enfeeble and cripple elocution. None but the most practised and accomplished rhetoricians and speakers, and these only in their happiest moods and most favorable circumstances, are able perfectly to overcome this difficulty, so as to speak, on the spur of the moment, with all the power of which they are capable.

§ 62. **Greater or less preparation is required according to circumstances, but as a general rule it should embrace a complete analysis of the discourse.**

The extent or thoroughness of the preparation required for extempore speaking, is greater or less, according as the mind of the speaker acts with more or less precision and rapidity. Too minute preparation resolves extempore into memoriter speaking, and instead of relieving the mind from the burden of sub-processes, only exchanges one class of them for another. The principle which will enable each one to decide this point for himself, turns upon the question, how far he can relieve himself from the labors of invention and style, without loading his memory. As a general rule, however, the speaker, whenever it is possible, ought to prepare beforehand, either mentally, or with the aid of the pen, a complete analysis of his discourse.

including the distinct statement of his proposition, the arrangement by co-ordination of the general heads, and by subordination of the secondary topics, together with a general statement of the thought contained in each paragraph. Such an analysis, which Rhetoric teaches us to prepare, may either be carried in the memory without loading it, or it may be committed to paper, and referred to while speaking, without any serious disadvantage. With a fine memory, the former method is to be preferred; with a poor memory, the latter. Thus the speaker will be fully master of the subject-matter, and of the general drift and arrangement of his discourse beforehand. The detailed elaboration of the thoughts, the construction of the sentences in advance, and the selection of the words, should be left to the inspiration of delivery; which, after some facility has been gained by practice, will enable him to carry on these operations strictly as sub-processes, unconsciously, and hence to suppress all their manifestations.

§ 63. **Such a mastery of the subject and discourse beforehand, relieves the mind from the most burdensome of the sub-processes, and from anxiety, and enables the speaker to employ his faculties in the proper work of delivery.**

1. *It relieves the mind from the most burdensome of the processes of invention and arrangement.*

These laborious intellectual operations, not being thrown upon the mind at the moment of speaking, cannot of course express themselves in the delivery; which is thus purged at once from all its worst

Mastery of the Subject. 121

faults, and most easily besetting sins. The speaker is thus left free to throw all his faculties and powers into those forms of activity which properly belong to the expression of thought, and the expression of which constitutes good delivery (§ 22).

2. *It relieves the mind from the paralyzing effects of anxiety and dread of failure.*

Being assured of his mastery of the subject, and, in substance, of what he wishes to say, the speaker is of course relieved from all distressing anxiety upon that score, and is enabled to avail himself of all the advantages which flow from a rational confidence (§ 28). Otherwise this anxiety may, in this method of speaking, easily amount to a paralyzing dread, and thus prove the most certain cause of entire failure. For such dread renders the speaker insensible to the power of the thoughts he wishes to express, and of the emotions which he would excite; it draws off all his faculties from the work of speaking directly to the audience; and it may even frustrate his power of invention. Under its influence he will be conscious of hardly anything but a desperate effort to find out what to say, and of paralyzing fear lest he should fail even in that. His delivery will consist of a painful expression of this and other such feelings, with all the vices of elocution therein implied. Even when the case may not be so bad as this, it will always approach it in the degree in which the processes of invention, and the dread of failure, predominate in the consciousness over those mental operations which properly belong to expression.

§ 64. **Such mastery of the subject and discourse enables the speaker to manage his time, pauses, pitch, transitions and force, in adaptation to his thoughts and sentiments, and to forecast the structure of his sentences.**

1. *The right management of these elements of expression is one of the chief excellences of speaking.*

The great power of elocution consists in the right management of these pauses, and transitions from one general or subordinate head to another; and in the delivery of the several parts more or less rapidly, and with greater or less force or stress of voice, with corresponding variations of pitch, according to the relative importance of each, and to the requirements of the ever-varying sentiment. All this depends obviously upon carrying in the mind at least some general knowledge of the drift and arrangement of the discourse, and of the character of the sentiments to be expressed.

2. *The want of this mastery of the subject occasions the following damaging faults.*

Without such knowledge of the general character of the discourse, the speaker is always liable to make his pauses too long between sentiments closely related, and too short between those more remotely separated; also, to exert his voice unduly on a subordinate passage, and hence to fail in force and animation where these are most required. Not knowing beforehand where his special points and telling passages are to come, he finds it almost impossible to deliver them with that due mental reference to their relative importance, and with that significant emphasis, which is no less essential to their proper effect, than the making of such points is to rhetorical power. The common effect of this, especially when the speaker is at no loss for words, is that he runs into a monotonous rant, rushing on from one topic, or sentiment, or paragraph, to another, without any of those significant pauses, and returns to the key-note, or middle pitch of the voice, and to the moderate or normal movement, or degree of rapidity, which are indispensable to mark the close of one topic or paragraph, and the commencement of another, and to give effect to the transitions of the thought.

3. *Such faults have the effect of a pointless discourse.*

These vices of elocution are extremely common, and no less fatal. For where the distinction of ideas and sentiments is thus lost in one monotonous stream of sound, the effect is similar to that which is produced in rhetoric by a discourse without points; that is, in which there is no distinction of general or subordinate heads, or topics, or paragraphs. In such speaking nothing stands out from the dead level; all is "flat," and soon becomes intolerably "stale and unprofitable" to the audience.

4. *Such mastery of the subject enables the speaker to forecast the structure of his sentences, with respect to clearness, emphasis, and other elements of expression.*

(1.) Forecasting the sentence is a sub-process,

more or less essential to the principal elements of expression. This forecasting of the structure of the sentence is properly a sub-process, but one which can hardly be carried on as such in extempore discourse, when the burden of all the operations which enter into it, is thrown upon the mind at the same time. Preparation beforehand is indispensable to the best success in it. Extempore speakers of the greatest power are sometimes wonderfully perfect in it, so that, whilst delivering one sentence, they are enabled to elaborate the next, in all its details. Others are less perfect; but probably it goes on in the minds of all, to a greater degree than we are commonly aware. Something of it is certainly indispensable to anything like a sustained melody of speech, to right emphasis, and to almost all the other elements of expression.

(2.) The want of it renders the speaking confused, and occasions false emphasis and intonation. For when the speaker has no conception beforehand of the structure of the sentence he is about to deliver, he knows not with what pitch, tones, or inflections to commence it, or to proceed with it, or to close it; and he has nothing to guide him in withholding or placing his emphasis. He can hardly fail, therefore, to deliver his sentences in a perplexed and unmelodious manner, and to beat the air with uncertain and unmeaning sounds. When the words upon which the emphasis ought to fall, are not anticipated by the speaker, it is impossible to deliver them with their due effect.

(3.) A good speaker always foresees his emphatic words. As the accomplished rider, in order to obtain a better view of the wall or ditch before him, raises himself in his stirrups, then settles himself again in his saddle, reins in his horse, gathers the animal's hind legs well under his body, and at the precise moment lifts his head with the bridle, applies the whip or spur, and launches himself over the obstacle, amidst the cheers of his more timid companions —so the accomplished speaker looks ahead for his emphatic words, and, as he approaches them, draws in his breath, and gathers up all his forces, and, at the precise moment, flings himself upon them, with all the impulse gained from the preceding restraint. A single word, spoken with such emphasis, will sometimes thrill a whole assembly. But nothing of all this is possible, of course, when the structure of the sentence is not foreseen, and the emphatic words cannot be anticipated.

§ 65. **Extempore speaking is more favorable than either of the other methods, to animation or vivacity, to the exercise of the sensibilities, to attention and sympathy, and to the consciousness of speaking directly to the audience.**

It would seem that the vulgar prejudice, as it has been regarded, against reading sermons, and in favor of extempore preaching, is not altogether a prejudice, but is founded on sound elocutionary reasons. For there can be little doubt that, with such preparation as has been indicated, extempore speaking is more favorable and conducive to good elocution, or power in delivery, than speaking either from manuscript or from memory. For although the sub-processes, in this method, seem to be more numerous and difficult than in either of the others, yet they are found by experience to be more manageable, and less damaging. The following are some of the particulars in which it is more favorable to good delivery than either of the other methods.

1. *It is more conducive to animation or vivacity.*

It has been well observed that "the least animated mode of delivering thought to others, is reading from a book the composition of another; the next in order is reading one's own composition; the next is delivering one's own composition from memory; and the most animated of all is the uttering of one's own thoughts, as they rise fresh in his mind."*

2. *To the exercise of the sensibilities.*

When a thought comes fresh into the mind, and chooses, as it were, at the moment, its own words, the meaning of these words is more present to the mind of the speaker, and their power is more felt, than when he recurs to them in the memory, or upon manuscript. In the same way, all the emotions in extempore speaking are more fresh and genial than when they are reproduced in the other methods. Hence "there is more natural warmth in the declamation, more earnestness in the address,

---

* Hints on Extemporaneous Preaching, by Henry Ware, Jr., Professor of Pulpit Eloquence and Pastoral Care, in Harvard University; an admirable little work, now out of print, but which ought to be republished.

greater animation in the manner, more of the lighting up of the soul in the countenance, and whole mien, more freedom and meaning in the gesture. The eye speaks, and the fingers speak, and when the orator is so excited as to forget everything but the matter on which his mind and feelings are acting, the whole body is affected, and helps to propagate his emotions to the audience."

3. *To the attention and sympathy of the audience.*

When the audience have the opportunity of following the thoughts of the speaker, as they germinate and spring up in his mind, and grow, and put forth their branches, leaves, blossoms and fruit, they feel an interest in the whole process, which they cannot feel when they know that everything has been "cut and dried" beforehand. And this interest of the audience reacts, as we have seen, by sympathy, to quicken all his faculties, and clothe his delivery with power.

4. *To the conciousness of speaking directly to the audience.*

When the thoughts of the speaker thus originate, and take on their peculiar forms, in presence of the audience, they naturally adapt themselves to the varying moods and states of mind, and to the different degrees of excitement, manifested by the audience, much more perfectly than is possible when they have all been written out beforehand. Hence the style in extempore speaking is commonly less abstract and involved, more simple and direct, than in other kinds. This directness of style naturally prompts to directness of speaking. The speaker more easily maintains himself in the conciousness of speaking directly to the people before him, and secures all the benefits which flow from this source of power in delivery.

CHAPTER VIII.

FACILITY OF REMEMBERING IN MEMORITER DELIVERY.

§ 66. A good memory is a source of power in all the methods of delivery, but most of all in memoriter speaking.

FACILITY of recalling what has been committed to memory, is necessary to the greatest power of elocution, in all the different methods of delivery. In the words of Quintilian, " it is not without reason that the memory has been called, the treasury of eloquence." But its most important relations, of course, are those which it bears to memoriter speaking, in which the whole discourse is delivered in the very words in which it has been prepared beforehand. In this method of delivery, it is indispensable that the discourse be so perfectly committed that it can be remembered without conscious effort; that every word shall seem to come of itself, in its proper place and connection. This might seem to be sufficiently evident, if the want of due attention to it were not extremely prevalent, and the cause of failure to many. It is necessary, therefore, to explain the influence of this source of power by applying again, in a manner precisely similar to that already employed in the case of extempore speaking, the fundamental principles of this art, as laid down in §§ 21—23.

§ 67. The sub-process of remembering and the fear of forgetting, in this method of speaking, when they predominate, render other sources of power unavailable, and the speaking consists of the expression of these mental operations.

1. *The predominance of these sub-processes is more damaging to elocution than those of invention and style.*

In this method of speaking the sub-processes, properly so called, are simply those of remembering what has been committed to memory. But in addition to these, which are extremely damaging when they become predominant in the consciousness of the speaker, from the fact that his speech has been imperfectly committed, he has to deal with the far more deleterious influence of anxiety, and dread of forgetting what he wishes to say. These influences are similar in their effects upon the mental state of the speaker, and upon his elocution, to those of invention and style, and of the dread of failure in finding out what to say, in extempore speaking. Commonly, however, they are much more enfeebling to the expression, for the reason that these sub-processes are more incompatible with the proper work of delivery.

2. *The predominance of these sub-processes in the consciousness of the speaker, renders other sources of power unavailable.*

Evidently when the speech has been imperfectly committed, or is remembered with difficulty, all the faculties of the speaker must be withdrawn from the proper work of delivery, that of speaking directly to the audience, and concentrated upon the mental toil of remembering what he has to say. Consequently he loses sight of the audience, and of the object which he aims to accomplish in their minds, and the desire to accomplish it ceases to be operative. He may have the best speech in the world, the greatest power of thought, and the most moving sentiments; but he cannot think of the matter of his discourse, because he is wholly occupied with the forms and sounds of the words which he is mentally struggling to lay hold of, and which threaten every moment to escape from his grasp. In this mental state the appropriate exercise of the sensibilities is paralyzed. He cannot feel the power of his thoughts, nor of the emotions which he wishes to communicate and excite in the audience, nor make the least effort to engage their attention or sympathy. He can exert no intellectual faculty but the memory. He can feel nothing but a horror of forgetting his speech, which enfeebles the memory itself, and often ensures the result which is most feared;—by overstrained effort to pump up the words into his mind, the pump itself often breaks down.

3. *It renders the speaking the expression of the mental operations of remembering, and of the dread of forgetting.*

When the speech is imperfectly committed, or remembered with difficulty, these are the mental states which predominate in the consciousness of the speaker, and which his speaking really expresses, with all the vices of elocution which this implies. The people before the speaker, being pushed out of mind, are pushed out of sight. His eye takes no note of their countenances, and cannot be employed in fixing their attention. It wanders around the room, or up to the ceiling, as if looking for something that it cannot find, or it is closed. In any case it loses all power of appropriate expression. Often it seems to be turned inwards, as if looking into the back of the head, in search of the words which the speaker is laboring to recall. In this case the countenance becomes so ludicrous that it makes one think of the words of a great comic writer, "Did you ever pick the lock of a cupboard to steal a bottle of wine? and did you ever think of the expression of your face while you were doing it?" In like manner, all the motions of the hands, arms and body, all the tones, inflections, articulation and emphasis, take on their peculiar forms, not from the mental operations which properly belong to speaking, but from these sub-processes; which ought not to manifest themselves at all, but which, being now the leading operations of the speaker's mind, it is impossible to suppress. All that he succeeds in expressing, and impressing upon the audience, is the mental toil of remembering words without meaning to himself, consequently without meaning to those who hear him; together with his torment of anxiety, and dread of forgetting what he wishes to say, and of breaking down in his discourse. The vices of elocution which are inseparable from this cause, it is not possible to enumerate, much less to describe

They are nearly all that are possible, and all in their most aggravated forms.

4. *It renders the training and practice of the art often ineffectual and injurious.*

Among the worst consequences of the predominance of these mental states, is that it renders a great deal of the training and practice of this art, not only ineffectual for good, but often productive of great harm. For where the teacher allows imperfectly committed exercises to be performed, all these vices of elocution are cultivated, instead of being corrected; and the faculty of speaking is dwarfed, instead of being developed. Prompting therefore ought never to be allowed. In all cases where the speaker cannot do without it, it would be far better not to speak at all. For this reason such exercises should be very short. On many other accounts also, a short speech is much better for training purposes than a long one.

§ 68. **The influence of this source of power upon the speaker and upon his delivery, is to render the other sources of power available, and to render the speaking expressive of those mental states which properly belong to delivery.**

1. *It renders the other sources of power available.*

By perfect facility of remembering, the speaker is relieved from all conscious effort of memory, and from the dread of forgetting what he wishes to say; and in this method of speaking, the processes of invention and style have no place. Consequently he is left free to throw all his faculties into the proper work of delivery. He can grasp in his mind the object which he aims to accomplish, and feel the desire of accomplishing it; he can hold himself in the mental state of speaking directly to the audience, with this object in view; and he can be moved himself with the power of the thoughts which he has to express, and of the emotions and passions which he wishes to excite. The natural flow of his sensibilities is unobstructed, and his mind is open to receive the whole volume of the sympathies of the audience, as it rolls in upon him. These, and in fact all other sources of power which are not inconsistent with this method of speaking, are thus rendered fully available.

2. *It renders the speaking expressive of those mental states which properly belong to delivery.*

The mental operations of remembering, being now carried on strictly as sub-processes, and so confidently as to give relief from anxiety and fear, have no tendency to manifest themselves in the delivery, which thus purges itself from the vices which they otherwise produce: whilst those operations which properly belong to the expression of thought, being predominant in the consciousness of the speaker, naturally express themselves; the speaking consists in the expression of them, and thus clothes itself with power. The speaker, having no occasion to withdraw his eye from the audience, even for a moment, can employ all its mysterious power to fix their attention, and to engage their sympathy. All his gestures, tones, inflections, articulation and emphasis, all the changes of force, pitch and time, in a word, all the elements of expression are now formed and governed by the sentiments which he has to express. Having the whole speech in his mind, he knows the relations of the several heads, topics and paragraphs to each other, and is thus enabled to graduate the degrees of force, pitch and rapidity of movement appropriately to every part; to return to the key-note and initial movement, as often as may be required, and to manage his pauses and transitions so as to produce their true and proper effect. And foreseeing the structure of every sentence, when he begins to speak it, he finds it easy to distribute his emphasis aright, and to deliver it in the most effective manner.

§ 69. **Memoriter speaking was the favorite method of the ancient orators, but, with a common memory, it is not so favorable to power in delivery as extempore discourse.**

Apart from experience, it would seem that, with due attention to its proper source of power, this method of speaking ought to be the most favorable of all to a good delivery. It is certain that it was the favorite method of the ancient orators; and it seems to have contributed much to their success in that forensic and deliberative eloquence, in which they have never been surpassed. But experience does not prove that this is the best method, but rather, except where the memory is naturally very superior, or has been very highly cultivated, that the sub-processes in this method are more unmanageable, and more incompatible with expression, than those of extempore speaking. Notwithstanding, its advantages are such that whoever aspires to become an orator, will do well to make full proof of his ability to follow it. If he should find his talents ill-adapted to extempore discourse, and can, by the most laborious culture, so develop and strengthen his memory that it will sustain him in this method, he will surely reap an abundant reward. It will be more likely to conduct such a man to excellence than any other. But if, after full proof of his memory, he should still find it inadequate, he can then apply himself to speaking from manuscript, which yet remains to be considered.

§ 70. The memory is capable of great development by exercise, of which we have many striking examples.

There is no faculty of the mind more susceptible of cultivation and improvement, and none which suffers more from neglect, than the memory. The ancient orators cultivated it to such a degree of excellence as is unknown, and almost inconceivable to us. Mithridates, king of Pontus, who held the Roman conquests in check for thirty years, in the first century before the Christian era, could talk with the people of twenty-seven nations under his government, in all their different languages. Quintilian gives us a number of instances of prodigious memory. Cicero informs us that Crassus, to whom he gives the palm of Roman eloquence, would sometimes dictate as many as six different parts of the same argument to six clerks at the same time, and then go immediately into court, and deliver the whole, without once looking at his papers. In the attainment of such results, they seem to have relied to some extent upon systems of artificial mnemonics, based upon the principle of the association of ideas, which, however, were not much approved of by some of their best writers, and which do not seem to be well adapted to our mental habits. No doubt, the most effectual means of cultivating this faculty, is to exercise it systematically in committing to memory the finest passages of eloquence. In committing our own discourses, we are greatly aided by such an analysis and arrangement as exhibits the closest logical connection between the thoughts.

CHAPTER IX.

FAMILIARITY WITH THE MANUSCRIPT.

§ 71. The importance of this source of power arises from the peculiar character of the sub-processes in speaking from manuscript.

THIS source of power refers exclusively to the method of speaking in which the speech is all written out beforehand, and read or spoken from the manuscript, either held in the hand, or lying under the eye of the speaker. Its importance arises from the fact that this method of speaking is one in such common use, especially among clergymen; and from the peculiar character and damaging effect of the sub-processes, whenever these become predominant in the consciousness of the speaker. In order to exhibit this latter point it will be necessary to make a third application of the fundamental principles laid down in §§ 21—23, precisely similar to those which have been made in extempore and memoriter speaking.

§ 72. The sub-processes in reading, and in speaking from manuscript, are the reverse of expression.

Reading, and speaking from manuscript, are so nearly allied, and the sub-processes in the two cases differ so little, and the light they throw upon each other is so important, that they require to be treated together. For in both the sub-processes are those of taking in the sense of the manuscript, or printed page, through the eye; and these processes are the reverse of those which belong to the giving out of the sense by the voice, and to the impressing of the thought and sentiment upon other minds. The mental operations of giving out, and of taking in the sense, are in the highest degree incompatible with each other. Certainly they cannot both go on together as leading states of the same mind; one or the other must fall into the rank of a sub-process. At least three of those leading states or mental operations, the expression of which constitutes good delivery (§ 22), namely, (*a*) the consciousness of speaking directly to the audience, (*b*) with the desire of accomplishing a given object, (*c*) which object is held firmly in the grasp of the mind, are diametrically opposed to the mental operations of taking in the sense through the eye. This opposition and incompatibility between these two classes of mental operations, both of which have to be carried on simultaneously, exhibits the great difficulty to be overcome in speaking from manuscript.

§ 73. **Reading, in which the sub-processes exercise a legitimate influence, is a more subdued, and a more difficult form of elocution than speaking.**

1. *The distinction between reading and speaking has never been precisely determined.*

Göthe, somewhere in Wilhelm Meister, has remarked that 'the limits between reading and speaking are very narrow,' but nowhere, it is believed, has he attempted to define them. In practice the two are often confounded. Speaking from manuscript commonly takes the form of a poor kind of reading, whilst reading not unfrequently merges in a wretched attempt at declamation. But the principles maintained in these Sources of Power, with respect to leading mental operations and sub-processes, will enable us to determine this point, and to understand precisely wherein these two forms of elocution differ from each other.

2. *Reading is a more subdued and quiet, speaking a more full and demonstrative form of elocution.*

This difference will be evident at once to any one who will compare the signs which each employs. For in reading, the tones are naturally less full and strong, the range of pitch and inflection is less extended, there is less variation in time and force, the articulation is less hard and sharp, the emphasis is less decided, and the gesture, if any be allowed, is less marked and striking, than in speaking. A reader in whom this quiet and subdued manner is wanting, who runs his reading into declamation, exhibits a want of taste, culture and refinement; whilst a speaker who simply reads his discourse, can exert but little power to impress his sentiments, or to inflame the audience with the emotions and passions which his words may be intended to express.

3. *The reason of this difference is that in reading, the sub-processes legitimately exercise a subduing influence, whilst in speaking, they require to be wholly suppressed.*

For it will be observed that in reading, we deliver the sentiments *professedly* as taking them in through the eye at the time, as gathering and reproducing them from the written or printed page before us; but in speaking, we deliver them as immediately our own, as welling up from within our own minds. Consequently in the former case, the elocution is *legitimately* affected and modified by the mental operations of taking in the sense, in which we are professedly engaged; whilst in the latter, no such influence or effect can be allowed. Good reading requires that these operations should not be wholly suppressed, but should exert a certain modifying influence upon the expression; whilst it is essential to good speaking that they should exert no influence upon the expression, but should be wholly suppressed. Now, as we have seen, these mental operations of taking in the sense through the eye, are precisely the reverse of those which belong to giving it out, and impressing it upon others; consequently the influence of these reverse mental operations legitimately affects the elocution in reading, as a negative quantity affects a positive one; that is, it reduces it from a more to a less full and demonstrative form of delivery. It is under this subduing influence that, in good reading, the tones are less full, the inflections less extended, the articulation less sharp and hard, the pitch, force and time less varied, the emphasis less pronounced, and the gesture less abundant, than in good speaking.

4. *Good reading is a more difficult form of elocution than good speaking.*

We should anticipate that this would be the case from the nature of the distinction between reading and speaking; and this anticipation is confirmed by all experience and observation. To read well any passage or author with which we are wholly unacquainted, is confessedly a very difficult thing. Hence we find many good speakers, for one good reader. The reason of this is the direct opposition and incompatibility between the mental operations of taking in the sense, and those of giving it out, at the same time. For although the former in reading do legitimately affect and modify the elocution, yet even in this case, if they become predominant in the consciousness of the reader, so as to overshadow and enfeeble the latter, the elocution is necessarily marred, or spoiled. The tendency to this is obviated, in some degree, by the great familiarity we attain with the forms, meanings and sounds of printed words, and by the wondrous perspicuity of the printed page, from which we are enabled to take in the sense, as the eye passes over it, with but little conscious attention or effort. In this way, the leading mental operations in good reading, continue to be those of giving out, rather than those of taking in the sense. A good reader, however, never undertakes to read in public a passage with which he is wholly unacquainted, except from necessity; nor then does he ever expect to do justice to himself, or his author. He always tries to familiarize his mind beforehand with the sentiments and words, in order to relieve himself as much as possible from the operations of taking in the sense, that he may be enabled to carry on these operations, in so far as they are indispensable, mostly as sub-processes, whilst his faculties are chiefly employed in the proper work of expression.

§ 74. **The degree of familiarity with the manuscript should be such as to enable the speaker to carry on all the operations of taking in the sense as sub-processes.**

In order to speak well from manuscript, it is indispensable that the mental operations of taking in the sense through the eye, should be suppressed altogether. Consequently much greater familiarity with the manuscript is required in this method of speaking, than with the printed page or manuscript in reading. In fact it must be such as to enable the speaker to carry on all these operations strictly as sub-processes, and for the most part unconsciously. If they become at all prominent in the consciousness, they cannot fail to manifest themselves in all the vices of elocution, to which this method of speaking is liable. Hence the speaker should never fail to make himself as familiar as possible, by previous study, with the matter of his discourse, including its structure, drift and general arrangement, so that the relations of the several parts to each other, and to the whole, may be carried in his mind. Also the first words of each general head, topic, paragraph and sentence, should be made so familiar in its relations to what follows, as to suggest its subject, object and principal thoughts. By a single unconscious glance at the first words of any sentence, the speaker should be able to possess himself of the whole of it, as nearly as possible in the words in which it is written. In the degree in which the speaker neglects this previous study, and his familiarity with his manuscript falls short of what is here required, in any of these particulars, will his delivery be enfeebled.

§ 75. **The influence of such familiarity with the manuscript enables the speaker to suppress the sub-processes, and to avail himself of all the other sources of power.**

This influence is similar to that of the last two sources of power, in the methods of speaking to which they respectively apply.

1. *It enables the speaker to suppress the sub-processes.*

By an adequate familiarity with the manuscript, and where a good degree of facility in this method of speaking has been acquired, all the mental operations of taking in the sense through the eye, are so reduced that they can be carried on strictly as sub-processes, of which the speaker is no more conscious than he is of standing on his feet, or changing his position, or of the motions of his lungs or diaphragm. He does not know when he turns the leaves of his manuscript, nor hardly that he has it before him. His glances at it are so momentary that they scarcely make a deeper impression upon his mind than the nictation of his eyelids. He is as unconscious of the use he makes of it as the skillful writer is of the manner of holding his pen, or the accomplished musician of fingering the keys of his instrument. Hence these mental operations are all suppressed; they have little or no tendency to express themselves in marring the delivery.

2. *It enables him to avail himself of the other sources of power.*

Being fully released from the embarrassment of these sub-processes, the speaker is enabled to throw all his faculties into the proper work of delivery. There is nothing to hinder him from entering, in the fullest manner, into the sentiments he has to express, nor to impede the flow of the emotions which the discourse, or the occasion, or the audience may be adapted to inspire. With only a momentary and unconscious reference to the manuscript, his eye and countenance are sufficiently free to exert their mysterious powers upon the audience, and to secure their attention and sympathy; whilst, in the full consciousness of speaking directly to them, he grasps them with his mind, and holds them up to the object which he aims to accomplish. Thus all the signs which he employs, both of voice and gesture, naturally take on their true forms, and the speaking is clothed with power.

§ 76. **The neglect of this source of power renders all others unavailable, and renders the speaking the reverse of true expression.**

The consequences of neglecting this source of power are similar, in most respects, to those which have been already exhibited, in the two preceding chapters; yet in one particular, at least, they are more damaging to elocution than any others.

1. *It renders all other sources of power unavailable.*

For where the previous study of the manuscript is neglected, the mental operations of taking in the sense through the eye, necessarily become predominant in the consciousness of the speaker; in which case, they either displace from the mind altogether, or degrade to a subordinate character, all those operations which essentially belong to the giving out, or expression of thought, and to impressing it upon other minds. Having his faculties pre-occupied, after a principal manner, with what ought to be wholly an unconscious sub-process, the speaker is unable to employ them in the proper work of delivery. Thus earnestness in speaking directly to the audience, for the accomplishment of his object, together with all the power which this gives to elocution, becomes impossible. The speaker cannot hold before his mind the object of speaking, nor feel the desire to accomplish it, nor be sensible of the power of the thoughts which he has to express; nor is his mind susceptible of sympathy with the audience, nor indeed of any other emotion which gives power to delivery. For there is no proper exercise of the emotional nature which corresponds to, or is consistent with the intellectual operation of spelling out the sense of a manuscript.

2. *It renders the speaking the reverse of true expression.*

(1.) This statement requires some qualification,

although its significance is not likely to be overestimated. For inasmuch as the mere utterance of the voice, and the pronunciation of words, in whatever manner, do necessarily imply something of the nature of speaking, these acts can never become in an absolute—but they do become in a qualified sense the reverse, or opposite of expression.

(2.) The reason is that the leading mental operations are the reverse of those which belong to expression. We have seen that the mental operations of taking in the sense through the eye, are the reverse of those which belong to giving it out, and impressing it upon other minds. Consequently, when the previous study of the manuscript is neglected, and these reverse operations become predominant in the consciousness of the speaker—that is, when he is wholly or chiefly occupied with the labor of transferring the sense of the words from the manuscript to his own mind—the speaking becomes chiefly expressive of this leading mental state; and hence it not only loses all proper adaptation to the communication of thought and feeling to other minds, but it actually consists, for the most part, of signs which are the reverse of expression.

(3.) This reason applies to all the signs employed. Hence all the phenomena of voice and gesture are not merely subdued, as in reading, where these reverse processes, from the greater plainness of the printed page, and other facilities, are still carried on subordinately (§ 73—4), but they actually become, in their characteristic elements, the reverse of all true expression. The eye, of course, is withdrawn from the audience, and confined to the manuscript, which signifies that the mind of the speaker is withdrawn from them, and from the work of speaking to them, and is otherwise employed. The expression of the countenance, when compared with the lighting up and glow of the features in eloquent delivery, becomes so absurd that Hogarth has chosen it for the subject of one of his masterly pictures, namely, that of the preacher spelling out the sense of his manuscript to a snoring congregation. In like manner, the motions of the hands, arms and body, all the gestures, and all the tones, inflections, articulations, and changes of time, pitch, force and movement, become, to a great degree, the reverse of those of an overflowing mind and heart, pouring out its fullness of thought and feeling, into the bosoms of an attentive and sympathizing audience.

(4.) The effect is like that of saying the Lord's Prayer backwards. Where these reverse processes thus become predominant in the consciousness of the speaker, their effect upon the speaking, and upon the audience, is very much like that of reading a passage of Shakspeare backwards; and in the pulpit, it may be compared to that of saying the Lord's Prayer backwards—a species of conjuring with sacred words, which, according to a popular superstition, has power to raise the devil. It is mournful to think how much of what is called preaching, is thus the reverse of all true expression. And where the case is not actually so bad as this, it is because these reverse processes do not become so prominent as to supersede all others, but are themselves held in check and modified by some remaining consciousness in the speaker, that he is yet talking to people, to effect some object in their minds.

§ 77. The chief temptation to neglect this source of power, which requires to be guarded against, is the security which the speaker derives from the manuscript.

1. *This temptation is very general and difficult to resist.*

The one great and sore temptation to neglect the previous study of the manuscript, which many speakers find themselves unable to resist, and which sometimes overcomes probably the best, arises from the very thing which gives this method of speaking its chief advantage, namely, that security which the speaker feels, with respect to the matter of his discourse, that he shall be able to reproduce it in some form, when he knows that he shall have it lying before him in manuscript, at the moment of delivery. It is necessary to guard against this temptation with the utmost vigilance, in order to avoid the most shameful failure, and in order to speak, in this method of delivery, with anything worthy of the name of power.

2. *Moral motives to resist it ought to be sufficient with clergymen.*

With all ministers of the gospel who speak from manuscript, the moral obligation which rests upon them, to neglect nothing which can aid them in impressing upon the people the great and precious truths which the Lord has put into their mouths, ought of itself to be sufficient to enable them to resist this temptation. For where this obligation is felt, and the importance of this source of power is duly appreciated, there is no difficulty. All that is required is a little time and labor, which grows less and less with every successive discourse. It would be easy to name examples of those who seem never to have neglected this source of power, and who have derived from it a rich reward of elocutionary power; so that from their delivery, one could hardly perceive that they had any manuscript before them, otherwise than from seeing them turn the leaves. But if the foregoing considerations should have no influence to remedy the enormous evil which arises from the prevalent neglect of this source of power, the church and the cause of Christ must continue to suffer, until a generation arises who shall have received from elocutionary training a better appreciation of its importance, or who shall be more faithful to their moral obligations.

§ 78. **The comparative advantages of this method of speaking are, that it relieves the mind from the laborious sub-processes of both the others, and enables the speaker, with due attention to its source of power, to employ all his faculties in the proper work of delivery.**

When the requisite degree of familiarity with the manuscript is secured, this method of speaking is nearly as favorable to power in delivery as either of the others. Indeed there can be little doubt that, for all who have not either the very highest endowments of memory, or at least a good faculty of extempore speaking, it is the best of the three. For it relieves the mind from all painful efforts of memory, and from the dread of forgetting, which are liable to prove so damaging in memoriter speaking; and from the vast labor of invention, arrangement and style, together with all the anxieties and fears to which these give rise, and which load the mind and delivery in extempore discourse. The perfect security which the speaker feels, when he has all that he wishes to say plainly written out before him, enables him to throw all his faculties and powers into the proper work of delivery. The sole difficulty which he has to overcome, is the necessity of some slight reference to his manuscript, which, with the requisite study of it beforehand, is, as we have seen, hardly any impediment. Nor will such a use of the manuscript give any offence to a moderately intelligent audience, after they have become a little accustomed to it. For when the speaker refers to it unconsciously, the audience soon cease to notice that he has any manuscript before him.

§ 79. A plain manuscript is of great importance in this method of speaking.

In order to facilitate the free and unconscious use of the manuscript, and to render this source of power available in the highest degree, it is evident that the discourse should always be written on the best of paper, and in the plainest chirography. For a plain and pure and perspicuous manuscript, not only facilitates greatly the mental operations of catching the sense by a momentary and unconscious glance, but also it encourages the esthetic feeling of the speaker, and makes it easier for him to feel confidence in what he has to say, in a similar way, though in a less degree, that beautiful paper and print enhances the beauty of the thoughts which are thus, as it were, appropriately dressed and adorned. On the other hand, a blurred, or blotted, or confused manuscript greatly increases the difficulty of these mental operations; and when the speaker relies upon gathering the sense of such a manuscript at the moment of delivery, he is liable to hesitate, and become puzzled, so that he must repeat the preceding words before he can succeed in spelling out his own meaning. What effect all this must have upon his elocution, and upon the audience, is known to those who have been bored by it, but which it is much easier to imagine than to describe. The only wonder is, that it does not have the effect ascribed to saying the Lord's Prayer backwards. It is well worth while therefore to rewrite a discourse, rather than to deliver it from a poor manuscript. Many a good sermon has been laboriously rewritten, chiefly for the purpose of purifying and perfecting the manuscript, in order to its more effective delivery.

CHAPTER X.

VITALITY, FAVORABLE MOODS, AND PHYSICAL REGIMEN.

§ 80. **Favorable moods are of great importance in delivery.**

ALL speakers have experience of favorable and unfavorable moods, which exert the greatest influence upon their elocution. So great is this influence that, after some experience, a good speaker would rather appear before an audience in a favorable mood with a feeble discourse, than in an unfavorable one with the best discourse he can possibly prepare. For in the former case, he is conscious of a certain inward fullness, from which his thoughts and feelings seem to overflow, like water from a full reservoir; in the latter, his mental and bodily action is feeble and slow, accompanied with labor and fatigue; in a favorable mood, he moves through his discourse as a stately ship through the water, when her sails are all filled with the favoring gale; in an unfavorable mood, he is like the same ship windbound, and thumping upon the shoals.

§ 81. **The favorable mood is chiefly dependent upon vitality.**

It is therefore a question of very great importance, how shall the speaker be enabled to command the favorable mood for each occasion of speaking? In order to answer this question, it is necessary to state that the favorable mood depends chiefly upon the condition and action of the vital forces of the physical organism. There is, indeed, a vitality of the intellect, of the sensibility, and of the will, as well as of the physical organism, but these cannot be regarded as independent of each other. For elocutionary purposes, they may all be conceived of as different modes of action, or forms of manifestation, of the one principle of life, health, strength and energy of body and mind. Now a full and healthy action of the vital forces will commonly, with due attention to regimen, enable the speaker to command the favorable mood for each occasion of speaking; whilst a defective, or exhausted, or obstructed vitality, arising from ill health, mental distress, fatigue, loss of sleep, excess in eating or drinking, or any other cause, will produce the unfavorable mood, and unfit the speaker for his work, just as in any other case which requires the most strenuous exertion of all the faculties and powers of body and mind.

§ 82. **A full vitality imparts to the voice its most effective qualities and powers, and a certain fullness and vivacity to the speaking; the want of it enfeebles the delivery in a corresponding manner.**

A full and healthy action of the vital forces is almost indispensable to these excellences of speaking, although it will not always secure them without the proper regimen. Its natural tendency is to these results.

VITALITY AND PHYSICAL REGIMEN.

1. *It imparts to the voice its most effective qualities and powers.*

Strength, purity, depth, compass and flexibility of voice are essential elements of power in delivery; and these depend upon a full and healthy vitality in the speaker, more perhaps than upon anything else. For although sometimes the most healthy and strong men have very poor and feeble voices, on account of abnormal defects in their vocal organism, and sometimes very feeble men have fine voices, yet there can be no doubt that a high degree of vitality is favorable, and a low degree is unfavorable to these qualities and powers of the voice, and to that easy management of it, which are essential to enable the speaker to endure the labor of addressing public assemblies without exhaustion or fatigue, and consequent feebleness in delivery.

2. *It naturally manifests itself in a certain fullness of utterance and delivery.*

This is a most excellent quality of elocution, in which the speaker's resources of physical strength, thought, feeling, voice, articulation, and all the elements of delivery, seem to be more than adequate to the demand. This at least is the impression which such fullness of utterance makes upon the audience. He seems to deliver himself without effort, constraint, or fatigue; or rather, it is not he that speaks; he opens his mouth, and it seems to speak itself. His thoughts speak, his emotions and passions speak; his whole delivery seems to overflow from an inexhaustible fullness. His tones are full and sonorous; his changes of pitch and inflection are full; that is, they rise and fall to the full pitch required by the sentiment; his articulation is full, distinctly enunciating every sound, without being labored, or overstrained; his emphasis is full, reaching the just measure of force and frequency; and the modulation or melody of his speaking is full, and satisfies the ear. In a word, fullness is the characteristic of the whole delivery.

3. *It imparts animation or vivacity to the speaking, for the want of which hardly any other quality can compensate.*

(1.) Vivacity is a beauty of motion, and depends upon vitality. As a beauty of motion it is allied to grace. Vitality, acting as keenness and rapidity of the intellectual operations, and as liveliness or quickness of sensibility, naturally manifests itself in those rapid, easy, sprightly, natural and expressive motions, in which vivacity consists. The motions in this case are those of the voice, in its changes of quality, force, pitch, inflection, time, emphasis and modulation; also those of the body, in its changes of position or attitude; those of the arms, hands and fingers, and of the features or countenance, but especially of the eye, which, in its amazingly quick, brilliant and varied expressions of the soul, is the most perfect type of vivacity. These are the motions in which animation in speaking consists, and by which a good speaker shows himself to be alive all over, even to his finger nails, and from which every part of his body seems to be no less eloquent than his words.

(2.) Animation, therefore, is a quality of speaking for the want of which hardly any other can compensate. For it is always interesting, and often charming, being almost sure to engage the attention and sympathy of the audience, and to bring out all the elocutionary power which is to be derived from that source; whilst a speaker without animation, however otherwise respectable, can hardly fail to put the audience to sleep.

4. *The want of vitality enfeebles the whole delivery.*

Where it is wanting, the speaker seems to be constantly overdrawing upon inadequate resources. The delivery is empty and dry; it lacks continuity, and sustained pressure upon the audience; it is labored, heavy and mechanical. The tones are dry and hollow, or rough; the inflections are either unnaturally extended, or they fall short; the voice is feeble, either too low, or strained to a high, shrill pitch; the emphasis is either neglected or artificial, and often misplaced; the articulation is either indistinct or overstrained; the general movement is either too slow or unnaturally rapid. The whole delivery is characterized by emptiness or hollowness, often making the impression of a want of sincerity and earnestness, and it renders the audience discontented and irritable. The speaking is consequently powerless to effect its object.

§ 83. Vitality and the favorable mood are dependent upon physical regimen, which varies for different speakers.

1. *The importance of such regimen arises from its influence upon the vitality.*

A high degree of vitality, and the favorable mood for speaking, are no doubt dependent to a considerable extent upon moral, but far more upon physical causes. Hence the importance of some physical regimen in preparation for each occasion of speaking. Some such preparation has been found indispensable by almost all great orators. It is impossible for any one who has never tried it, to be at all aware how much aid it will afford in exciting the requisite vitality, and in securing the favorable mood. It is a pity, therefore, that so many speakers who might otherwise excel, allow themselves to neglect it; for in consequence of this neglect, they are seldom able to bring more than half of their actual resources to the work of delivery.

2. *Such regimen varies for speakers of different temperaments and constitutions, so that only general rules can be laid down.*

Every speaker ought to make careful experiments for himself, to determine what may be best in his own case. There are, however, at least two general rules, by the observance of which it will commonly be found possible for healthy persons to command the requisite amount of vital force, and the favorable mood, for almost every foreseen occasion of speaking.

§ 84. The first general rule is that the speaker, in preparation for speaking, should eat less than usual, and the food which is taken should be nourishing and easily digested.

1. *The vital forces will not inspire the brain, and grind in the stomach, at the same time.*

The vital forces are hardly ever sufficient to inspire the brain with that intense energy and activity which public speaking demands, at the same time that they are employed in digesting a stomach full of food. Hence it is necessary to tax them as lightly as possible in the work of digestion, when they are all required for the expression of thought.

2. *In feeble constitutions this rule sometimes requires to be reversed.*

It holds good chiefly for healthy speakers. Where the general health is enfeebled, it may require to be reversed. It is related of the younger Pitt, that in the later years of his life, when his physical constitution was broken down, he always found it necessary, before delivering one of his great speeches in Parliament, to brace himself up with a hearty meal, and at least a couple of bottles of wine. Some of our greatest American orators also, as is well known, have required to be very highly stimulated before speaking. But these are examples fatal to imitate.

3. *The food should be nourishing and easily digested.*

Probably in most cases some food is necessary, but it should always be taken in a highly concentrated form, such as the yolks of soft-boiled eggs, so that as little in bulk and quantity as possible may yield sufficient nourishment.

4. *The best regimen for a healthly speaker is to abstain altogether from solid food.*

Where the physical strength is abundantly adequate, as it ought to be in all young and healthy speakers, the best regimen, approved by a copious experience, is total abstinence from solid food, and a cup of tea or coffee taken immediately before commencing to speak. This last particular may seem to be a small matter, but the genial and inspiring influence of a cup of tea upon an empty stomach, is much greater than one would suppose; and, rightly considered, nothing is unimportant which tends in the least to increase the speaker's power before an audience. When the physical strength is not fully adequate, some food should always be taken, or the consequence may be a greatly enfeebled vitality.

§ 85. The observance of this rule acts favorably upon the intellect, sensibilities, and physical organs; the neglect of it enfeebles all these.

1. *Its beneficial effects are as follows.*

These will be found, in a very short time, to be such that the speaker will never willingly neglect his regimen. For when the stomach is not overloaded with food, the intellectual operations are more keen and rapid, the sensibilities more easily excited, especially the affections are more tender and susceptible, than at other times. Also there is more room for the play of the breath, and lower organs of the voice. In fact the most marked effect of this regimen is upon the voice, which is rendered more deep and full and strong and flexible; so that in most cases its power will be found to be more than doubled.

2. *The evil consequences of neglecting it are the following.*

These are far more damaging than any one would believe who has never tried it. For it is almost impossible to speak well with one's belly full. It impedes the intellectual operations, dulls the sensibilities, clogs the affections, and thus renders the speaking dull and heavy and sluggish. It enfeebles the voice, renders it inflexible and unmanageable, and its deepest and richest tones unavailable. Often it manifests itself in forms hardly to be distinguished from total want of earnestness and unction. Accordingly we often find in the recorded experience of clergymen, such language as the following: "Yesterday, I preached twice to my beloved people; but oh! I was empty, empty—my wheels were taken off, and I dragged heavily through both the services." One can hardly read such a passage without wishing for an opportunity to reply, Ah! my friend, you were not empty, or it would have been much better for you and your people; neither were your wheels taken off—you were too full, you were overloaded—that was your trouble.

§ 86. The second general rule is that the speaker, in preparation for speaking, should take plenty of rest, and exercise in the open air.

1. *Fatigue implies the destruction of life.*

The physiological cause of fatigue, whether of body or mind, is always the destruction of life in a large number of the vital cells, of which the brain and nervous tissues, and in fact the whole organism of the body are composed. This destruction always takes place from strenuous and prolonged effort, whether of the intellect, sensibility, or will, or of the muscles of the body. In mental activity especially, and most of all, in that which is accompanied with anxiety, or grief, or watchfulness, this destruction of life, and consequent exhaustion of the vital forces, is very rapid and prostrating. But howsoever it is produced, it leaves the animal matter of which the defunct life-cells are composed, in a decomposed state, in which it is deposited in the blood, rendering this vital fluid thick, sluggish and pale.

2. *In a state of exhaustion, therefore, it is impossible to speak well.*

For when the speaker comes to his work, having his blood thus loaded with dead animal matter, all his faculties of body and mind are necessarily clogged and dull and sluggish. Evidently to speak with feeling, animation, or any other element of power, in such a physical and mental condition, must be the next thing to impossible.

3. *Hence the necessity of rest and pure air.*

For the blood in this corrupt state is poured into the lungs, where the dead matter is absorbed by the breath, and exhaled, or carried out of the system. Hence the absolute necessity, previous to speaking, of adequate rest, and of inhaling large draughts of pure air, in order to purify the blood, and restore its exhausted vitality. This implies, of course, that every cause of fatigue should be avoided, and that some time previous to each occasion of speaking should be spent in the open air, which should also be accompanied with more or less, but never fatiguing exercise of the voice.

4. *This rule is of special importance to clergymen.*

The extensive and laborious intellectual and moral preparations for speaking which are required of clergymen, and which render their observance of this rule somewhat difficult, render it also of far greater importance for them than for other speakers. Abundant experience proves its necessity, and that it brings a rich reward of increased power in delivery. For the reason that clergymen are compelled to speak twice or three times on Sunday, they ought never to leave the study later than at noon on Saturday. The remainder of the day should be devoted to rest, and gentle exercise in the open air, and the night to sound and refreshing sleep. In like manner, the intervals between the Sunday services should be devoted to rest. For by such adequate refreshment and renovation of the vital forces, the preacher may make the latter services as animated and interesting as the former, which is the more desirable in order to overcome the increasing temptation of church-goers to stay at home in the afternoon.

5. *The neglect of this rule by clergymen is both a folly and a sin.*

The habit in which so many clergymen indulge, of sitting at the study table until late on Saturday evening, thus rendering the few hours of unrest which follow, totally inadequate to restore their exhausted vitality, cannot be too strongly condemned. No necessity of intellectual preparation, whether theological or rhetorical, can justify it; for thus a vast proportion of the fruits of such preparation is thrown away, from inability to deliver with any power what they have prepared. This habit is a sin, as well as an inexcusable folly—in many cases the consequence of previous sin and folly, namely that of neglecting their study work on the earlier days of the week—sins and follies, which receive their just punishment often in such feebleness of delivery as renders the attempt at preaching the gospel on the part of those who are guilty of them, a miserable failure; and which not unfrequently result in the early ruin of their health, and blasting of all their hopes of usefulness. For whatsoever is worthy of the name of preaching requires the exercise of the whole vital force of a sound and healthy man. To preach the gospel takes all there is or can ever be in any man.

CHAPTER XI.

SELF-CONTROL.

§ 87. Self-control is essential to the consciousness and manifestation of reserved force in speaking—'the spirit of the prophets must be subject unto the prophets.'

THIS divine precept teaches us that the prophets were not allowed to lose the entire control of themselves, even in their inspired revelations, and ecstatic visions. The orator also is a prophet in a true though limited sense, and it is equally necessary that his ardor and passion, however high they may rise, should never be allowed to get the better of reason and propriety. He must never allow himself to be transported wholly out of himself, but there must always be a clear method in his prophetic raptures. It was said of Demosthenes, that even in his most impassioned eloquence, he never was known to lose control of himself; and this enabled him to control and direct the storm which he raised, and on which he rode. In like manner, all truly great orators, in their noblest flights, whilst transporting their audiences, keep the mastery of the situation by remaining masters of themselves. Their speaking is always characterized by a certain consciousness and manifestation of reserved force, by temperance and propriety or becomingness of utterance and gesture, which are essential to genuine and sustained power in delivery.

§ 88. **The consciousness of reserved force enables the speaker to feel secure; in its natural manifestations it awakens the confidence of the audience, and the want of it enfeebles delivery.**

1. *The consciousness of power is itself a source of power.*

This consciousness of reserved force applies to thought, feeling and utterance. It is practically the same thing as the consciousness of power. A very large proportion of the power in delivery, which is exerted by great orators, results simply and directly from this consciousness of power, or from the sense of security inseparable from it, which they have acquired by successful practice. Feeling that they carry within them, while speaking, abundant resources of thought, emotion and utterance, which are as yet untouched, they are enabled to exercise that rational self-confidence which is essential to the employment of their faculties in the proper work of delivery (§ 28—1).

2. *Its influence upon the speaking is as follows.*

It enables the speaker to forecast his emphatic passages and words, to graduate the amount of force and time which may be appropriate to the several parts of the discourse, to manage his pauses and transitions with their proper effect, and to speak with due deliberation and right emphasis.

3. *It awakens the feeling of security in the audience, and excites their imaginations.*

This consciousness of power, or reserved force, in its natural manifestations, produces upon the audience a great effect. For the feeling of security in the speaker awakens a corresponding feeling of security in them. They follow him with confidence, who leads them with confidence. They follow him with expectation, because he seems to be leading them into a region of inexhaustible abundance, of which as yet they have had only glimpses from a distance. When they see that he is rather restraining than exerting himself, they feel the greater interest in, and ascribe a higher value to what he actually says, than they would if they saw that he was giving out, at every step, all that there was in him. Their imaginations are more excited, and their sensibilities are more deeply affected, by what is veiled or held back, than they would be if all were openly and fully expressed. For in elocution, as in rhetoric, partial and judicious suppression is one of the most powerful forms of expression. The stifled sob of the bereaved mother, at the grave of her dead child, is more affecting than the loud and boisterous wail of uncontrolled anguish.

4. *The want of this consciousness of reserved force confuses and enfeebles the elocution, and begets distrust in the audience.*

When the speaker feels that he is exerting himself to the uttermost, and has nothing to fall back on, this renders him anxious and uncertain, which enfeebles all his faculties. In case he is at no loss for words, he will speak too rapidly, piling sentence upon sentence, and paragraph upon paragraph, without due deliberation, pauses, or discreteness in his delivery. In other cases, his timidity and anxiety will be so great as to cause hesitation and confusion. His voice now trembles; his tones, inflections, articulation, emphasis and gesture, are hurried and flurried. His whole delivery becomes uncertain, confused and ineffectual. By such signs the audience soon perceive that the speaker is drawing upon all his resources, that he cannot rise, and must soon decline, consequently their expectations are all unfavorable, their sensibilities are chilled, and their imaginations are paralyzed. They now follow him, if at all, with a feeling of insecurity; he seems to them to have less and less power the longer he speaks; and they experience a sense of relief, instead of regret, when he comes to a close. It is only in his peroration that the speaker can safely exert himself to the utmost, and leave himself without the consciousness of reserved force.

§ 89. **The loss of the control of himself causes the speaker to lose control of his audience—when overcome by emotion he should pause.**

When the speaker loses control of himself through excess of feeling, the sympathetic relations between himself and his audience are broken up, and thrown into confusion. His emotions, being so much deeper and more powerful than theirs, become incomprehensible to them; they can see no good reason why he should be so deeply moved, and consequently they are unable to sympathize with him. Not only then does his passion fail to excite in them corresponding emotions, but it produces a contrary effect. Thus, as we have seen (§ 45—3), weeping, or other signs of grief or sorrow, in excess, or when there does not seem to be sufficient cause, has the effect of drivelling. Whenever, therefore, from such excessive emotion, the speaker loses control of himself, he necessarily loses control of the audience. He can no longer grasp them with his mind, nor hold them in his mental grasp up to the object which he aims to accomplish. Excessive feeling, moreover, soon exhausts the vital forces, and renders the delivery of the subsequent parts of the discourse tame and feeble, both in itself, and by contrast with that which has preceded. If, however, in spite of himself, the speaker should at any time be overmastered by a flood of emotion, his only safe course is to pause until he recovers his self-control; in which case, if the pause be not too long, it may prove the most effective part of his delivery.

§ 90. **Self-control is essential to propriety in speaking, which consists in the adaptation of the delivery to the character of the speaker, the sentiments, the occasion, and the circumstances, and which is of great importance in elocution, as in all art.**

1. *Propriety, the* UT DECEAT, *as understood by the ancient authors, and by Shakspeare, depends upon self-control.*

(1.) Cicero insists much on propriety, as one of the chief essentials to power in oratory; but he gives us little aid in determining wherein it consists, or how it is to be attained. His directions are often reiterated in such words as the following : " In most things [pertaining to oratory] that which is most useful is, I know not how, the most becoming."

(2.) Quintilian is more full and explicit, where he tells us, in substance, that propriety consists in the adaptation of the delivery to the character of the speaker, the sentiments, the occasion and circumstances of speaking. This seems to cover the whole ground.

(3.) Shakspeare teaches us that the chief element of this excellence has its source in self-restraint, or self-control. In the passage cited below (§ 91), he gives us the following direction : " Suit the action to the word, and the word to the action ; with this special observance, that you o'erstep not the modesty of nature.... For in the very torrent, tempest, and, as I may say, whirlwind of your passion, you must acquire and beget a temperance that may give smoothness." We see in this that the most glaring violations of propriety arise from the loss of self-restraint, and consist in thus ' overstepping the modesty of nature.'

2. *In all art nature requires to be imitated with a certain modest reserve.*

Truth to nature does not consist in copying her material forms with servility, or minute particularity. Often this will produce nothing better than a caricature. For such is the eternal distinction between nature and art, that we reverence in nature what we cannot tolerate in any attempt at the imitation of her sacred mysteries. That which in nature is simple truth, will often, when minutely copied, become an outrage on propriety. A certain creative freedom is characteristic of all true art. For nature can be truly imitated only by generous spirits, who sympathize with her inner life; never by servile copying of her mere material forms.

3. *This modest reserve is one of the most important lessons of ancient art.*

So imbued with it were the Greeks, and so keen was their sense of propriety with respect to it, that they seem to have regarded it as a fundamental esthetic law. Hence in expressing even the most violent passions, such as the despair of Niobe, the grief and anguish of the father of Iphigenia at Aulis, and the physical torment of Laocoön and his sons, the whole exhibition is subdued, and kept within the strictest limits of propriety. The Greek artists have, indeed, been criticised for the rigor of their works in this respect, as being untrue to nature; for nature often expresses herself in very unlovely forms. Despair, *e g.* grins, gnashes the teeth, and tears the hair. Yet the Greeks were right, and their critics are wrong.

4. *The principle applies in all its force to elocution.*

For it is certain that whoever, in speaking, should attempt to portray the anguish and despair of lost souls, by showing us how they grin, and gnash their teeth, and tear their hair, would 'overstep the modesty of nature,' would outrage all propriety, and instead of producing the impression at which he aimed, would excite disgust or ridicule; and all this, for the reason that the sacred mysteries of nature require to be imitated or expressed in art with a certain reverent modesty, and delicate reserve.

§ 91. Propriety is the principal point insisted on in Hamlet's direction to the players.

This whole subject of propriety, in its relations to self-control, is that which is chiefly insisted on by Shakspeare, in that masterly direction to the players which he has given us in the Hamlet, and which for its own intrinsic excellence, no less than for the weight of the great poet's authority, ought to be carried in the memory of every student of elocution, and of every public speaker. It has, indeed, far greater value for the orator than for the actor, for the reason that violations of propriety, that is to say, violations of truth and nature, ought to be, if they are not, more offensive in public speaking upon grave and momentous occasions, than they can be in play-acting. This whole passage is therefore reproduced here:

"Speak the speech, I pray you, as I pronounced t to you. But if you mouth it, as many of our players do, I had as lief the town crier spoke my lines. Nor do not saw the air too much with your hand—thus, but use all gently. For in the very torrent, tempest, and, as I may say, whirlwind of your passion, you must acquire and beget a temperance that may give it smoothness. Oh! it offends me to the soul to hear a robustious, perriwig-pated fellow, tear a passion to tatters, to very rags, to split the ears of the groundlings; who, for the most part, are capable of nothing but inexplicable dumb shows and noise. I would have such a fellow whipped for o'erdoing Termagant. It out-Herods Herod. 'Pray you avoid it. . . . . Be not too tame neither; but let your discretion be your tutor. Suit the action to the word, and the word to the action; with this special observance that you o'erstep not the modesty of nature. For anything so overdone is from the purpose of playing [speaking]. Oh! there be players [speakers] that I have seen play [speak], and heard others praise, and that highly—not to speak it profanely—that neither having the accent of Christians, nor the gait of Christian, pagan, nor man, have so strutted and bellowed, that I had thought some of nature's journeymen had made men, and not made them well, they imitated nature so abominably."

§ 92. The means of acquiring self-control in elocution are the same as in other things.

The means of cultivating the power of self-control do not come within the province of elocution. They are in speaking the same as in every other department of life, viz: practice and familiarity, in the circumstances and sphere of activity in which we most desire to exercise it, together with the feeling of our moral responsibility with respect to it, and of its indispensable importance to success, not only in speaking, but also in everything else For without self-control, man is not man, but only a fractional part of the vast and fatal forces of nature.

§.93. Conclusion of the sources of power in delivery.

It is hoped that the views which have now been presented, will tend to obviate the prejudices against this art, which have arisen out of the attempt to construct it from the nature and laws of the organs of speech, and of articulate sounds, without reference to the sources of its power, in the intellectual, moral and esthetic states and workings of the mind and soul of the speaker. It is hoped and believed, also, that the study of this noble and beautiful art, as here laid down,—so far from having any tendency to generate coldness, mannerism, or a mechanical style of speaking, which to some extent have been the fruits of the study of it, conceived as an art of mere manner, without reference to the states of the soul which it is intended to embody, symbolize and express,— will so stimulate and quicken the faculty of speaking and of eloquence, that the student will be enabled to derive the greater benefit from the studies which are to follow, of the manner and forms which are characteristic of eloquent speaking, that is to say, of the Elements of Power in delivery.

PART II.

THE ELEMENTS OF POWER IN DELIVERY.

  I.—Articulation.
  II.—Accent.
  III.—Pronunciation.
  IV.—The Qualities of the Voice.
  V.—The Powers of the Voice.
  VI.—Pitch and Inflection.
  VII.—Time and Pause.
 VIII.—Force.
  IX.—Emphasis.
  X.—Gesture.

CHAPTER I.

METHOD OF TREATMENT.

§ 94. The treatment of the elements of power in delivery includes phonology, and the laws of expression.

1. *Phonology is the science of vocal sounds.*

The principles and laws of this science are exhibited in the chapters on the vocal organism, articulation, accent and pronunciation. It is hoped that these chapters may have an interest for the scientific phonologist, independently of their bearing upon the art of Elocution. For the objects of this art, however, they of course include a discussion of the general relations of phonology to expression.

2. *The laws of expression include the applications of phonology to the expression of thought and sentiment.*

These laws are treated of chiefly in the chapters on the qualities and powers of the voice, pitch and inflection, time and pause, force, emphasis and gesture. The Elements of power in delivery, moreover, are properly divided into those of the voice, and those of gesture; of which the former are beyond all comparison the most important, and constitute nearly the whole of what is commonly included in Elocution.

§ 95. **The following treatment of the Elements aims at more perfect generalization, and greater simplicity, than have been hitherto attained.**

The Elements, as distinguished from the Sources of power in delivery, have been copiously and ably treated, both by European and American authors. Most of these works, however, are characterized by great minuteness of analysis and detail, and contain a vast multitude of special rules and precepts. The author of this work, in addition to the original views presented, especially in phonology, has carefully reworked, and brought to the test of experiment, whatever he has retained from previous writers. He has also aimed to effect a more thorough and perfect generalization and simplification of whatever he has found wrought out to his hand; whilst, at the same time, he has excluded a great amount of what, in his judgment, has been overdone, and thereby rendered practically unavailable.

§ 96. **The treatment here proposed is founded upon Dr. Rush's Philosophy of the Human Voice.**

1. *This is a work of the greatest value.*

This author, it is believed, has done more to lay open what was before veiled and mysterious in speech, and to explain the phenomena of power in delivery, than any other, whether of ancient or modern times. His work ought to be patiently studied by every one who would become acquainted with the nature, powers and adaptations of that wondrous vocal instrument, which is brought into play in every spoken word. In fact, before it was pub-fished, anything like a scientific exposition of the vocal elements of expression was hardly possible. Consequently all subsequent writers, at least in this country, who are worthy to be consulted, have drawn from it, sometimes with, and sometimes without acknowledgment, both their materials and most of their results.

2. *But the work is ill-adapted to the wants of practical students.*

For those whose only and immediate aim is the attainment of power in delivery, this work can seldom be of much service. For few persons, except the most earnest teachers, or physiologists led by a purely scientific interest, can be expected to master its difficult and often obscure details; and even where this seems to have been accomplished, as in the case of some teachers, the result has not always been satisfactory. For the author's plan embraces only the treatment of the Elements, excluding entirely the preceding Sources of power, from which, as we have seen, the very life and spirit of delivery must be derived. Consequently the tendency of the work, if the student be not on his guard, is to displace from his consciousness those mental operations which properly belong to the giving out or expression of thought and feeling; to render predominant in his mind the rules and precepts of the art, together with all those other mental actions which, in good speaking, are carried on strictly as sub-processes; and thus, to cherish and develop the vices of elocution, rather than to correct them.

3. *The evils which have arisen from the various attempts to reduce it to practice, are here guarded against.*

The great difficulty with the work of Dr. Rush, then, is not that it is not true, but that it is limited to the discussion of the Elements of power, and that it is too minute and abstruse for practical use. The system here exhibited is founded upon it, for the reason that otherwise truth and nature must have been violated: whilst the evils which have arisen from previous attempts to reduce its minute and obscure statements to practice, are sufficiently guarded against, it is hoped, by the preceding exhibition of the Sources of power; by avoiding, as far as possible, the multiplication of rules and precepts, and by insisting upon comparatively a few general principles.

CHAPTER II.

THE VOCAL ORGANISM IN RELATION TO VOCAL CULTURE.

§ 97. Great importance of vocal culture.

1. *The voice is of paramount importance in delivery.*

This would seem to be sufficiently obvious. If it were not, we might refer to the following authoritative declaration of Cicero: "For the effectiveness and glory of delivery, the voice, doubtless, holds the first place."

2. *It is capable of as great improvement for speaking as it is for singing.*

The wonderful improvement of which the voice is capable, is well understood, and fully appreciated by the teachers and proficients in the sister art of music; but it is not so · generally understood that it is capable of equal development, by systematic training and exercise, for purposes of oratory. Yet every teacher of elocution can refer to numerous instances, in which voices very inferior by nature, have attained, in a short time, by a few simple exercises, to great excellence; have, in fact, doubled, tripled, and even quadrupled their speaking power. There would seem to be no instances in which diligence in such exercises, with due care to guard against overstraining the organs, has not resulted in great improvement; whilst it may be said, in general, that the untrained, or uncultivated voice, is worth little more for public speaking than it is for singing.

3. *The culture of the voice was highly appreciated by the ancients.*

Among the Greeks and Romans there was a distinct class of teachers, called *phonasci*, or *vocists*, who devoted themselves wholly to the training of the voice, and who carried their pupils through a most laborious and protracted course of exercises. In order to develop strength of voice, e. g. they prescribed declamation whilst walking, running, climbing, and lying upon the back; and in this last position, with weights on the chest. The results which they attained have been already alluded to (§19) as exemplified in the thunder-words of Demosthenes, and in the sweetness, compass and power of Cicero's voice. Similar pains are taken in vocal culture, and similar results are obtained by the great singers and tragedians of modern times.

4. *Modern neglect of vocal culture for public speaking is inexcusable.*

In consequence of this neglect it is a rare thing to hear a public speaker with a voice of great purity, compass and power. And this in clergymen especially, is the more inexcusable, because they have to rely upon the same instrument, namely, that of oral speech, which was so assiduously cultivated by the ancient orators, for infinitely higher and holier purposes than were ever conceived of either by Cicero or Demosthenes.

§ 98. **Some knowledge of the vocal organism is essential to the greatest success in the culture of the voice.**

Some general acquaintance with the physiological structure and functions of the vocal organs, is found by experience to be a great help in elocutionary training. We might expect that this would be so, for such reasons as the following.

1. *Many of the organs are strictly voluntary.*

A large class of these organs are immediately under the control of the will. Such *e. g.* are the lips, tongue, and breathing muscles. Some knowledge of these, in their more important functions, is of great utility. For one of the most common and fruitful causes of poor speaking, is that these organs either have never been reduced under the complete and facile control of the will, or that this control has become impaired, or well-nigh lost, from careless or slovenly habits. Hence, in order to attain, or to recover such control, it is found necessary that the attention of the student, in his exercises, should be directed to their functions and modes of operation, that the power of his will may be brought to bear immediately upon them.

2. *Many other of these organs are semi-voluntary.*

It is difficult to impart the necessary information with respect to the voluntary organs, without taking into view some of the more important of those which are semi-voluntary. These are such as the soft palate, and the vocal chords, which perform their functions in speaking in part according to vital laws, to a certain extent like digestion and nutrition; which, indeed, never operate better than when the whole physiological process is unknown. Yet even in the case of digestion, where it has become impaired, the knowledge of its laws is found to aid in its restoration. Similar aid, but much greater in degree, do we find in the knowledge of the structure and functions of the semi-voluntary organs of speech, which, though not immediately, are yet mediately and indirectly under the control of the will. These organs are put in operation by acts of the will, directed not immediately upon them, but upon the utterance of the sound, or the speaking of the word, which is in the mind. When such a volition is put forth, they instinctively respond to the action of the will, thus assuming the positions, and performing the actions, which the word or sound requires, although their functions and operations, and even their existence, may be unknown to the speaker. But even this instinctive action of the semi-voluntary organs is aided, in no small degree, especially where it is imperfect, by a competent knowledge of their structure and functions. Experience fully verifies this fact, however difficult of explanation it may be.

3. *A minute acquaintance with the physiology of the organs is not required.*

It seems to have been supposed by some authors, that a minute and technical knowledge of the physiology of all the vocal organs, was indispensable to successful training and practice in elocution. But that this is not the case, is proved by the facility with which we learn to speak in our earliest childhood, and by the unquestionable success of the ancient *phonasci*, who can hardly be supposed to have had much acquaintance with this department of modern science.

§ 99. **The principal vocal organs are the diaphragm, the lungs, the bronchial tubes, the trachea, the larynx, the vocal chords, the mouth, and the ear.**

A complete analysis would exhibit more than thirty distinct organs, each of which performs important functions in the speaking of every word. These here enumerated, however, are the principal ones, and the exposition of them will suffice to impart the necessary information in the training and practice of elocution. The subject is one of considerable difficulty, upon which physiologists have not come to a perfect agreement among themselves, and to them the student is referred for a more full and detailed exposition of the vocal organism.

§ 100. **The diaphragm is an elastic muscle of the abdomen, one of the principal organs of breathing, and capable of being brought under complete voluntary control.**

1. *The diaphragm is the lowest in position of all the vocal organs.*

This organ is a very elastic muscle which divides the stomach below from the lungs above. Hence it has been called, "the roof of the stomach, and the floor of the lungs."

2. *Its principal vocal function is that of expanding and contracting the lungs in respiration.*

This function it shares with the pectoral muscles, not necessary to be described here. When the diaphragm is feeble, the speaker is incapable of drawing in a full breath, and of expelling it again with adequate force. When it is not under perfect voluntary control, he is unable properly to economize his breath; whence impurity of tone, unnecessary fatigue, and exhaustion in speaking. When it is fully developed, and under good control, neither breath nor voice will commonly be found wanting.

3. *It is capable of great development, and of being brought under perfect control.*

That this organ is capable of being brought under perfect voluntary control, any one may perceive for himself, by voluntarily distending and contracting the abdomen, without allowing the air to enter or escape from the lungs. But apart from the exercise which Elocution prescribes for this object, this control of the muscle is commonly very imperfect. It is also capable of great development by the proper exercises, for want of which it is often very feeble.

4. *The exercise required is that of expanding and contracting the muscle by the direct action of the will.*

The object of this exercise is to develop the organ in size and strength, and to bring it under the most perfect control of the will. The exercise should be performed, sometimes whilst holding the breath, at other times whilst drawing in and expelling it;

now, as slowly and equably as possible, in order to obtain the utmost length or duration of each respiration—again, more and more rapidly and forcibly, in order to obtain the greatest possible force of breathing. These exercises should be performed once or twice a day, for a half or a quarter of an hour at a time, with the waist free from stricture, the clothing loose, and the stomach empty, or but little distended with food. From such exercises, the waist soon begins to increase in size, and this increase measures the development and increased power of the diaphragm, and other breathing organs. We see from this, that hardly any more effectual means for injuring their voices could be devised, than the tight lacing of the ladies.

§ 101. The lungs depend for their power as a vocal organ upon the quantity of breath which they are capable of receiving.

1. *The lungs are composed of hollow cells for containing the breath.*

This organ is the next in order above the diaphragm. It consists of two lobes, which are composed of a vast multitude of vesicles, or little hollow cells, into which the breath pours when the chest is expanded, and from which it is expelled when the chest is contracted, by the expansive and contractile action of the diaphragm and pectoral muscles. The greater or less quantity of breath which the lungs are capable of containing, is, then, other things being equal, the measure of their power as a vocal organ. Large and capacious lungs, therefore, as commonly indicated by a broad and full chest, are a grand desideratum for the public speaker; as a narrow chest and small lungs are extremely unfavorable.

2. *The lungs are capable of great development.*

The reason of this is that a considerable proportion of the air cells, of which they are composed, are not, commonly, even in perfectly healthy persons, brought into use; that is, they are not expanded or filled with air in respiration, but they lie in a collapsed state; and those, moreover, which are utilized, are not expanded to their utmost capacity. Now, by the proper exercises, the former class are brought into use, and the latter are increased in size and capacity.

3. *The exercise required for the development of this organ, consists in inhaling the largest possible draughts of pure air.*

This exercise should be performed whilst standing in an upright position, or leaning back and thrusting out the chest; also, whilst walking, running, and declaiming out of doors. In this way the girth of the chest is much increased; by which is measured the increase in number and capacity of the utilized air cells, and the development of this organ, together with the breathing apparatus.

§ 102. **The bronchial tubes and the trachea are the pipes which convey the breath to and from the lungs, and give resonance to the voice.**

1. *These organs are shaped like an inverted tree.*

They are next in position above the lungs.

Taken together with the larynx, the next to be considered, they constitute what is called the windpipe, which resembles, in its external form, an inverted tree. The bronchial tubes are the inverted twigs and branches; the trachea is the trunk, and the larynx, the upturned root. The bronchia are a great number of little air-pipes, whose lower extremities, the tips of the twigs, are inserted into the upper surface of the lungs. These tubes, as they ascend, are all brought together so as to form two principal branches, which, as they continue to ascend, are finally consolidated in one main or trunk. This is the trachea, which ascends through the neck to the throat, and terminates in the larynx, the root of the inverted tree.

2. *These organs have two vocal functions, that of airpipes, and that of resonant cavities.*

Both of these functions are of the greatest importance. The first is that of conveying the breath to and from the lungs and the mouth, the second is that of giving resonance to the lower tones of the voice. This resonance, or re-echoing of the sound, in the cavities of these organs, is that which gives their peculiar character and force to the low tones, or, as they are often called, the chest tones of the voice. Hence the larger and more capacious these organs, the greater the depth, fullness and volume of the vocal sounds in speaking.

3. *The exercises for their development are the same as those prescribed for the diaphragm and the lungs, together with that of sounding the low tones.*

These organs are very liable to become obstructed by secretions from colds and bronchial diseases, which soon destroy the powers of the voice for public speaking. In order to guard them from such injuries, and to develop them to their greatest possible capacity of resonance, they should be much exercised in breathing large draughts of pure air, and in sounding the lower and lowest tones of the voice. In this latter exercise, however, extreme care is necessary not to overstrain the organs; otherwise the voice may be irreparably spoiled. Moderately exercised as above, these organs rapidly attain a great increase of their capacity and power. Such exercise, moreover, will often cure inveterate bronchitis, which is caused by inflammation of the tubes, when all other remedies have failed.

§ 103. **The larynx and vocal chords are the organs for generating the sound of the voice.**

1. *The larynx is a bell-like cavity, in which the sound of the voice is generated.*

The position of this organ is that of the root of the inverted tree, of which the trachea is the trunk, and the bronchia are the branches. It is formed by an expansion of the trachea, and causes that protuberance in the throat which is called "Adam's apple." One of its principal vocal functions is that of resonance.

2. *The vocal chords are the organ by which the sound is generated.*

The larynx is crossed about the middle of its bell-like cavity, by two parallel muscular chords, the *chordæ vocales*, the extremities of which are fastened to its sides, and which are capable of being lengthened or shortened, with increase or diminution of their tension, by the muscular action of the organ. These chords are made to vibrate in unison by the breath, as it is expelled from the lungs; and by these vibrations the breath is converted into sound. Thus the sound of the voice is generated. The contrivance is precisely similar to that of a double-stringed Æolian harp. The sounds thus produced derive their peculiar human character from the resonance which takes place in the bell of the larynx, also in the windpipe, mouth, and cavities of the nostrils.

3. *The force or loudness of the sound depends chiefly upon the amplitude or breadth of the vibrations.*

When the breath is expelled from the lungs with greater or less force, it causes the vocal chords to vibrate through a greater or less breadth; and these vibrations, according to their amplitude, produce a sound of greater or less force or loudness. Hence the loudness of sound of which the voice is capable, depends ultimately upon the strength of the diaphragm and pectoral muscles, by which the breath is expelled. It depends also in no inconsiderable degree upon the size of the resonant cavities, inasmuch as the same concussion will produce a louder sound in a large bell, than it will in a small one.

4. *The pitch of the sound depends upon the number of vibrations in a given time.*

The vocal chords are capable of being tightened or relaxed by the muscular action of the larynx; thus the number of vibrations in a given time is increased or diminished, and the sound thereby produced, is made either higher or lower in pitch. The chords in women and children are normally about a third shorter than in men; and whilst the common range of the human voice is about three octaves, the pitch of the child's, and of the female voice, is an octave higher than that of the adult male. The lowest tone which the ear perceives, is due to about thirty vibrations in a second; in the highest, the vibrations run up to as many as four thousand.

There are other vocal organs, such as the pharynx or swallow, immediately connected with the larynx, and sharing, to a certain extent, its function of resonance, but which do not seem to require any exposition.

5. *The exercises for these organs are the same hereafter prescribed for the cultivation of the ear and voice* (§§ 105—4; 174).

These exercises are of great importance to preserve these organs in a healthy state, and, especially, free from the secretions produced by the various affections of cold. For among other effects of these is that of *aphonia*, or voicelessness, in which the person is unable to speak, except in a whisper, and which is produced by the inflammation and clogging of the vocal chords, so that they cease to **vibrate.**

By the action of those interior and exterior organs of the mouth, which are employed in articulation, namely, the soft and hard palates, the tongue, gums, teeth and lips, the volume of sound is still further differentiated into those elemental sounds of human speech, which are represented by the letters of the alphabet, and which compose syllables and words. The amazing power of differentiation possessed by these organs, appears from the fact that by their action the volume of homogeneous sound, which streams from the vocal chords, is differentiated into all those innumerable particular sounds, and combinations of sounds, out of which the whole structure of human speech is built up, and which express all the thoughts, and shades of thought, and all the infinitely diversified sentiments, of which the human mind is capable.

4. *The exercises required for this organ should aim to develop its resonant and differentiating capacities.*

There is no doubt about it, a large and well formed mouth is a great advantage to the public speaker. In general, the larger the internal cavities, the better the resonance of the voice. Often, however, the resonant capacities are not half utilized; and they are capable of considerable development by the conscious effort to speak with a full voice. The organs of differentiation should be exercised systematically, for the purpose of bringing them under the most perfect and facile control of the will, and of obtaining the greatest possible precision in the formation of all the sounds of speech. More specific directions will be given in the exercises prescribed for articulation (§ 114).

§ 105. The ear is the organ of perception and discrimination of sounds.

1. *Hearing is essential to speaking.*

The importance of the ear, in its relations to speech, is evinced by the fact that persons born deaf are also dumb. This statement hardly needs qualification from the artificial, feeble and confused articulation which such persons, with laborious effort and instruction, may sometimes acquire. For properly we learn to speak in no other way than by imitating the speaking sounds we hear from others (§ 12—3). It is by the ear alone that the mind acts in the perception, and discrimination from each other, of those numberless modifications of sound, of which the speech of man is composed, so as to enable the other vocal organs to reproduce them at pleasure.

2. *The functions of the ear in speaking are the same as in singing.*

The excellences and defects of this organ, with respect to speaking and singing, are precisely the same. Its chief excellence in both consists in fineness, or keenness, or delicacy of discrimination from each other of the different sounds, with respect to quality, force, pitch and time. For it is in the infinitely various modifications of sound, with respect to these particulars, that both speaking and singing chiefly consist. To these, however, must be added articulation, which is essential in speaking, but not absolutely essential in singing. Accurate discrimination of sounds, therefore, is at least as indispensable in speaking as it is in singing.

3. *The most faulty speaking implies the discrimination of sounds.*

When in teaching elocution an illustration is drawn from music, we often hear from the pupil some such reply as this, " O, I know nothing of music. I have never been able to distinguish one sound from another." Now this, as we here see, is always a mistake; and if it were true in any case, that person could never have learned to speak. For it is no less an essential function of the ear to discriminate, than it is to perceive sounds. Let the student turn his attention to this point, and he will find that he has been distinguishing sounds from each other all his life, with respect to all those modifications of them which enter into music, except that of concord or harmony. For with this exception, all the modifications of sound which belong to music, are employed in speech, and can be represented by the notation of the musical score (§ 3; 13—2).

4. *The training and practice which the ear requires are the same for speaking that they are for singing.*

The elementary exercises prescribed by the teachers of vocal music, are the best possible for the training of the ear, as also for the development of the qualities and powers of the voice, for public speaking. These exercises, moreover, are hardly of less importance in the one case than in the other. For one of the main causes of feebleness in delivery, is that the ear is dull by nature, or has become so from inattention and careless habits, and requires to be trained up to discriminate with delicacy and facility. Many, it is true, fail to recognize the importance of these exercises, from the fact that good speakers may never have learned to sing, and good singers are often miserable· speakers. But it must be remembered that what is here stated and enforced, does not rest upon an assumed identity, but upon the obvious analogy, between these kindred and sister arts, and upon abundant experience. These exercises should be continued at least until the student is able to ascend and descend the diatonic scale with accuracy, and to distinguish with facility the principal intervals of the second, fifth and eighth. Even without this, much may be accomplished in elocution, but it is hardly possible to attain the best results; and there are few persons whose ears are so dull that they cannot learn to do all that is here required with very little trouble.

CHAPTER III.

ARTICULATION.

§ 106. Articulation is the formation, and jointing together into syllables, of the elementary sounds of speech.

ARTICULATION properly includes both these operations. The above definition is strictly according to the etymology of the word, which is derived from *articulus*, signifying both a little member, and a little joint. The articulating organs come into full play, both in the formation of the elements, and in jointing them together into syllables; as also in forming syllables into words; but their use in this last case belongs under the head of pronunciation, of which articulation, strictly taken, is the fundamental and controlling element.

§ 107. The first division of the elementary sounds is that of vowels, semi-vowels, and consonants.

1. *Analysis of the sounds is indispensable.*

In order properly to exhibit articulation as an element of power in delivery, and to afford the most effectual aid in acquiring it, we shall find it necessary to analyze and classify the elementary sounds of the English language, and to determine precisely by what organs, and by what position or action of these organs, they are formed. Such classifications may be made in different ways, with some special utility belonging to each. The first and most common of these is that which is here given.

2. *The principle of this division is that of vocality.*

The word, vowel, *vocalis* in Latin, signifies a vocal sound, that is, a sound made by simply vocalizing the breath. The vowels, therefore, are those elementary sounds which have the highest degree of vocality, or a perfect vocality. The semi-vowels, according to the signification of the word, are those which have a lower degree of vocality. The consonants are those of such feeble vocality that they are supposed in this nomenclature, though falsely, as we shall see, to be incapable of articulation by themselves, and to require for this purpose to be joined with vowels.

3. *This division is neither accurate nor complete.*

No strict definition can be given of any of these classes; they are not distinguished from each other by any sharp dividing lines, or exclusive differential characteristics. This is evident from the name, semi-vowels, denoting a class of sounds which are neither one thing nor the other, but a mixture of vowel and consonant. The word, consonant, is altogether objectionable, not only because it includes, as we shall see, sounds which are fundamentally different, but also because it intimates that such sounds cannot be formed or articulated by themselves, which certainly is not true. In addition to this, a number of the sounds classed as vowels are in reality diphthongs, or double vowels; whilst several of those commonly represented as diphthongs, are nothing but simple vowels. Notwithstanding, this classification is often convenient, and cannot be wholly dispensed with.

§ 108. A rigorous classification of the elements is impossible, for the reason that they are a series from the greatest openness to perfect closure of the organs.

It would seem that a perfect classification of the elementary sounds upon the above, or any other one principle, is not possible. The reason of this is that they constitute an irregular and complicated series, from the greatest openness to the most perfect closure of the organs of articulation. The sounds which are made with these organs in the most open position, naturally have the highest degree of vocality; those with the organs brought nearer together, a less degree of vocality; and those with the organs closed, the least, or none at all. But this series is irregular and involved, so that the sounds cannot be arranged in an unbroken order. It is easy, indeed, to fix the extremes. On the side of the greatest openness and strongest vocality, we have the sound of a as in far; and on that of perfect closure, those of b and p. But these last two letters represent two wholly different classes of sounds, of which the former have an imperfect vocality, the latter none at all. The extremes in the vowel series are, on the one hand, a as in far, and on the other i as in pin. All the other vowels and diphthongs have less vocality than the former, and greater than the latter; but a as in all is formed by an openness very different in the position of the organs, from that of i as in pine. After these come the sounds which are formed by the organs in near approach, but not in actual contact; such as y, w, r; next, those formed by a partial contact, such s, z, v, sh, th; and finally those formed by perfect closure of the organs, such as m, l, g, k, d, t, b, p. Now there is no point in this irregular gradation from the greatest openness to perfect closure, at which the series can be divided with rigorous precision. This difficulty cannot be entirely overcome, but there are other classifications of much greater practical utility than the preceding.

§ 109. **The second division of the elements is that of tonic, subtonic, and atonic sounds.**

This classification, upon the same principle, is more nearly accurate and complete, and of far greater practical utility, than the former. The principle is the same also with that of the division into *surd* and *sonant*, first established by the native Sanskrit grammarians, and now of universal application in linguistic science. The tonics correspond to the vowels and diphthongs, and consequently have the highest degree of vocality. The subtonics have a lower degree of vocality, and include the semi-vowels, together with all the consonants which have any vocality at all. They are the sounds represented by the following signs, y, w, wh, r, l, z as in zone, and as in azure, th as in then, j, v, ng, nk, n, m, g, d, b. Both the tonics and subtonics are included in the class of sonants. The atonics are altogether destitute of vocality; they are mere articulations which check or stop off the whispering breath. They correspond to the class of surds, and are as follows: h, th as in thin, sh, s as in see, f, k, t, p. We shall find that these distinctions will enable us to simplify the rules of English pronunciation, and to explain a great number of its apparent anomalies.

§ 110. The subtonics and atonics are again divided into hard, soft and feeble checks.

The principle of this division is the degree in which the sound or breath is checked by the organs of articulation. From the fact that all these sounds are more or less checked, as to the outward flow of the vocalized or non-vocalized breath, by contact, or a near approach to contact, of the articulating organs, it is found necessary to classify them upon this principle. The special utility of this classification is that it directs the attention of the student to the peculiar checking action of the articulating organs, and thus enables him to obtain a more perfect control over them, in the performance of this function. The feeble checks are those articulations by which the sound or breath is checked in the least degree, either by a very slight contact, or a near approach to contact, of the articulating organs. They are the sounds represented by y, w, wh, r, l, h. The soft checks are those in which the contact is soft or partial, yet such as to restrain the sound or breath in a sensible manner. They are represented by z as in azure and zone, th in then and thin, j, v, sh, s in see, f. The hard checks are those in which the outflow of the sound or breath through the mouth is entirely stopped off by the hard or firm contact of the organs. They are represented by ng, nk, n, m, g, d, b, k, t, p.

§ 111. **The subtonic hard checks are divided into nasals and subnasals.**

The principle of this division is the degree in which the resonance of the sound is thrown into the nasal cavities. These sounds are all properly hard checks, because the outflow of the sound through the mouth is perfectly stopped off by a hard contact of the mouth organs. But in the nasals, the resonance of the sound takes place along the whole line of the nasal cavities. They are represented by ng, nk, n, m. In the subnasals, the resonance is in the back cavities of the nostrils, where these open into the mouth. They are represented by g, d, b.

§ 112. **The number of the elementary sounds in the English language is forty-five.**

The number of these sounds is estimated by Prof. Day at thirty-two, by Dr. Rush, at thirty-five, and by Mr. William Russell, a practical elocutionist and teacher of the art, at forty-three. But none of these estimates is anything more than an approximation. In fact the elementary sounds may be regarded as more or less numerous, according as they are more or less minutely analyzed. For the shades of difference, especially between some of the vowels, are often extremely fine, so that it is a nice question whether they are to be regarded as the same, or different; whether *e. g.* a as in all, and o as in nor, whether i as in pin, and y as in folly, are distinguishable or not. The number here given is preferred not so much for its rigorous accuracy, as for its superior utility in the training and practice which Elocution prescribes. There are, moreover, certain transitional sounds, which enter into the formation of syllables and words, and which will require consideration hereafter (§ 148—4). The elements, as arranged in the table below, are represented by the italics.

TABLE OF THE ELEMENTS.

TONICS.		SUB-TONICS.			ATONICS.	
arm	*eve*	Feeble Checks. { *yet* / *way* / *when* / *ray* / *lay*	Hard Checks. { *azure* / *zone* / *then* / *joy* / *vile*	Nasals. { si*ng* / bli*nk* / *nay* / *may* / *gay* / *day* / *bay* } Sub-nasals.	F.C. { *h*ay	Soft Checks. { *th*in / *sh*un / *s*ee / *f*ee
all	*not*					
ask	*nor*					Hard Checks. { *k*ey / *t*ell / *p*ay
hat	*old*					
care	*hut*					
fate	*full*					
pine	*rule*					
pin	*use*					
err	*oil*					
pet	*our*					
20		17			8	

§ 113. The elementary sounds are all capable of voluntary modification.

The foregoing anylysis does not pretend to exhibit all the differences between the elementary sounds, for they are all capable of voluntary modification. Thus the tonics and subtonics may all be deprived of their vocality, and reduced to atonics, by voluntarily stopping off the vibrations of the vocal chords; in other words, they may all be articulated in non-vocal, or whispering breath. If this were not so, it would be impossible to speak in a whisper. Again, there are other differences between subtonics and atonics, besides that of vocality; otherwise it would be impossible to distinguish the cognates, b, p,—d, t,—g, k, when uttered in a whisper, from each other. For the position of the organs in the formation of each pair of these cognates, is very nearly, if not precisely the same. So also the hard, soft and feeble checks may be, and often require to be articulated in a more or less hard, soft, or feeble manner; the breath, whether vocalized or not, requires to be expelled more or less forcibly, and the organs to be placed in contact, and separated again, more or less abruptly. This voluntary modification of the elements is of the utmost importance, in order to express all the distinctions of thought, and all the varieties and shades of the gentle, tender, elevated and passionate, or violent emotions.

§ 114. **The proper exercise in the elementary sounds consists in forming them with the utmost precision, both separately, and in their easier and more difficult combinations.**

1. *These exercises are of great importance.*

The student should not fail to exercise his articulating organs in the formation of all the elementary sounds. These exercises should be continued until the breathing, vocalizing and checking organs are brought under perfect control, and to the highest degree of efficiency and facility, in the formation of every sound.

2. *The attention should be directed to the position and action of the organs in the formation of each sound..*

For this purpose, the aid of a teacher should be secured, if possible, to explain the position and action of the organs in each case, and to exemplify the correct sounds, together with the student's errors and defects. Where a teacher canot be had, reference should be made to the description of the position and action of the organs in the formation of each sound, which is given under the head of pronunciation. For we find by experience that where all other attempts fail to correct faults in articulation, this method commonly succeeds.

3. *The exercises should be upon the sounds in their several classes, according to the preceding analysis.*

The common rule, "Take care of your consonants, and the vowels will take care of themselves," though it expresses an important truth, is not altogether a safe one. The student should be careful to practice on every sound by itself, especially the semi-vowels and consonants without vowels attached, paying no attention to the notion, that a consonant cannot be articulated without the aid of a vowel, which groundless notion it is difficult to imagine how people with ears should ever have entertained.

(1.) The tonics should be carefully rendered with the precise distinctions between those that are most nearly alike.

(2.) The subtonics should be formed with as full a vocality as can be given them.

(3.) The atonics, with no vocality at all, *i. e.* with the non-vocalized, or whispering breath.

(4.) The hard, soft and feeble checks must be carefully formed, with the exact position and action of the organs, with the precise degree of contact required by each class, so that the vocal or whispering breath may be perfectly stopped off, or partially, or very slightly checked.

(5.) The nasals and subnasals require to be practiced on with special reference to the resonance of the voice in the nasal cavities, and to the different resonance in the two classes, as being in the former class along the whole line of these cavities, and in the latter, confined to that portion of them where they open into the mouth.

4. *Exercises in whispering breath are of great importance.*

There is no more important exercise in articulation than that which consists in speaking in a whisper. The reason is that thus the distinction of vocality and non-vocality is eliminated, and the only way of making one's self understood, is by the strength and precision of the articulation. The attempt to speak in a whisper to persons at a little distance thus brings out all the speaker's articulating powers.

5. *Exercises in the more difficult combinations of the elements.*

In addition to the above exercises, the student should practice his organs in the more difficult combinations of the elementary sounds, repeating them in succession as rapidly as possible. The following are examples of such difficulties.

> That morning, thou that slumbered'st not before.
> Nor slept'st, great ocean, laid'st thy waves to rest,
> And hush'dst thy mighty minstrelsy.

But the best possible examples for this purpose, are those with which children amuse themselves, in practicing and gaining control over their articulating organs, such as the following.

> Theophilus Thistle, the thistle-sifter,
> Sifted a sieve of unsifted thistles.
> If Theophilus Thistle, the thistle-sifter,
> Sifted a sieve of unsifted thistles,
> Where is the sieve of unsifted thistles,
> That Theophilus Thistle, the thistle-sifter, sifted?

§ 115. **A syllable consists either of one elementary sound, or of several combined.**

The sound which is represented by the letter a, forms a perfect syllable by itself in the indefinite article; on the other hand, the word, helm, composed of four distinct elementary sounds, is yet but one syllable. In the formation of syllables, whether of single elements, or of many thus jointed together, the voice obeys certain laws, which depend, in great part, upon the nature of the elements, as exhibited in the preceding analysis. These laws require now to be unfolded.

§ 116. **A syllable is an articulate sound formed by a single impulse of the voice.**

It is the distinctive character of a syllable, that it is formed by a single impulse or movement of the voice. This is equally the case whether the syllable consist of a single elementary sound, as a in aright, or of several in combination, as the word, strands, composed of seven distinct elements. If this latter word be incorrectly pronounced in two syllables, str-ands, as such words often are, it will be found that it takes two such impulses. This characterization of the syllable we owe to Dr. Rush.

§ 117. **The division into syllables is caused sometimes by the strength of vocality in the tonics, sometimes by the relation of different elements to each other, and sometimes it is arbitrary.**

A great deal has been written in answer to the question, what causes the division of the elements into syllables? and much confusion has arisen from the attempt to reduce this phenomenon to one cause. The truth is that there are at least three such causes, which operate either separately, or in combination with each other.

ARTICULATION. 211

1. *The principal cause is the strength of vocality which belongs to the tonics.*

The strength of vocality in the tonics is such that no two of them can be fully sounded with a single impulse of the voice. In the case of a diphthong indeed, two of the tonics are blended in one, and articulated by one impulse; but this is done by withholding from the latter of them its full tonic vocality, and making it coalesce with the former. If the full tonic vocality be given to the latter tonic, the diphthong will be resolved, and two syllables will be the result. Thus oi as in oil is a diphthong; but if the full tonic vocality be given to i, the diphthong is resolved into two syllables, and articulated with a double impulse of the voice. Hence the word, navy, *e. g.* is of two syllables, and cannot be of more or less, because it contains two tonics, and no more, each with its full tonic vocality. It follows from this that there cannot be more than one full tonic in one syllable.

2. *A second cause is the relation of different elements to each other.*

This relation is often such that no single impulse of the voice can be made to comprehend some of the elements in combination with others; in other words, the change of position of the organs, in passing from one to another, is often so great as to necessitate the closing of one vocal movement, and the commencing of another. This cause, together with the preceding, operates in the case of the word articulation, *e. g.* which is of five syllables, and cannot be pronounced in less, because it contains just five tonics (io of the last syllable, representing u), and because the relation between the sounds of ar and ti, ti and cu, cu and la, la and tion = shun, is such that no two of them can be joined together in a single phonetic impulse. This cause operates on the most open sounds, *i. e.* those which are made with the organs in the most open position, equally with the closest sounds. Thus in the artificial combination, i o e u a, there are necessarily just as many syllables as there are elementary sounds, because these elements are all tonics, and because the relation between them in juxtaposition, is such that no two of them can be made by a single vocal impulse.

3. *The division into syllables is sometimes arbitrary.*

This is the case in such words as higher, flower, goer, mower, and many others, which may be pronounced correctly in two syllables, or incorrectly in one, so as to be indistinguishable in sound from hire, flour, gore, more. Accordingly in poetry, they are freely used as one or two syllables, according to the requirement of the metre.*

---

* It is with no little regret that the author feels obliged to differ here, and on other still more important points, from that eminent scholar and phonologist, Prof. Wm. Whitney, from whose masterly criticisms upon the Standard Alphabet of Prof. Lepsius, valuable aid has been derived in the foregoing analysis of the elementary sounds. Prof. Whitney maintains (Trans. Am. Or. So. vol. viii. pp. 359-60) that the above characterization of the syllable, as an articulate sound formed by a single impulse of the voice, "is not of the slightest value." "Just as much," he says, "is a whole word, or a whole sentence, uttered by a single impulse of the voice." The true reason why the word *navy*, e. g, is of two syllables, he says, "is clearly this: among the four sounds of which it is composed, there are two which are of so much more open position, more sonorous and continuable, than the others with which they are connected, that they make upon the ear the impression of two phonetic impulses." But this impres

ARTICULATION. 213

§ 118. **Every syllable is composed of a radical and a vanishing sound.**

We are indebted to Dr. Rush also for our knowledge of this curious fact. The commencement of every syllable is its radical, and the close is its vanishing sound. The latter naturally rises through a whole tone of the musical scale above the former. Let the syllable, fate, *e. g.* be spoken without emo-

---

sion is fallacious, because "the distinction of syllables is primarily made, not by the mouth of the speaker, but by the ear of the hearer."

COMMENTS.—1. The learned professor teaches us here that the distinction of syllables depends upon the juxtaposition of open and close sounds. Now this is probably the first explanation that occurs to every inquirer, but it is soon found to be untenable. Take, *e. g.* the combination given above, i o e u a, which includes all the most "open" and "sonorous" sounds in the language, and it is found impossible to articulate them in a less number of syllables than there are elements. But if Prof. Whitney's explanation were correct, they might all be articulated as one syllable.

2. In the word *navy*, the sounds, *n* and *v*, are just as "continuable" as *a* and *y*; in fact they are all alike capable of indefinite prolongation. This only remaining reason, therefore, can have nothing to do with the distinction, any more than those which are expressed in the words "open" and "sonorous."

3. Why should the two syllables of the word *navy* uniformly "make upon the ear the impression of two phonetic impulses," if there be nothing in the manner of their formation which corresponds to this impression? and why should the ear of the hearer make the distinction of syllables, if no such distinction is made by the mouth of the speaker? It would seem that here is a uniform effect without any cause at all. Is not this uniform impression, made upon the ear, of two phonetic impulses, good evidence that the cause of this impression is the fact of two such impulses? If not, what becomes of the principle, which none knows better than Prof. Whitney himself, but which he seems to have forgotten for the moment, that speech consists wholly of sound, and that we truly apprehend its nature by the ear alone?

4. In fine, let Prof. Whitney apply his sharp and cultivated ear to the syllabic distinction between *vile* and *vial*, *cream* and *create*, and he can hardly fail to perceive the single vocal impulse in the monosyllables, and the double impulse in the dissyllables; and consequently that the juxtaposition of open and close sounds has nothing to do with the matter. Or, to take a still stronger case, let the sounds *pa-a*, with *a* as in *far*, be articulated in two distinct syllables. Here now is a simple repetition of the most "open" and "sonorous" sound in the language, with no close sound to divide the word into two syllables, and yet the two are just as distinct as those of *apple* or *battle*.

tion of any kind, and, upon close attention, it will be perceived that it opens with a full impulse of the voice, and closes with a *vocule*, or vanishing sound, which rises in a continuous slide, a whole tone above the opening pitch. But on monosyllabic words, on all accented syllables, and on the last syllable of every word, this *vocule* may fall instead of rising from the radical pitch; and it may rise or fall through more than one tone or interval. Whether it rise or fall, and whether through one or more intervals, depends upon the character and strength of the emotions to be expressed. This fact, as we shall see hereafter, is of primary importance in the expression of all the emotions and passions.

§ 119. A tonic, or a strong subtonic, enters into every syllable, and in no syllable can there be more than one such sound.

1. *A full tonic sound forms the basis of every syllable.*

In order that an elementary sound should be capable of forming a syllable by itself, or in combination with feeble elements, it must be either an open sound, *i. e.* one formed without contact of the organs, or one which, in spite of slight contact, has nearly or quite a full tonic vocality; consequently, it must be capable of indefinite prolongation. The reason of this is that only such sounds can take the full radical and vanish, with which every syllable opens and closes. Hence a syllable cannot be formed of atonic sounds, such as t k s p f, either separately, or in any possible combination with each other. Hence also a syllable cannot be formed of those subtonics which, by reason of the strength of their articulation, or check, have but a feeble vocality, such as b d g z j, either separately, or in any possible combination with each other, or with atonics. But each of the tonics is capable of forming a syllable; so also are those subtonics which are formed without, or with a very slight contact, or which, by reason of their anomalous nasal character, have a full and strong vocality. The subtonics which are thus capable of forming syllables, are y, w, r, l, n, m, which, therefore, are the true and proper semi-vowels of the language. Examples of their forming syllables will be given under each of these elements in pronunciation.

2. *There can be but one tonic in each syllable.*

This is strictly true of the tonics as enumerated in the table (§ 112). But it must be borne in mind that several of these are properly compound tonics, or diphthongs. Thus, a as in fate, i as in pine, and oi as in oil, are diphthongs, all closing with the sound of i as in pin. O as in old is also regarded and treated by the Sanskrit grammarians as unquestionably a diphthong, composed of a and u; and hence in French, one of the branches of the great Sanskritic family, it is still represented by au, as in baume, pronounced, bome. Ou as in our represents to the eye the elements of which it is composed. With this explanation, there must be as many syllables in every word as there are tonics. The reasons for this have been already given (§§117

1, 2); viz. the vocality of the tonics is so full and strong that each requires a separate impulse of the voice; and their relation to each other is such that no two of them in juxtaposition, can be formed by one and the same impulse. Thus no such combination as ao, eo, eu, io, oa, ua, uo, can form a single syllable. In order that any of these signs should represent a single syllable, either one of its elements must be suppressed, as e in euphony and yeoman, or one of them must represent some other sound, as u represents w in persuade.

§ 120. **All the sounds which are capable of forming syllables by themselves, are essentially variable in length.**

Properly there is no such thing as an essentially long or short vowel. For not only all the vowels, but all the sounds which are capable of forming syllables by themselves, are essentially variable in length, and capable of being prolonged or shortened indefinitely. Thus a as in fate, commonly regarded as an essentially long vowel, is long in fate and face, but short in fatu'itous and face'tious. Again, the so-called short vowel i as in pin, is short in minute', but as long as the longest in sing'ular; whilst the so-called long vowel u as in use, in the same word, is as short as the shortest. In like manner, a as in all, and e as in eve, are long in al'tar, and de'viate and short in auspi'cious and educe'.

ARTICULATION. 217

§ 121. The length and strength of syllables depend upon accent, emphasis, and the number and vocality of their elements.

We shall find hereafter that syllables are made long by the temporal accent, and are still further lengthened by emphasis. But besides these two causes, the length of a syllable depends upon the number of elementary sounds of which it is composed. When several additional sounds come after the tonic, their power to lengthen the syllable gives us the explanation of the rule in Latin prosody, that a vowel is long by position; for even when the following consonants are not in the same syllable as written, they often are as it is uttered by the voice. Thus the syllables, length, strength, starch, flash, wasp, are essentially long, because they are composed of a large number of elementary sounds; whence they cannot properly be made to stand in the place of short syllables. But, on the other hand, syllables composed of few elements, are not necessarily short, because they may be lengthened by the accent or emphasis.

The strength of syllables, though depending in part upon the same causes, is capable of being distinguished from their length. A strong syllable is one which is composed of a number of elements which have a strong vocality. Thus again, the syllables, length, strength, worm, bang, whang, loud, wrong, are essentially strong, by reason of the number of vocal elements, tonics and subtonics, which compose them. On the other hand, pet, pit, kit, sit, are essentially feeble, because their tonics have the feeblest vocality, and their other elements are few, and have no vocality at all.

The importance of all this in metre and style is obvious; and the errors which arise from neglect of it are frequent and damaging:—in metre, by the interchange of long and short syllables; and in style by the attempt to express a strong thought in a word of feeble sound, or an insignificant thought in a sonorous word.

§ 122. The principal causes of bad articulation are, confusion of thought, defective organs, want of control over the organs, nervous timidity, careless habits, and too much care.

The causes of bad articulation are very numerous and complicated. Only the most important are here enumerated.

1. *Confusion of thought, or inarticulate thinking.*

We have seen (§ 27) that the character of the thinking constantly tends to characterize the vocal expression of it. Hence clear and articulate thinking naturally forms or expresses itself in clear and articulate speaking. As soon as a man begins to think with sharpness and precision, instinctively he begins to bite off his words precisely. In fact it is the influence of such thinking which brings the organs of articulation under the perfect control of the will. It exerts in time a marked influence even upon the physical constitution, size, and shape of these organs. Consequently, indiscriminate and blurred thinking naturally forms or expresses itself in indistinct and blurred articulation. Hence the articulation of stupid people, and of tribes in the lowest state of barbarism, is commonly very imperfect. The Boobies of the island of Fernando Po, communicate with each other in what can hardly be called an articulate language. Even the physical organs of such people remain unformed and uncontrolled. The coarse thick tongue, and ill-defined blubber lip, of every undeveloped or degraded type of mankind, seem to be sufficiently accounted for by the fact that for thousands of years they have been without any sharp distinctions in their thoughts, destitute of culture and refinement. Hence we may expect that civilization and educated thinking will in time purify the organization, and reduce the size of their lips, tongues, and other organs of speech, and give them that sharp outline and flexibility, which are so characteristic of the European and civilized man.

2. *Defective organs.*

A defective ear, that is, a sense of hearing which fails to discriminate accurately the different elementary sounds from each other, is a prevalent cause of bad articulation. Hence the different tonics, and different classes of sub and atonics, are constantly liable to be confounded and interchanged. Thus many persons fail to distinguish a as in far, from a as in ask, and this latter again from a as in hat. In this way, also, l and r, d and t, b and p, w and wh f and v, th in then and th in thin, are frequently confounded. The remedy for this defect is the exercises prescribed for the training of the ear (§ 105—4). In like manner, undue thickness of the lips and tongue, enlargement of the tonsils and soft palate, imperfect circulation of the breath through the nostrils, and other similar defects, often produce indistinct and impure articulation. Such defects, however, seldom present insuperable difficulties, provided the organs be adequately trained to their work.

3. *Imperfect control over the articulating organs.*

There are all degrees of control over the organs of speech, and few persons have it in perfection. Yet the very highest degree of it is necessary to articulate with precision and facility the various combinations of the elementary sounds in English, many of which are extremely difficult.* Such combina-

---

* In some languages, as *e. g.* in the Welsh, and other dialects of the Old Celtic, in the Greek to a very limited extent, and in the Sanskrit perfectly, such difficult combinations of the elementary sounds are avoided by euphonic rules, so that whenever two sounds of difficult combination come together, either one of them is changed, or a euphonic element is inserted between them just as we change *a* into *an* before a vowel or a silent *h*. The word, Sanskrit, itself, which is exactly translated by our word *perfect*, is an example, the s in the middle of the word having no significance whatever, being simply a euphonic insertion, to avoid a difficult combination. These rules in Sanskrit are so comprehensive and particular that every combination of sounds, whether difficult of articulation, or unpleasant to the cultivated ear of the Brachman, is eliminated from the language. In English, also, to a far greater extent than is commonly supposed, euphonic influences have determined the combinations which actually occur. Thus the word, diphthong, is rightly pronounced *dipthong*, in order to avoid the unpleasant combination of $ph = f$, and *th* as in *thin*. But the combinations, once established by the authorized pronunciation, are the same in English, wherever the word occurs ; we have to take them as they come, whether difficult or easy. Nor is this any disadvantage to our mother tongue for the highest and best purposes of human speech ; for the Sanskrit, though vaunted as 'perfect,' is greatly enfeebled by its euphonic over-refinement, as might easily be shown.

ARTICULATION. 221

tions *e. g.* as the word, strength (often on account of its difficulty pronounced, strenth) stcpt'st, hush'd'st, ask'd'st, cannot be perfectly articulated without a high degree—and when several of them occur in rapid succession, without the most perfect control over the articulating organs. Where this is wanting, moreover, the different classes of sub and aton ics are constantly liable to be confounded and interchanged with each other.

4. *Nervous timidity.*

The articulation of many speakers is marred by undue haste or hurry, arising from nervous timidity and agitation. When thus flurried, instead of articulating every element with deliberateness and precision, they throw out whole mouthfuls of vowels and consonants, all jumbled up together. For speaking to a great audience, as the most practiced and eloquent orators have always felt, is something terrible; it is like hunting the lion single handed. But this terror must be overcome by the firm and steady exercise of self-control (§ 87). "One must be sure of himself before he can be sure of the lion."

5. *Careless habits.*

One of the most fruitful causes of bad articulation is mere carelessness, or slovenly habits, in speaking. When such habits are once formed, they are, like all others, extremely difficult to correct. For the speaker becomes entirely unconscious of his faults, even when they are so numerous and aggravated as to render a large proportion of his words unintelligible. But whoever can be careless or slovenly in addressing a public audience, may thereby know that he is naturally incapable of speaking well.

6. *Too much care.*

Sometimes the articulation is marred by over nicety, rendering it finical, pedantic and affected. This fault appears most frequently in sounding silent letters, the t *e. g.* in such words as often, soften, epistle, apostle, thistle (§ 166–2, (5)). Such faults are worse than many that arise from carelessness, because they attract more attention, and because pedantry or affectation in any form is fatal to eloquence.

§ 123. The qualities of good articulation are correctness, distinctness, purity, ease and elegance.

These qualities are not always logically distinct, but, for the most part, they overlap or imply each other.

1. *Correctness* refers chiefly to the formation of the elementary sounds, and requires that they should be rendered, in all their combinations, with the utmost accuracy and precision.

2. *Distinctness* characterizes that clear and sharp distinction of the elements from each other, which necessarily results from their precise and accurate formation.

3. *Purity* requires that the vocal elements should be formed of pure tone (§ 168), without admixture of noise from the expulsion of non-vocalized breath,

or from the unskillful and harsh operation of the articulating organs.

4. *Ease* or *facility* is, of course, the opposite of a labored or difficult working of the articulating organs, arising from inadequate voluntary control over them.

5. *Elegance* or *beauty* of articulation results from all the foregoing qualities combined. It implies also a certain smooth or liquid flow of the sounds, and is in fact the crowning perfection.

§ 124. **Good articulation is an essential element of power in delivery.**

The importance of good articulation as an element of power in delivery, cannot be overestimated. This may be evinced in the following particulars.

1. *Articulation is the differential character of human speech.*

The word, language, in its most comprehensive sense (§ 2—1), includes not only speech, but also written and printed and other symbolical representations of human thought. Hence each of the arts, such as music, painting, sculpture and architecture, has its own language. In distinction from all these, and also from the inarticulate voices or cries of the irrational creation, articulation is the special characteristic of human speech. Hence "the articulately speaking men" of Homer, expresses the conception which the Greeks, the greatest practical masters of speech the world has ever seen, formed of humanity. The articulate word of a man is his rational nature in its most full and perfect revelation —a revelation which is dim and obscure in the degree in which his articulation is defective.

2. *Good articulation is necessary in order to speak and to be understood with ease.*

The question whether the public speaker can deliver himself without exhaustion, so as to be understood by large audiences with facility, turns upon the quality of his articulation, even more than upon the strength of his voice. Good articulation will enable him to speak with comparatively little effort, or fatigue, or expenditure of vital energy, so as to be understood with ease by the most numerous assemblies. In such assemblies, and more especially if they are in the open air, he cannot make himself understood without great distinctness and purity of articulation; his speaking will be unintelligible; or if not absolutely so, yet the effort on the part of the audience to understand will be so great that they will soon become wearied, and cease to give their attention. In the meantime, the strain upon his own organs, especially those of the breath and throat, will be so great that it may inflict upon them irreparable injury, and break down the strongest health.

3. *Distinct articulation is essential to the expression of the distinctions of thought; and in this, the consonants are of more importance than the vowels.*

The distinctions of sound made by the articulating organs, are the most significant of all symbols, whether natural or artificial, for the expression of the distinctions of thought, *i. e.* all the various states and operations of the intellect. For this purpose, the consonants are of far greater importance than the vowels, for the reason that the differentiating action of the organs in the formation of the consonants, is greater than in the vowels. Hence the consonants require to be formed with the utmost precision and distinctness, and to be jointed together in syllables and words with the utmost purity, in order to symbolize and express the subtle distinctions of precise and articulate thinking. Feebly rendered, they express feebleness of the intellectual operations. The omission of any of them, as that of f = v in of, or one of them put for another, as b for p in baptism, or w for wh in why and when, or a confused and blurred utterance of them, is the natural symbol and expression of the want of discrimination and precision of thought (§ 122—1).

4. *Good articulation is essential to the adequate expression of emotion and passion; and here the vowels are of the greatest importance.*

It is true, indeed, that the gross and sensual and violent passions may be expressed, to a certain extent, by inarticulate cries, such as those of mere animals. Uncontrollable passion naturally runs into confused articulation. But all the delicate modifications and distinctions of emotion, all its nicer shades and variations, and all passion that is held under control—in a word, all feelings which are distinctively human, require for their adequate expression, the purest and most perfect articulation. Thus anger, scorn, contempt, hatred, and all such passions, when not uncontrollable, express themselves by sharpening and hardening the consonantal sounds; whilst love, pity, sorrow, and all the tender and gentle emotions, give these sounds a peculiar softness and smoothness, and a certain liquid flow to the whole utterance. In the expression of emotion and passion the vowels are more significant than the consonants. One reason of this is that they correspond to the nature of emotion more closely, as being less sharply distinguished from each other than the consonants; which more properly correspond to the sharp and precise distinctions of thought. Hence it is by means of the vowel sounds, in all their ever varying qualities of voice, and changes of pitch, time and force, that the passions of the speaker's soul pour themselves forth, and are communicated to the audience, with the greatest fullness and power.

CHAPTER IV.

ACCENTUATION.

§ 125. Accentuation consists in giving distinction or prominence to particular syllables, by increasing the time, or stress, or by raising the pitch, of the accented syllable.

THERE are at least these three ways of rendering any particular syllable more prominent than the others with which it is immediately connected; and each of these methods may be employed separately, or any two, or all of them, may be combined in one and the same accent.

§ 126. The temporal accent consists in giving an increase of time to the syllable; it is preferred by syllables which end in tonic sounds.

Thus in the words, dai'ry, ju'ry, vo'cal, it will be readily observed that about double the amount of time is given to the former syllables, as compared with the latter. All syllables which end in tonic sounds have a decided preference for this form of the accent; in other words, this is their leading or predominant form. The reason is that all the tonics, being open sounds, that is, formed by the organs not in contact, and having the highest degree of vocality, are capable of being indefinitely prolonged. This reason applies also to the subtonic feeble checks, and to the nasals, though with less force, inasmuch as they have a lower degree of vocality; and hence syllables which end in these sounds, frequently take this form of the accent, as in the words, an'vil, bev'el, beam'ing. The temporal accent readily combines with that of increased stress, and sometimes with that of the raised pitch.

§127. The stress accent consists in giving increased stress of voice to the syllable; it is preferred by syllables ending in subtonic sounds.

Thus we give about double the ordinary stress or force of voice to the accented syllables of the following words, bab'ble, mad'der, bag'ging. This is the leading form of the accent in syllables that end in subtonic sounds, especially those which cannot be indefinitely prolonged, and which have therefore a comparatively feeble vocality. Instinctively the voice seems to make a greater effort, in anticipation of its being so soon and suddenly checked, or stopped off, by the strong articulation in which the syllable ends. Increased stress is the most apt way of distinguishing syllables which end with such sounds. These, however, are not incapable of the temporal accent in combination with their own, for the reason that the increase of time can be laid upon the tonic which precedes the closing subtonic sound.

§ 128. **The pitch accent consists in raising the pitch of the syllable; it is preferred by syllables which end in atonic sounds.**

In this case, the pitch of the syllable is raised a full tone, or one degree of the musical scale, above the other syllables. This also may be readily observed in such words as bat tle, capit′ulate, refrac′tory. This is the leading form of the accent in syllables which end in atonic sounds, for the reason that such sounds having no vocality, and being formed by mere articulations of the whispering breath, are extremely unpleasant when unduly prolonged, where they are capable of it, and when too much distinguished by increased stress. Yet this form of the accent may be combined with either or both of the others, by laying the increased time, or stress, or both, upon the tonic of the syllable.

§ 129. **Accents are of primary, secondary and tertiary degrees of time and stress.**

Besides the preceding distinctions, the accent may be of greater or less increase of time and force; and from the fact of such variations, we have the distinctions of primary, secondary and tertiary accents.

1. *The primary* is the accent of greatest increase of time, or stress, or of both these combined. Words of two syllables take only this accent, as in the words, man′ly mer′cy caprice′.

2. *The secondary* accent is one of less increase, and is, as it were, the echo of the primary. It occurs on words of three syllables, when the primary is on the first or last, and on words of four or more syllables; as in the following, prac″tical′, pal″pitate′, pur″ify′, accent″uate′, facil″itate′, com′pensa″tion.

3. *The tertiary* is of the least increase, and is as if the echo should repeat itself in a still feebler form. It occurs on words of five, six, or more syllables, as in tran″substan′tia‴tion.

This image of the echo, however, is so far inaccurate, that the primary accent does not always precede, but is often preceded by either or both the others. The primary is, of course, the most important, and is the one always meant when the accent is spoken of, except when either of the others is specified.

§ 130. The accent has four functions; it gives unity and variety to the sound of words, expresses their different and contrasted meanings, and constitutes the principal element of rhythm.

1. *It gives to words of more than one syllable unity and variety of sound.*

This is the most important function of the accent. For every such word in English takes one, and but one primary accent, which gives distinction or prominence to the accented syllable over all the others, and draws them into a certain relation of subordination, and dependence upon it. This unifies the sound of the whole word, and thus enables it to symbolize and express that unity of thought, which, as we shall hereafter see, is an essential character of words. Consequently in the English language, such words have a far higher degree of unity, and in so far are more perfect as words, than in those other languages which are properly destitute of the accent. The manner in which the different accents, primary, secondary and tertiary, with their various elements of time, stress and pitch, contribute to that full and rich variety of sound, which is characteristic of English words, is sufficiently obvious.

2. *It expresses the different meanings of words which, without the accent, would have the same sound.*

We have a large class of words in English which are composed of precisely the same elementary sounds, and are represented by the same alphabetic symbols, but which differ widely in their grammatical character and meaning. Such are all the words which are used both as nouns or adjectives, and as verbs. Now this whole difference of character and meaning is commonly, and the tendency of the language is such that probably, in no long time, it will be uniformly, expressed by accenting the words differently. We have examples of this in the words, tor'ment and torment', fre'quent and frequent', in'terdict and interdict', at'tribute and attri'bute.

3. *It expresses the contrasted meanings of similar words.*

When the meanings of any two similar words in the same sentence are contrasted, or opposed to each other, the accent enables us to express this contrast or opposition in a corresponding difference of sound. This function is of such importance that it justifies and requires a change of the accent from its normal position on one or both of the words, as in the following expressions : " He must in'crease, but I must de'crease;" jus'tice and in'justice, giv'ing and for'giving, prob'ability not plau'sibility.

4. *It is the principal element of rhythm.*

The rhythm, both of prose and poetry, depends in English chiefly upon such a distribution of accented and unaccented syllables as is adapted to the expression of the sentiment, and as makes a pleasing impression upon the ear. We see this in the following prose sentence from the address of the Apostle Paul to the Athenian Areopagus : " Whom', there'- fore, ye ig'norantly wor'ship, him' declare' I un'to you ;" also in the following words of the Queen in Hamlet, strewing funereal flowers upon the corpse of Ophelia.

Sweets' to the sweet'—farewell'.
I hop'ed thou should'st have been' my Ham'let's wife ;
I thought' thy bride'-bed t' have deck'ed, sweet maid,'
And not' t' have strew'ed thy grave'.

The change of a single accent in these quotations would essentially mar their superb rhythm. Accent enters deeply also into the nature and effects of melody and harmony in discourse, by which the sonnd of the words is made to fall musically upon the ear, and to symbolize and echo, as it were, the sense which they are intended to express.

§ 131. The accent gives the En lish language a great superiority over others which are destitute of it.

This fourfold function of the accent gives to the English language a vast superiority over the French, and all others which are destitute of this element of expression. For it imparts to all words of more than one syllable, a much greater unity and variety of sound—it renders them much more precise and perspicuous in meaning—it renders contrasted words and phrases far more antithetical and expressive—and it gives to the rhythm, both of poetry and prose, far greater fullness, richness and symbolical power —than were otherwise possible.

§ 132. Rules for placing the accent express the tendencies of the language.

It is hardly possible to lay down precise and invariable laws of accentuation; but there are certain tendencies of the language, which approach more or less nearly to the nature of laws, and which require to be exhibited.

§ 133. Monosyllables commonly take no accent.

This rule requires to be qualified in the four following cases.

1. *Monosyllables which are essentially long*, from the large number of their elementary sounds (§ 121), such as dart, harm, realm, are undistinguishable from syllables which are lengthened by the temporal accent.

2. *Monosyllables essentially strong*, from the strong vocality of their elements (§ 121), such as mourn, glean, blaze, are undistinguishable from syllables with the accent of increased stress.

3. *Emphatic monosyllables* include the accent in their emphasis.

4. *Rhythm sometimes requires the accentuation of monosyllables.*

This is true of the rhythm both of prose and poetry. In the latter, however, it is very necessary to guard against error.* For where perfect regularity in the rhythm requires a monosyllable to be accented, it is often the intention of the poet to leave it without the accent, in order to secure a more full and copious rhythmic variety. This remark applies chiefly to articles, prepositions, conjunctions, pronouns, adverbs, and all the monosyllabic forms of substantive and auxiliary verbs. An unskillful reader would be likely to spoil the poet's rhythm in the following lines, by accenting the words, is and in.

> There' is a pleas'ure in the path'less woods';
> There' is a rap'ture on the lone'ly shore'.

§ 134. All words of more than one syllable are accented.

The only exception to this rule is that rhythm sometimes requires an insignificant word of two syllables to stand without the accent; as the word, upon, in the following line.

> Since' upon night' so sweet' such aw'ful morn' could rise'.

§ 135. Words of Anglo-Saxon origin commonly take the accent on the root syllable.

Of course, these are not the only words which are thus accented, but this rule applies to them more generally than to others. This is one of the causes of the superior strength of the Anglo-Saxon elements of the language; for it always enfeebles a word when the accent falls on any other than its radical syllable. The following are examples under the rule.

Above', adown', affright', ba'ker, back'wardly, black'ness, care'ful, death'liness, eat'ing, fear'ful, ga'ble, heart'ily, i'dleness, jum'ble, kind'liness, land'less, mar'ketable, nip'ple, own'er, pic'kle, quirk'ish, rag'ing, scan'ty, thiev'ish, ud'der, wretch'edly, without,' youth'ful.

§ 136. Dissyllables transferred* from the French commonly take the accent on the last syllable.

Also a large number of polysyllables of the same origin are accented on the last syllable.

Allies', balloon', brocade', burlesque', cartouch', cartoon', coquette', dessert', detail', discourse', escheat', finance', finesse', grimace', halloo', illume', juppon', lampoon', maintain', morass', oppose', parterre', research', resource', romance', severe', tinaile', vendue'.

§ 137. Dissyllables, which as nouns or adjectives are accented on the first syllable, are as verbs frequently accented on the last.

This is the case also with a number of words of more than two syllables. The analogy of the rule

---

* Transferred *i. e.* adopted with little or no change.

applies, moreover, in changing the accent on some words, where it does not transfer it to the last syllable, as in at′tribute and attrib′ute, ar′senic and arse′nic, coun′terbalance and counterbal′ance. In the case of arsenic, and some other words, it distinguishes nouns from adjectives. It is necessary, however, to guard against this clear tendency of the language, so as not to apply the rule to words which, according to the best usage, have not yet been brought under it; such as the words, per′fect and content′, in which the accent is the same in all cases. Contents, in the plural, will bear the accent on either syllable. The following words are examples of this change of accent, that is, they are accented either on the first or last syllable, according to their grammatical character and meaning; thus ab′ject or abject′, and so of the others.

<small>Abject, absent, abstract, accent, affix, augment, bombard, cement, colleague, collect, compact, complot, compound, compress, concert, concrete, conduct, confine, conflict, conserve, consort, contest, contract, contrast, convent, converse, convert, convict, convoy, countercharge, countercharm, countercheck, countermand, countermarch, countermine, counterpoise, countersign, desert, descant, discount, digest, escort, essay, export, extract, exile, ferment, foretaste, frequent, import, impress, incense, inlay, interchange, interdict, insult, object, overcharge, overflow, overmatch, overthrow, perfume, permit, prefix, prelude, premise, presage, present, produce, project, progress, protest, rebel, record, refuse, reprimand, subject, survey, torment, traject, transfer, transport, undress, upstart.</small>

§ 138. Words terminating in **ia, iac, ial, ian, efy, ify, ety, ity, eous, ious, sion, tion, athy, acal, ical, fluent, fluous, gonal, graphy, itude, logy, loquy, meter, metry, parous, phyl-**

ACCENTUATION. 237

ious, tomy, (together with tive and commonly ic, preceded by a consonant) take the accent on the preceding syllable.

There are a few exceptions to this comprehensive rule, such as ad'jective, ar'senic, arith'metic, bish'opric, cath'olic, chol'eric, elegi'ac, ephem'eric, her'etic, lu'natic, pol'itic rhet'oric, splen'etic, sub'stantive, tur'meric, and perhaps, pleth'oric, which, however, according to the best authorities, should be accented, pletho'ric.

The following are examples under the rule.

Af'fluent, algebra'ic, alphabet'ical, ammo'nia, anat'omy, aph'yllous, attrac'tive, barba'rian, biol'ogy, cheru'bic, climacter'ic, conta'geous, conten'tious, coura'geous, cu'bical, declara'tion, demo'niac, demoni'acal, diag'onal, dissen'sious, diph'yllous, diver'sity, ed'ify, epidem'ic, epidem'ical, empir'ic, fanat'ic, fanat'ical, farina'ceous, for'titude, geol'ogy, geolog'ical, geom'etry, geomet'rical, geom'eter, geog'raphy, geograph'ical, harmon'ic, harmon'ical, heli'acal, heteroph'yllous, homeop'athy, impe'rial, invec'tive, jacobin'ic, jacobin'ical, liberal'ity, malleabil'ity, merid'ian, metal'lic, mol'lify, mu'sical, Noa'chian, ovip'arous, presump'tive, phlegmat'ic, quan'tity, rar'efy, scientif'ic, scorbu'tic, scorbu'tical, sol'itude, solil'oquy, super'fluous, sym'pathy, sympathet'ic, triph'yllous, vivip'arous.

139. Words of three or more syllables terminating in eal, erous, orous, inous, ulous, take the accent on the preceding syllable.

There are a very few exceptions to this rule, such as cano'rous, sono'rous, and, perhaps, deco'rous, indeco'rous, which, however, on good authority, may be accented as in the following examples.

Bo'real, corpo'real, carniv'orous, cu'neal, dec'orous, empyr'eal, ethe'rial, fune'real, herbiv'orous, heteroge'nial, homoge'nial, indec'orous, incorpo'real, lac'teal, lin'eal, or'deal, sed'ulous, vocif'erous, volu'minous.

§ 140. Words accented on the first syllable.

Accessary, accessory, admirable, advertise, aggrandizement, aperture, behemoth, Bernardine, blasphemous, capillary, character, characterize, compromise, complaisance, corollary, construe, contrary, contumacy, contumely, deficit, designate, desultory, desuetude, disputable, disputant, diverse, dynasty, exemplary, exercise, exquisite, epocha, fallacy, gratitude, harass, impetus, industry, integral, interest, interested, interesting, judicature, lamentable, legislative, legislator, legislature, maxillary, mercantile, miscellany, mischievous, oasis, pedestal, perfected, posthumous, presbytery, puissant, recognize, recreate, recreative, repertory, sepulchre, sinister, specialty, speculative, towards, vehement, vehemently, yesterday.

§ 141. Words accented on the second syllable.

Abdomen, advertisement, albumen, alumen, acumen, anchovy, antipodes, aroma, aruspice, aspirant, asylum, Augean, bissextile, bitumen, camelopard, catastrophe, centrifugal, centripetal, ceramic, Cerberian, cerulean, clandestine, clandestinely, committee, compensate, component, computable, concentrate, condensate, condolence, confiscate, consummate, contemplate, contemplative, coquetry, decorum, defalcate, demonstrate, deponent, devastate, diploma, diplomacy, diplomatist, distribute, divertise, divertisement, enervate, exponent, extirpate, fraternize, Herculean, horizon, idea, imbecile, inculcate, inculpate, indisputable, inquiry, irrefragable, interpolate, interstice, intrepid, liceum, marmorean, misanthropy, museum, obdurate, obduracy, opponent, Orion, pantheon, philanthropy, pilaster, precedence, Promethean, promulgate, pygmean, recital, recusant, remonstrate, respiratory, respirable, restorative, retributive, sequestrate, subsidence, Tartarean, tiara, ubiquist, vesicular, xerodes, zygoma.

§ 142. Words accented on the third syllable.

Atheneum, Atlantean, acquiescent, bastinado, benefactor, circumjacent, coadjutor, coriander, colossean, colosseum, convalescent, desperado, empyrean, Epicurean, European, evanescent, hyperborean, hymenean, ignoramus, literati, simultaneous, subterranean, ultimatum.

CHAPTER V.

PRONUNCIATION.

§ 143. Articulation and accentuation are the two elements of pronunciation; the former is the more controlling element.

WHEN a word is properly articulated, and properly accented, it is rightly pronounced. Articulation, however, is the more fundamental and controlling element. The formation of the elementary sounds, and of syllables, is obviously the most essential element of the formation of words. Also the articulating organs come into play in jointing syllables together to form words, as truly as in forming the elementary sounds, and in jointing them together into syllables. Moreover, a great number of words in English are monosyllables, in which case, articulation is identical with pronunciation. Notwithstanding, however, that articulation and accentuation, taken together, are precisely equivalent to pronunciation, the propriety, and even the necessity of treating pronunciation under a separate head will be obvious from what is to follow.

§ 144. Pronunciation is the oral speaking of words.

We have seen that language, in the deepest sense of the word, is identical with oral speech. Hence it is that what we have to keep our minds intent upon, in all linguistic studies, is the sounds themselves, as distinguished from their literal symbols. This is the clue which guides us to the true nature, and inmost secret of language. For the letters of the alphabet are mere symbols (often extremely clumsy, and always inadequate) of the elementary sounds of which words are composed. And even a perfect symbolization, if that were possible, would be only a mechanical contrivance, of which the highest use would be that of serving as a means of reproducing the sounds represented. But speech is an organic and vital development of the laws of thought— thought striving to embody itself more and more perfectly in oral sounds. When, therefore, the literal symbols are regarded and treated as elements and powers in the formation of words, language becomes incomprehensible.

§ 145. Pronunciation ought not to be conformed to the symbolization.

There is no more fruitful source of errors in pronunciation than the attempts, which are constantly made, to conform the sounds to the spelling of the words. All such attempts proceed upon a false principle, and are essentially impracticable. This may be evinced from the following considerations.

1. *Such attempts reverse the original method of procedure by which language was reduced to writing.*

Every language, before it was reduced to writing, had its own pronunciation as fully developed and perfected as it became afterwards. The original procedure of writing down a language at first, is, of course, that of conforming the symbolization to the sounds, not the sounds to the symbolization. The attempt to conform the pronunciation to the spelling, therefore, reverses this whole process, and hence it can never fail, in the degree in which it is successful, to mar and deform the language.

2. *Pronunciation cannot be fixed in any symbolization.*

Speech, because it is an organic and vital development, is always in a process of change; it is always moving on the line of the development of thought and life. Hence the pronunciation of a language can never be permanently fixed; and if it could, it would tend to arrest human progress. The symbolization, on the contrary, because it is a mere conventional and mechanical contrivance, constantly tends to become indurated, and difficult of modification. Hence the necessary divergence, in the course of time, of the pronunciation from the symbolization. The causes which produce this effect are always at work in living tongues which have been reduced to writing. Their ultimate result is that the written becomes a dead language; for the life of a language always follows the sound, and not the symbol. Under the influence of these causes for thousands of years, the spoken language and dialects of China have become so different from the written and classical Chinese, that the most perfect knowledge of either is hardly an introduction to the other. For beyond a question, when the sounds of the classical Chinese were first reduced to writing (and for ages subsequently) the written language was the same with the spoken; but the pronunciation gradually receding from the symbolization, the present result has been at last reached. The case is precisely similar with the classical Sanskrit, and the living dialects of that family which are now spoken by the people of India. Thus it was also that the Latin became a dead language, and that the Romance tongues grew up under it. And the same causes have been at work for centuries in these last mentioned tongues, until now in French *e. g.* the spelling is hardly any clue to the pronunciation. What would be the consequence if the French people should attempt to pronounce their words as they are spelled!

§ 146. The symbolization ought to be conformed to the pronunciation.

This is now becoming so obvious to those who have given the subject adequate attention, as to leave little doubt that the change, with whatsoever temporary inconvenience it may be attended, cannot be much longer delayed. The objections which have been urged against it are rapidly giving way in the minds of our ablest scholars, such as Max

Müller, and Professor Whitney, before a more full recognition of the fundamental principle that the essence of language is significant sound, and before the urgent necessity pressing more and more heavily upon us. For it is now demonstrable that if this change be not effected, we must in time have a written language totally different from the spoken one, like the Chinese; in other words, classical English must become a dead language. Our symbolization, having been radically defective at first, has become a perfect chaos, which defies all attempts to reduce it to order, and from which it is not only impossible to gather the true sounds, or pronunciation of the words, but which exerts a mighty influence to lead us all astray. For we have, in the first place, a vast number of symbols, which represent no sound at all, that is, silent letters; few of which, if any, were silent when the language was first reduced to writing. In the second place, most of the symbols represent each a variety of different sounds; and, in the third place, the same sound is often represented by a great number of different symbols. The sound of i as in pin *e. g.* is represented by as many as fifteen different signs; and the case is nearly as bad with each of the other nineteen or twenty vowels and diphthongs in the language. All the peculiar difficulties of English pronunciation arise from this chaotic state of our symbolization. For there is no such confusion in the sounds themselves. Here we shall find law and order and beauty, as in all the developments and manifestations of organic life—a regularity and certainty, in fact, like that of instinct. For oral speech is a true product of the instincts of reason in man.

§ 147. A word is an articulate sound expressing a single thought.

A single articulate sound expressing a single thought, is the differential character of a word.

1. *A word expresses a single thought.*

A sound which does not express any thought or sense, is not a word; nor can any word express more than one thought at the same time, or in the same connection. This one thought, however, may be composed of any number of different elements, but these will always be expressed in a unified or generalized form, as in such words as horse, man, world, thing.

2. *The means of expressing this unity of thought is a corresponding unity of sound.*

In order that this unity of thought may be adaquately expressed, it requires a corresponding unity of sound, which, therefore, is essential to the nature of a word. But this unity of sound, as in the case of the thought which it expresses, may be composed of many different elements, as in the words, flail, education, polysyllable.

§ 148. There are four causes of unity of sound in words, the single impulse of the voice, the primary accent, the pause before and after the word, and the transition sounds.

Of these four distinct causes of unity of sound in

words, the first is limited to monosyllables, the second to polysyllables, and the last two are common to all words.

1. *Monosyllables are pronounced with a single vocal impulse.*

This fact has been already exhibited in the discussion of the syllable (§116). It is the most influential cause of all that contribute to give unity of sound to words; and taken together with the others that co-operate with it to produce the same result, it gives the highest degree of unity to monosyllables, and thus renders them the most perfect of all words.

2. *Polysyllables take but one primary accent.*

This cause gives unity of sound to all words of more than one syllable. After what manner it does this has been already explained in treating of the functions of the accent (§ 130—1).

3. *Every word is preceded and followed by a pause.*

This is the case in all connected English speaking. The pause may be very slight, so as to be almost insensible, but it is still there, and may commonly be perceived by a good ear, with close attention. It is admirably symbolized in writing and printing by the little blank spaces between the words. Its function is to separate each word from the others with which it stands connected in speech, to circumscribe it, so to speak, and thus to give it a defined unity of sound. This cause of unity is, of course, common to all words.

4. *The elements of each word are cemented together by transition sounds.*

These transition sounds, which are produced by the voice in passing from one element to another, have never been treated of. Professor Day supposes himself to be the first who has ever alluded to them. Yet they constitute a considerable proportion of the sound of almost every word. We shall find that they will enable us to explain a great number of the apparent anomalies of English pronunciation.

(1). Transition sounds are made by the voice in passing from one element of a word to another. That there are such sounds becomes evident upon a little attention. For whilst the organs are passing from their position in the formation of one element to that of the next in the same word, the voice or breath is not suspended, but continues to flow out, except in the case of the hard checks, g, d, b, k, t, p. Thus in the word, ear, the a being silent, the sound of e passes into that of r by a vocal transition, which is neither that of e nor r, but partakes of the nature of both. Between different syllables the transition sound is still more sensible, as between e and a of the word, create. Frequently these sounds are identical with some of the elements themselves, in which case they are sometimes expressed. Thus in the word Iowa *e. g.* w represents nothing but the transition sound made by the voice in passing from o to a, and the word is pronounced **exactly** as if it were spelled Ioa. Commonly, however, these sounds are not represented at all in the spelling. Thus in the words, nature, virtue—pronounced, natshure, virtshue—the transition sound between the two syllables is precisely that of sh, but it does not appear in the spelling of either word. These transition sounds are aptly symbolized by the little intermediate strokes which connect the different letters in current writing; and it would seem that printing would be a more perfect symbol than it now is, if its letters were joined together in a similar manner

(2.) A principal function of these transition sounds is to give unity to the sound of each word. These transition sounds are never heard between one word and another, or only in faulty articulation; otherwise there would be no pause before and after every word. But between the different elements and syllables of each word they are very frequently, and often necessarily introduced. The effect of this is to cement the elementary sounds and syllables together, thus giving wholeness and unity to the sound of every word, as the bricks or stones of a building are cemented together with mortar. This cause of unity is also common to all words.

§ 149. **Pronunciation is an important element of power in delivery.**

A correct and elegant pronunciation is an element of power in delivery which can hardly be overestimated. It has been said that it makes the words of a speaker like new gold coin, as they drop from the mint, bright and clean-cut, with their legends or superscriptions so plain that they can be read without effort, and the value of the coin recognized at sight; whilst bad pronunciation makes the words like old, rusty, defaced coin, with their legends blurred or worn away, so that it requires the study and skill of an antiquarian or numatist to determine their value.

§ 150. The pronunciation here given follows the best English and American authorities.

English pronunciation, when considered apart from the totally inadequate and chaotic symbolization, is not of so uncertain or anomalous a character as is commonly supposed. Almost all its apparent anomalies arise from the groundless notion that somehow the sounds ought to be conformed to the spelling, instead of the spelling to the sounds. Considered apart from this cause of difficulty, it is probably as regular, and as capable of being reduced under general euphonic laws, as that of any other language. The examples given below to establish such laws, are selected mostly from words that are often mispronounced, of which the true pronunciation is here given. But it should be distinctly understood that no new or unauthorized pronunciations have been introduced, except in a few cases of apparent inadvertency of the best English and American authorities, which, with this exception, have been uniformly followed. But where these authorities differ among themselves, and it has become necessary to choose between them, the laws of euphony have been allowed to influence the choice. What authorities have been followed in any particular case, may commonly be seen by reference to Worcester's large dictionary; which is here recommended as, upon the whole, the best exhibition of the orthoëpy of the language.

§ 151. **The tonics in a, from the greatest to the least openness of the organs, are as in arm, all, ask, hat, care, fate.**

These six tonics are here arranged in a regular series (except in the case of a as in all) with the organs constantly flattening and approaching to contact. The exception might properly be placed in another series, but is retained here for reasons given below. The sign here chosen for these sounds, namely, the letter a, has been found the most convenient for practical treatment, although they are not unfrequently otherwise represented.

1. *A as in arm, represented by a, au, e, ea.*

This sound is formed with the mouth simply open, the organs in their natural position, and farther apart than in any other sound of the language. Consequently it is least modified by the action of the organs, and has the strongest vocality of all. It is often confounded with a as in care, and in all, and with o as in nor; as in psaalm or psawlm, for psalm, and port, stort, for part, start. The signs by which it is represented in the following examples are in italic letters.

*A*re, *a*unt, *a*vant, b*a*lm, b*a*th, c*a*lf, c*a*lm, clerk, cr*au*nch, d*au*nt, d*au*ntless, emb*a*rk, fl*au*nt, g*a*pe, g*au*nt, g*au*ntlet, gu*a*no, gu*a*rd, h*a*lf, h*a*lve, h*au*nt, h*au*nch, h*a*rk, h*ea*rken, imp*a*rt, j*au*nt, j*au*ndice, kn*a*rl, l*au*gh, l*au*ndry, l*au*ndress, M*a*, m*au*nch, m*au*nder, n*a*rd, P*a*, p*a*riah, p*a*lm, ps*a*lm, qu*a*lm, r*a*jah, r*a*gout', s*au*nter, sergeant, st*a*nch, st*au*nch, sult*a*'na, t*au*nt, upb*a*r, v*a*rnish, y*a*rd, zen*a*'na.

2. *A as in all—a, au, aw, oa, ou.*

Formed by rounding the aperture and cavity of the mouth a very little from the position of the preceding a as in arm, and by throwing the resonance of the voice farther back. The sound is very nearly related to o as in nor. It is placed here because it is formed by a very slight modification of the position of the organs from the preceding, and because it is most frequently represented by a, either alone, or in combination with other signs.

*A*lder, *a*lderman, *a*lmanac, *a*ltar, *a*lterative, app*a*ll, *au*dacious, *au*spicious, *au*ght, *a*vaunt, *aw*l, b*a*ll, b*aw*l, b*ou*ght, br*ou*ght, br*oa*d, c*a*ll, c*a*lk, ch*a*lk, d*au*b, enthr*a*ll, f*a*ll, f*a*lcon, f*ou*ght, gr*oa*t, h*a*ll, h*a*le, h*a*lter, h*au*l, j*aw*, l*aw*, m*aw*, n*au*ght, n*ou*ght, *ou*ght, p*a*ll, p*aw*, p*au*nch, qu*a*rt, qu*a*rter, r*aw*, s*au*cer, s*ou*ght, th*ou*ght, v*au*lt, v*au*nt, w*a*nt, wr*ou*ght, y*aw*l.

3. *A as in ask—a, au.*

Formed by flattening the mouth cavity a very little from its position in a as in arm, and by drawing the corners of the mouth a little farther from each other—an intermediate sound between a in arm, and a in hat. It is most frequently followed by nasal or atonic sounds, except when it ends a syllable. An unaccented a at the end of a word usually represents this sound. In some sections of the country it is confounded with a in arm, in others with a in care.

*A*ft, *a*fter, *a*ghast, *a*las, *A*nna, *a*nswer, *a*nt, b*a*sk, b*a*sket, bl*a*nch, br*a*ss, c*a*st, c*a*stle, cl*a*sp, cr*a*ft, d*a*nce, dr*a*ft, dr*au*ght, *e*nch*a*nt, ex*a*mple, f*a*st, fl*a*sk, gh*a*stly, gr*a*ft, gr*a*nt, gr*a*ss, h*a*ft, h*a*sp, id*ea*, l*a*nce, l*a*st, m*a*sk, m*a*ss, m*a*st, n*a*sty, p*a*nt, p*a*ss, p*a*ssable, p*a*stor, qu*a*ff, r*a*ft, s*a*mple, sl*a*nder, sl*a*nt, t*a*sk, v*a*st, w*a*ft.

4. *A as in hat—a, ai.*

Formed by a position of the mouth organs differing from the preceding precisely as that differs from a in arm. It is about as far removed, on the same line of change, from a in ask, as that is from a in arm. It is often confounded with the preceding, and with the following.

*A*bba, *a*bbey, *a*pple, *a*ctual, *a*dapt, *a*g'ile *a*pparel, *a*re'na, b*a*de, b*a*nd, b*a*nk, bl*a*nd, bl*a*ndish, bl*a*nk, cab*a*l', c*a*n, c*a*nt, d*a*ndle, d*a*ndy, er'r*a*nt, f*a*n, fl*a*nk, fr*a*nk, fr*a*ntic, g*a*ther, gl*a*cier, h*a*nd, j*a*m, kr*a*'al, l*a*mb, l*a*nd, m*a*n, m*ai*ntain', n*a*tional, or'de*a*l, Or-le*a*ns, p*a*rentage, p*a*tent (noun), p*a*tronage, pl*ai*d, r*ai*lery, r*a*n-dom, r*a*nt, r*a*tional, s*a*crament, s*a*crifice, syll*a*b'ic t*a*ndem, v*a*ntage, Z*a*nte.

5. *A as in care—a, ai, ay, e, ea, ey.*

Formed by still further flattening the mouth, and drawing the corners a little more apart—differing very slightly from the preceding. The distinctive character of this tonic seems to be mostly due to the influence of the peculiar subtonic r, by which it is nearly or quite uniformly followed.

*A*ir, *a*pparent, b*a*re, b*ea*r, ch*ai*r, ch*a*ry, d*a*re, decl*a*re, *e*'er, f*ai*r, f*a*re, gl*a*re, h*ai*r, h*ei*r, imp*ai*r, l*ai*r, m*a*re, n*e*'er, p*ea*r, pr*ay*er, r*a*re, rep*ai*r, sc*a*re, sc*a*rce, st*a*re, sw*ea*r, t*ea*r (verb) th*e*re, wh*e*re, wh*e*refore, w*ea*r.

6. *A as in fate—a, aa, ae, ai, ao, ay, e, ea, ei, ey.*

Formed by carrying the change of the preceding a little further—the flattest of all the tonics in a, but differing from all the others in that it is clearly a diphthong, which terminates with the sound of i as in pin. Hence, notwithstanding the near approach of the organs to contact, it has a strong vocality. In words transferred, with little or no change, from the Latin and Greek, it is often confounded with a as in arm, contrary to the best English usage.

*A*aron, *a*ble, *a*erie, Atè, *a*fflatus, *a*ncient, *a*ngel, *a*udacious, b*a*ne, b*a*thos, bim*a*'nous, C*a*naanite, ch*a*mber, ch*a*nge, ch*a*sten, com'r*a*de, d*a*te, d*a*ta, d*a*tum, d*ai*ry, d*a*nger, dec*a*'dence, dec*a*'dency, dr*a*ma, err*a*'tum, err*a*'ta, *ey*ry, f*ei*gn, fr*ei*ght, g*au*ge, g*ao*l, H*a*des, h*ei*nous, h*a*lo, inv*ei*gh, J*a*nus, K*a*lif, liter*a*ti, liter*a*tim, M*a*gi, m*a*nage, m*a*tins, m*a*tron, mess*a*ge, missionary, n*a*tion, or*a*nge, P*a*rian, p*a*tent (adjective) p*a*triot, p*a*triotism, p*a*tron, P*a*'ternoster, P*a*'tripassian, Ph*a*roah, pl*ai*t, pr*a*y, qu*ai*l, r*a*nge, r*ai*l, r*a*tio, s*ai*l, s*a*line, secret*a*ry, sol'*a*ce, st*ai*n, sw*a*the, tête-à-tête th*ey*, v*a*'demecum, verb*a*tim, v*a*g*a*'ry, v*a*gr*a*nt, vor*a*cious, voy*a*ge, y*ea*, w*ei*gh, z*a*ny.

§ 152. **The tonics in i are as in pine, pin.**

These two sounds may seem to be very different, but they stand in the closest relations to each other. Hence they are interchanged more frequently perhaps than any others. It would take a very long list of words to correct only the more common mispronunciations which arise from this cause.

1. *I as in pine—i, ai, ei, ey, eye, ie, y, uy.*

Properly a diphthong or slide, commencing with

the organs in a very open state, with the roof of the mouth raised considerably higher than in the most open of the preceding tonics, and with the corners of the mouth drawn farther apart. Thus commenced, it continues in a slide, the tongue and the roof of the mouth constantly approaching each other, until it closes with the sound of i as in pin.

*A*isle, ad'vertise, b*i*nd, b*i*og'raphy, b*i*ol'ogy, brig'antine, b*uy*, cho*i*r, ch*i*rog'raphy, col'umb*i*ne, crys'tall*i*ne, c*y*n'osure, decli'nature, despite', detri'tus, diam'eter, d*ie*, di'verse, dio'cesan, echi'nus, edif*y*, *ey*'as, *eye*'lash, fe'l*i*ne, fe'r*i*ne, flu'or*i*ne, gent*i*le, g*uy*, he*i*ght, heli'acal, h*y*drom'eter, h*y*per'bole, *i*'odine, *ia*m'bic, g*y*ration, k*i*nd, l*i*lac, literat*i*, m*i*'crocosm, m*i*'croscope, m*i*nus, M*i*thras, mus'cad*i*ne, n*i*h*i*l, ni'hilism, obl*i*ge, obl*i*que, pan'tom*i*me, pari'etal, p*i*ratical, p*ri*me'val, qu*i*escent, rhinoc'eros, respi'ratory, sacrif*i*ce, sac'char*i*ne, sat'urn*i*ne, ser'pent*i*ne, s*i*necure, sp*i*kenard, th*y*me, tribu'nal, tri'logy, tri'lobite, u'ter*i*ne, v*ie*, v*i*rus, w*i*se'acre, z*y*mol'ogy.

2. *I as in pin—i, ai, ei, oi, ui, e, ee, ey, ia, ie, a, ay, o, u, y.*

Properly a section cut off from the end of the preceding tonic, the organs being in precisely the same position in forming this, as at the close of that. It is one of the feeblest of the tonic sounds, for the reason that it is formed with the organs very near together. It will be observed that we have here no less than fifteen different signs representing the same sound; and besides this, the sound is often omitted where the sign remains. Thus the letter i is almost always silent when preceded by the sound of sh, or z as in azure, and followed by a, e, o; as in anxious, fashion, nation, partial, patient, precious, vision, pronounced, angshus, fashun, nashun, parshal, pashent, preshus, vizun (z as in azure).

Adaman'tine, adver'tisement, agile, aquiline, bargain, been, breeches, busy, business, carriage, certain, chime'ra, chimer'ical, chrysalis, cowardice, conduit, dis'cipline, diver'tise, duc'at, England, fa'vorite, fidelity, finance', finesse', forcible, foreign, forfeit, fran'chise, galley, gen'uine, hos'tile, hypochon'driac, irritability, irresistible, intes'tine, ju'venile, lettuce, lib'ertine, mar'itime, mer'cantile, mas'culine, marriage, min'ute, minute', mir'acle, mirac'ulous, mirror, mountain, myr'iad, mythol'ogy, nec'tarine, Pal'atine, philan'thropy, philol'ogy, philos'ophy, prac'tice, pretty, pu'erile, rally, rallied, ra'pine, Sunday, Monday, etc. tally, tor'toise, tribune, tyranny, unit, valley, villain, virulent, whim, women, xi'phias, zinc.

§ 153. **The tonics in e are as in err, pet, eve.**

These three sounds also are here placed in regular series from the greatest to the least openness of the organs. They are all, however, of comparatively feeble vocality.

1. *E as in err—e, ea, i, y.*

Formed by raising the tongue a little from its position in a as in arm, by slightly contracting the mouth cavity, and by throwing the vocal resonance a little higher up. This sound is very nearly the same with that of u in but, with which, therefore, it is frequently comfounded. Like the sound of a in care, it is almost always followed by r, the peculiar influence of which seems to determine its character.

Alert, berth, birth, birch, certain, der'nier, dirge, dirk, dirt, earl, early, earnest, earth, expert, fern, fertile, first, germ, gird, girl, guerdon, her, herb, heard, hearse, immerse, jerk, kernel learn, mercer, mercy, mirth, mirky, myrrh, myrtle, nerve, perch, person, quirk, re'pertory, serve, servant, serpent, sir, sir'loin, squirm, stir, stirrup, syrup, term, terse, therefore, verge, vernal, virtue, were, yearn, zerda.

2. *E as in pet*—*e, ea, ei, eo, ey, a, ai, ay, ie, oe, u.*

Formed by flattening the mouth cavity a very little from its position in the preceding, the tongue being a little more raised towards the roof of the mouth. The letter e, where otherwise it would represent this tonic, is frequently silent. The following are the most important cases, although not without exceptions.

(1.) At the end of syllables and words, as in ace, careless, time, sublime, wake.

(2.) In closing unaccented syllables when followed by l, n; as in drivel, even, grovel, harden, heaven, mantel, navel, ousel, ravel, seven, shekel, shovel, shrivel, snivel, weasel; pronounced, drivl, evn, gravl, hardn, heavn, etc.

(3.) In ed not preceded by d, t, at the end of verbs and participles; as in feared, praised, tossed, pronounced feard, prazd, tost. The e has its full sound, however, in the following participles used as adjectives, beloved, blessed, cursed, learned. Thus we say, He learnd well, and became a learned man. It has its full sound also in adjectives ending in ed, as in horned, naked, ragged, striped, winged.

This tonic is frequently confounded with e in err, or u in but. Thus American, error, chicken, children, herald, are mispronounced, Amurica, urror, chickun, childrun, hurald.

Ag*ai*n, ag*ai*nst, am*e*nity, *a*te (did *ea*t) assafœtida, b*e*rry, b*e*ryl, b*e*vel, b*u*ry, car*e*less, car*e*lessness (in *less* and *ness*, wherever they occur) cel′ibacy, ce′ment, cer′ebral, chimer′ical, def′icit, defalcation, deluge, departmen′tal, dep′recate, deprivation, der′elict, descant, des′tine, des′ultory, des′uetude, det′onate, det′riment, devoir′, dreamt, edible, endeavor, enemy, error, errand, evolution, feof, feofment, felon, fetichism, forget, friend, get, genealogy, herald, heroine, heroism, imbe′cile, inherit, instead, jeopard, jeopardy, jealousy, let, lev′ee, many, men′ace, measure, nonpareil′, parl*i*ament, peasant, petal, pl*ea*sure, poem, prebend, predicate, preface, prelate, presage, presentee′, prestige, question, quæstor or questor, realm, rec′reant, rec′reate, recreation, reg′imen, ren′dezvous, said, saith, ster′ile, ster′eoscope, ster′eotype, tepid, terror, treble, very, weapon, yellow, yes, yet, yesterday, zealot, zealous.

3. *E as in eve—e, ee, ea, ey, ae, i, ie, oe, uay.*

Formed by carrying the change of the mouth organs, described in the preceding tonic, a little further. The position of the organs is almost identical with that which they occupy in the formation of i as in pin; hence there is very little difference between the two sounds, and they are frequently confounded.

Æge′an, beard, breach, caprice, chime′ra, courier′, deduce′, degrade, de′viate, devious, *ea*st, *ee*l, *ea*r, educe′, e′dile, either, fe′line, fe′rine, fetich, fœtus or fetus, fierce, fretum, frequent, gleam, grega′rious, hear, heat, heave, heathen, heather, implead, jejune′, k*ey*, leap, leaped, leisure, lenient, lever, l*ey*, lineage, lineal, memoir, mien, neither, niece, or′deal, Or′leans, œsoph′agus, petrol, pique, pre′fect, pre′fix, q*uay*, query, quie′tus, ravine′, rear, receive, receipt, recluse′, research′, resource′, seine, sheik, shire, siege, sleek, treason, veal, weal, yeast, zeal.

§ 154. The tonics in o are as in not, nor, old.

In these three tonics, here arranged in series, as in the preceding cāses, there is a constant approach to a circular position of the lips, corresponding to the form of the letter which represents the sound.

1. *O as in not—o, ou, ow, a, au.*

Formed by rounding the mouth cavity, and the aperture of the lips, a very little from their position in a as in arm. There is a large class of words, chiefly such as have o followed in the same syllable by nasal or atonic sounds, in which it is differently pronounced, both by good orthoëpists, and good speakers. Thus the words gone, lost, shone, soft, are pronounced with the o either as in not, or in nor. The weight of authority, however, greatly preponderates in favor of the former, which accordingly is here followed, although the common practice in this country is in favor of the latter. This letter is often silent in on without the accent, at the close of dissyllables; as in bacon, cotton, deacon, iron, pardon, reason, weapon, pronounced, bacn, cotn, deacn, irn, pardn, reasn, weapn.

Allot, aloft, adopt, atrocity, beaumonde', bonnet, boss, brocade', broth, caul'iflower, cloth, closet, coffee, col'lier, cough, conserve (in *con* always) cost, cross, dem'agogue, dialogue, docile, dog, dogma, donkey, doll, domine, Donatist, dross, emboss, floss, forehead, frost, froth, gloss, gone, gong, grovel, hog, loft, Lombard, long, loss, lost, mock, Moslem, mosque, moth, off, offer, offspring, oft, often, omelet, orange, plot, process, product, progress, protest, prong, quadruped, quality, quandary, quantity, quarrel, scoff, shone, sol'ace, strong, swath, thong, trough, volley, wallet, wand, wander, wrong, wroth, yon, yonder.

2. *O as in nor—o, eo.*

Formed by rounding the aperture of the lips a

little from their position in the preceding, and by enlarging the back cavity of the mouth, so as to throw the vocal resonance a little further down. This sound differs hardly in a perceptible manner from a in all, with which consequently it is often confounded. It is almost always followed in the same syllable by r, except when it forms a diphthong with *i, y.*

Ad*o*rn, b*o*rn, c*o*rn, d*o*nor, d*o*rmant, eff*o*rt, f*o*r, f*o*rfeit, Ge*o*rge, h*o*rse, ind*o*rse, J*o*rdan, l*o*rn, m*o*rn, m*o*rning, m*o*rsel, m*o*rtal, n*o*rth, *o*rdain, p*o*rtion, rem*o*rse, res*o*rt, sn*o*rt, s*o*rcery, t*o*rn, w*o*rn.

3. *O as in old*—*o, oo, oa, ou, ow. ao, au, eo, eau, ew.*
Formed by rounding the mouth cavity and lips into a circle. It is properly, however, a diphthong or slide from a as in arm to u as in rule. Followed by r in the same syllable, it is often confounded with a as in all, or o as in nor, as in glaury for glory; and when it is correctly sounded in such words, there is a sectional tendency to suppress the following r, as in foth, cose, for forth, coarse.

Ad*o*re, al*o*ne, atr*o*cious, batt*eau*', b*o*re, b*ou*rn, b*eau*fet, br*o*'cage, br*oo*ch, c*oa*t, c*oa*rse, c*o*rse, c*o*re, c*ou*rt, c*ou*rt'ier, c*ou*teau, d*o*mes'tic, d*o*nor, d*oo*r, d*ou*gh, fl*oo*r, f*o*rge, f*o*rce, f*o*rt, f*ou*r, f*ou*rth, f*o*rth, g*oa*t, gl*o*ry, g*o*re, g*o*ry, h*au*tboy, h*oa*r, h*oa*rd, h*oa*rse, h*oa*ry, h*o*me, impl*o*re, j*ow*l, j*ow*ler, kn*o*ll, l*oa*th, l*o*th, l*ow*, mell*ow*, m*ou*rn, n*o*'-menclature, *o*nly, *o*pinion, p*o*rt, p*o*rter, p*o*rtly, p*o*rtion, p*o*rtrait, p*o*rtray', p*ou*r, p*ou*ltice, p*ou*ltry, Phar*ao*h, p*o*'tentate, res*ou*rce', rev*o*lt, r*oa*r, s*ew*, s*ew*er, sh*ew*, str*ew*, sh*o*re, sl*o*th, sn*o*re, s*ou*l, s*ou*rce, st*o*ne, sw*o*rd, t*o*'wards, tr*o*phy, tr*ow*, upr*oa*r, wh*o*le, w*oa*d, w*o*n't (will not), w*o*rn, y*eo*man, z*o*ne.

§ 155. **The tonics in u are as in hut, full, rule, use.**

These four tonics are arranged here in series from greater to less openness of the lips. They are all nearly related to the tonics in o, and consequently most of them are represented by o as often perhaps as by u. They are distinguished from each other by slight shades of difference; hence are frequently confounded; but the best speakers are careful give to each its precise value.

1. *U as in hut—u, ou, o, oe, eo.*

Formed by relaxing a very little the circular position of the lips, from that which they occupy in o as in old, and allowing them to recede a little further from each other. When followed by r in the same syllable, this tonic is taken by some orthoëpists for a different one; as if u in burn were different from u in but. This distinction, however, seems to have arisen from ascribing to the tonic something which is really due to the influence of the peculiar subtonic r. The case is somewhat similar to that of a in care, as distinguished from a in fate, and to that of o in nor, as distinguished from a in all; but the difference, in this case, does not seem to be sufficient to warrant a distinction. This sound is often confounded with o in not.

Above, atom, bulge, burden, burr, column, come, comely, comfit, comfort, companion, conduit, couple, covenant, cover, covetous, Cromwell, does, done, donjon, dost, doth, double, dove, duc'at, dungeon, dust, emulge, fulsome, glut, govern, grievous, gum, hiccough, hover, journal, journey, joust, love, money, mongrel, mother, motion, nation, none, of, one (pronounced wun), oven, plover, ronion, shove, shovel, sloven, smother, some, son, southern, sovereign, supple, touch, union, wonder, wont (accustomed) word, world, worm, worth.

2. *U as in full—u, o, oo, ou.*

Formed by bringing the lips a little nearer together than in the preceding—often confounded with it, and with u as in rule.

Book, bosom, brook, bull, could, crook, good, hood, hook, look, mistook, pull, pullet, pulley, push, put, shook, should, stood, took, wolf, wolverene', Wolsey, woman, wood, wool, would.

3. *U as in rule—u, ue, ew, o, oo, oe, ou, oeu, wo.*

This tonic differs in formation from the preceding as that differs from the one that immediately precedes it. The signs u, ue, ew, when preceded by r in the same syllable, always represent this sound. Some orthoëpists maintain that it is represented by these signs also whenever they are preceded by l in the same syllable; but the weight of authority is against them, and in favor of u as in use. A middle ground appears to be the true one. Accordingly when these signs are preceded by l combined with another consonant in the same syllable, they are taken to represent this tonic, as in flute, glue, slew, pronounced, floot, gloo, sloo. This is the common practice in England and this country, though it is different in Scotland and Ireland. The difficulty of pronouncing such words with u as in use, is such as to make it nearly certain that it will be entirely superseded by the pronunciation here given. But the difficulty is not so great when these signs are preceded by l alone; consequently, in such cases, the sound of u as in use has been retained, according to the best authorities.

Accou′tre, accrue′, amour′, behove′, blue, bousy, brew, canoe, clue, courier′, couteau′, crew, cruel, doom, drew, flew, flue, food, glutinous, groom, hoof, hoop, lose, loose, manoeu′ver, move, noose, ooze, plume, prove, prune, root, route, rou′tine, rue, ruby, ruse, shrew, soon, soot, stoop, to, too, tour, tourney, tournure′, true, two, who, whom, whose, wound, you, yours.

4. *U as in use*—*u, ue, ui, eau, eu, ew, ieu, iew.*

Properly a diphthong commencing with y as in yet, and closing with u as in rule. It originated in the attempt to form, with English organs, the peculiar sound of the French u, introduced by the Normans; which itself is formed by placing the tongue in the position of i as in pin, and then sounding u as in rule. The English substituted y for i—two sounds so nearly related that they are constantly interchanged—and thus formed u as in use. Hence this is a characteristic English sound, unknown in any other European language; and as such it should be carefully preserved wherever it properly occurs. For there is a strong sectional tendency to drop the y from this sound, wherever it is preceded in the same syllable by d, l, n, s, t, th, and thus to confound it with u as in rule. But the force and beauty of English speaking are greatly marred and enfeebled, when such words as allure, new, induce, enthusiasm, assume, tune, are pronounced as if they were spelled, alloor, noo, indooce, enthoosiasm, assoom, toon.

Adieu, assure, attitude, beauty, collude, constitution, delude, dew, due, during, elude, feud, few, grandeur, hew, hue, illude, juice, knew, lucid, lurid, lu′natic, Matthiew, news, opportunity, pew, presume, pur′lieu, purview, pursue′, relume′, resume′, sinew, sue, suit, suicide, superb, superfi′cial, stew, student, tube, tui′tion, tulip, Tuesday, value, voltigeur′.

§ 156. **The tonics in oi, ou, are as in oil, our.**

These are the only diphthongs in the language that are represented each by two signs; but they are not more truly diphthongal sounds than a in fate, i in pine, and o in old.

1. *Oi as in oil—oi, oy.*

This sound is vulgarly confounded with i as pine, as in jine for join, spile for spoil; also with o in nor, as in oshter for oyster.

Ann*oy*, ass*oi*l, b*oi*l, b*oy*, c*oy*, c*oi*l, desp*oi*l, f*oi*l, j*oi*st, j*oy*, l*oy*al, m*oi*l, n*oi*se, *oi*ntment, p*oi*nt, qu*oi*t, r*oy*alty, s*oi*l, t*oi*l, v*oy*age.

2. *Ou as in our—ou, ow.*

Formed by a slide from a in arm to u in hut. In some sections of the country this tonic is vulgarly mispronounced by placing a, e, before it; as in haouse, keow, for house, cow.

Acc*ou*nt, all*ow*, b*ou*gh, b*ow*, c*ow*, d*ou*bt, d*ou*ghty, en*ow*, fl*ou*r, g*ow*n, h*ou*se, kn*ou*t, l*ou*d, m*ou*nd, n*ow*, *ow*l, pr*ou*d, pr*ow*, r*ou*nd, r*ou*t, shr*ou*d, s*ou*nd, t*ow*n, w*ou*nd (did wind).

§ 157. **The subtonics are formed by a more full and varied operation of the articulating organs than the tonics.**

In the formation of this class of sounds, the organs of articulation are more active, and their work in differentiating the volume of sound is much more effective, than in the tonics. Hence they have a lower degree of vocality—being formed of the vocalized breath more or less checked, or stopped off, by a more decided action of the organs.

§ 158. **The subtonic feeble checks, y, w, wh, r, l, next to the tonics, have the strongest vocality.**

The vocality of these sounds is less than that of the tonics, because they are formed by 'a near approach to contact of the articulating organs; it is stronger than in the other subtonics, except the anomalous nasals, for the reason that all these sounds except l, are formed without actual contact. Hence they are all, except wh, properly semi-vowels, and as such are capable of performing all the functions of full tonics, in the formation of syllables (§ 119).

1. *Y as in yet—y, i, j, u.*

This subtonic sound connects itself immediately with the tonic i as in pin, being formed with the organs in the same position, except that the middle of the tongue is raised a little nearer the roof of the mouth. Hence in a strict arrangement, the i as in pin would have been the last of the tonics, and this would have come immediately after it. The two are so nearly related that the letters i, y, represent either sound indifferently.

(1.) It is represented by y followed in the same syllable by a tonic, that is, at the beginning of syllables and words; as in yellow, youth, beyond, steelyards. In all other circumstances (except in the word, hallelujah; pronounced, halleluyah), y represents i an in pine, or pin; as in by, my, folly, merry.

(2.) It is frequently represented by i preceded by an accented syllable ending in l, n, t, and followed by a, o; as in banian, biliary, bilious, million, pillion, poniard, scullion; pronounced, banyan, bilyary, bilyus, milyun, pilyun, ponyard, sculyun.

(3.) It is represented by u preceded by g, and followed by a tonic; as in guard, guardian, guerdon, guess, guest, guide, guile, guise, guilt; pronounced, gyard, gyardyan, gyerdon, gyess, gyest, gyide, gyile, gyilt. Exceptions to this are Guelf, guiniad, and their derivatives; pronounced, Gwelf, gwiniad.

(4.) It often enters as a transition sound after g, k (however k may be represented) before a as in ask, hat, and before i as in pine, pin, and before e as in err; as in cat, gat, casket, gasket, girl, gird, kind; pronounced, cyat, gyat, cyasket, gyerl, gyerd, kyind. The correct pronunciation of such words brings the organs into the position in which y is formed, although the dictionaries do not always indicate it. There is, however, a sectional tendency to introduce this transition sound before a as in arm, and vulgarly before e as in err when preceded by p; as in car, garland, perch, pert; mispronounced, cyar, gyarland, pyerch, pyert.

(5.) The manner in which this consonantal sound enters into u as in use, pronounced, yoose, determines the point that the indefinite article before it should stand without the euphonic n. We should always say, a useful, not, an useful thing. This latter is as incorrect as, an youth, an yellow flower.

(6.) This sound is often improperly suppressed, as in east for yeast; and often vulgarly inserted where it does not belong, as in yearth for earth, yearn for earn.

2. *W as in way—w, u, o.*

This sound connects itself with u in rule, in a manner similar to that in which y is connected with i in pin. It is formed by the organs in the same position in which u is formed, except that the lips are drawn a little closer together.

(1.) It is represented by w in precisely the same circumstances in which the preceding sound is represented by y; that is, at the beginning of words and syllables, when it is followed immediately by a tonic; as in awake, beware, war, well, worth. In all other cases, either it forms a diphthong with another tonic, as in cow; or it becomes the full tonic u, and is so represented in modern English orthography; or it is suppressed, *i. e.* the letter is silent.

(2.) It is represented by u preceded by q, g, and sometimes by s, when followed by a tonic in the same syllable; as in assuage, conquest, desuetude, frequent, mansuetude, persuade, quarrel, quiet, suavity, suite; pronounced, asswage', cong'kwest, des'wetude, fre kwent, man'swetude, perswade', kwarrel, kwiet, swavity, sweet. It is also represented by w in buoy, pronounced, bwoy. Exceptions to this rule are found in words transferred from the French, as in coquette', conquer, liquor, masquerade', in which the u is silent.

(3.) It is represented by o in the word choir, pronounced, kwire; also o is vulgarly pronounced w in some sections of the country in such words as gwine for going.

(4.) As a transition sound, it is, in most cases, inserted before oi, in such French words as boudoir, devoir, reservoir, soirée, pronounced, boudwor', devwor', reservwor', sworay'. It is always so inserted after o, u, before a, e, i, in different syllables of the same word; as in coadjutor, fluent, going, pursuant, poem, proem, ruin, pronounced, cowadju'tor, flu'went, go'wing, po'wem, pro'wem, pursu'want, ru'win. For in all such cases, the articulating organs, in passing from o, u, to a, e, i, necessarily come into the position in which w is formed: we cannot avoid making this sound, except by a pause, or interruption of the voice, between the syllables of the word, which would essentially mar its unity of sound (§ 148—4).

(5.) It is always heard before o in one, pronounced wun; and hence, as in the case of y in u as in use, the indefinite article should always stand before this word without the euphonic n. Such an one is as incorrect as such an wail, or such an wind.

(6.) W is always silent at the beginning of words and syllables before r, and sometimes before h; as in wrath, writhe, wrong, who, whom, whose, whole; pronounced, rath, rithe, rong, hoo, hoom, hoose, hole; also in the word, answer.

3. *Wh as in when.*

This sound commences with an expulsion of the whispering breath, the lips being in the position in which w is formed; the breath is then gradually vocalized. The atonic h can hardly be said to form any part of it. The difficulty of representing it by any of the letters of the English alphabet, has caused it to be differently noted at different times; formerly by huw, as in huwen for when, afterwards by hw, as in hwen, and at present by wh, as in when.

(1.) The w of this sign is silent before o, oo, and then the h resumes its atonic character; as in whoop, pronounced, hoop (§ 158—2, (6)), except in whorl, whortleberry, and their derivatives.

(2.) This sound is often confounded with w in way; as in when, which, why, mispronounced, wen, wich, wy. This is a very damaging fault, as it greatly enfeebles English speaking. In the following words, and all their derivatives, the sound of wh should be articulated in all its strength.

*Wh*ack, *wh*ale, *wh*arf, *wh*at, *wh*eat, *wh*eel, *wh*eedle, *wh*eeze, *wh*elk, *wh*elm, *wh*elp, *wh*ere, *wh*erry, *wh*et, *wh*ether, *wh*ey, *wh*ich, *wh*iff, *wh*ig, *wh*ile, *wh*im, *wh*ip, *wh*irl, *wh*isk, *wh*isker, *wh*isper, *wh*ist, *wh*istle, *wh*it, *wh*ite, *wh*ither, *wh*ittle, *wh*orl, *wh*ortleberry, *wh*y.

4. *R as in ray.*

Formed with the mouth open, nearly as in a in arm, and with the middle of the tongue raised up towards the roof, and the tip of the tongue turned up so as nearly to touch it at the highest point of the arch. Sometimes in the formation of this sound, there is a broken or trembling contact between the tip of the tongue and the roof of the mouth, which produces what is called the "roll" of the r. A slight degree of this is thought by many good speakers to impart greater force to the words in which this sound occurs.

(1.) It has great strength of vocality, because, like y, w, it is formed without contact of the organs and unlike wh, its vocality is pure, or unmixed with the atonic breath. Hence, in Sanskrit, it is regarded and treated as a vowel, or full tonic. In English also it frequently performs all the functions of a full tonic in the formation of syllables; as in the terminations, cre, chre, in acre, mas'sacre, sep'ulchre, in which the final e is silent. Thus also its vocality is so strong in such monosyllables as flour, hire, lore, more, roar, soar, that careful articulation is required to prevent them from running into dissyllables, so as to become undistinguishable respectively from flower, higher, lower, mower, rower, sower. It is, moreover, in consequence of this strength of vocality that it commonly produces, as we have seen, a marked effect upon the preceding tonic (§§ 151—5; 153—1; 154—2; 155—1).

(2.) It is sometimes articulated in too hard a manner, by bringing the root of the tongue too near the roof of the mouth, and holding it there too firmly; as in darrk, marrk, for dark, mark.

(3.) It is sometimes vulgarly added to a at the end of words, as in idear, Mariar, sawr, for idea, Maria, saw.

(4.) It is often improperly suppressed; as in hoss, or ho'se, for horse, and in cose or co'se, for course; and in the following additional examples.

Absorb, adorn, car, corn, core, door, drawer, endorse, effort, for, forego, force, fourth, guard, hair, jar, learn, mercy, nerve, observe, pear, quirk, rare, short, tear, vernal, warm, worm, yearn.

5. *L as in lay.*

Formed with the mouth open, about in the position in which e as in err is formed, by placing the tip of the tongue in contact with the front roof of the mouth, yet so as to allow the sound to escape freely on both sides of the point of contact. The fact that there is this actual contact, might seem to be a good reason for excluding this sound from the class of feeble checks, and placing it with the soft or hard. But it is retained here for the reason that the point of contact is so slight, and allows the vocality to escape on each side of it with so much fullness, that, in this respect, it is hardly, if at all, inferior to r, with which it stands in the very closest relations, and like which it is regarded and treated in Sanskrit as a vowel.

(1.) It often forms a perfect syllable by itself, or with other sub-tonic or atonic sounds, especially in the terminations el, il, le, in which e, i, are silent; as in able, addle, bottle, cattle, cradle, devil, diddle, dingle, drizzle, evil, fiddle, griddle, grizzle, higgle, jumble, kindle, little, middle, muzzle, pickle, puzzle, riddle, stickle, wrinkle; pronounced, abl, bottl, devl, evl, etc.

(2.) It is often suppressed before another consonant in the same syllable; as in alms, balm, calf, calm, calve, chalk, could, half, halve, palm, psalm, should, would; pronounced, ams, sam, etc.

§ 159. The sub-tonic soft checks, z in azure, z in zone, th in then, j, v, have the next strongest vocality.

In forming these elements, the organs require to be held firmly in such a degree of contact as allows of an indefinite prolongation of the sounds. The breath of which they are formed is very partially vocalized, which, as it escapes through the organs in partial contact, gives them all a certain buzzing character. Their vocality is less than that of the preceding class, because they are formed by actual contact; and it is greater than that of the following hard checks, except the nasals, because the contact is soft or partial.

1. *Z as in azure—z, g, s, ss.*

Formed of the partially vocalized breath, by placing the flat surface of the tongue in soft contact with the roof of the mouth, with the teeth brought almost together. The sound thus produced is a sort of buzz, precisely identical with that of soft g in French, and that of s in measure.

(1.) It is seldom represented by z, except when z is followed by u as in use, or by ie in unaccented syllables; as in azure, razure, seizure, brazier, glazier, grazier.

(2.) It is represented by g in many words transferred from the French, as menage', mena'gerie, giraffe', regime', rouge.

(3.) It is commonly represented by s after an accented tonic, and followed by ia, ie, io, iu, u; also, by ss in the words, scission, obscission, recission. The following are examples under this rule.

Ambrosia, ambrosial, Asia, brasier or brazier, Carte'sian, closure, cohesion, collision, composure, contusion, osier, crosier,

PRONUNCIATION. 271

deci*s*ion, deri*s*ion, displea*s*ure, divi*s*ion, eccle*s*ia, eccle*s*iastic, Eli*s*ian, Eli*s*ium, enclo*s*ure, enthu*s*iasm, eva*s*ion, exclu*s*ion, expo*s*ure, Fri*s*ian, gra*s*ier, ho*s*ier, illu*s*ion, inci*s*ion, inci*s*ure, lei*s*ure, le*s*ion, mea*s*ure, mispri*s*ion, persua*s*ion, plea*s*ure, preclu*s*ion, protru*s*ion, ra*s*ure, ro*s*ier, trea*s*ure, vi*s*ion, u*s*ual.

2. *Z as in zone—z, x, c, s.*

Formed of the partially vocalized breath, by placing the end of the tongue in soft contact with the upper front gums, the teeth being almost closed. This sound, which is a proper buzz, is closely cognate with the atonic s, with which therefore it is frequently confounded.

(1.) It is always represented by z, x, at the beginning of words, as in zodiac, zumic, Xenophon, xiphoid. It enters also, together with g as in gay, into the sound of x in certain other circumstances (§ 162—1, (2)). Both these sounds of x are heard in Xerxes, pronounced, Zergzez.

(2.) It is represented by c where c stands for s and s would represent this sound; as in discern, sice, suffice, sacrifice; pronounced, dizzern, size, suffize, sacrifize.

(3.) The cases in which it is represented by s are very numerous and complicated, so that they cannot be reduced under certain rules. The following are the most important.

(*a.*) In some derivatives to distinguish them from their primitives; as in use, abuse, close, grease, rise, (verbs) usage, greasy, gaseous, gooseberry; pronounced, uze, abuze, cloze, greaze, rize, uzage, greazy, gazeous, goozeberry.

(*b.*) In the plural of nouns and third person singular of verbs, when preceded by a tonic or subtonic; as in arms, bonds, cause, digs, heads, rings, churches, boxes, prices, charges, teaches; pronounced, armz, bondz, cauze, digz, headz, ringz, churchez, boxez, pricez, chargez, teachez.

(c.) Preceded by the inseparable prepositions, ob, de, pre, re, and followed by a tonic; also in usurp, and in all its derivatives; likewise in absolve, but not in all its derivatives.

Desert, deserve, desiderate, design, desire, desist, observe, present, preserve, preside, presume, resemble, resent, reserve, reside, resign, resile, resist, resolve, resort, resound, result, resume, resurrection.

(d.) It should be represented by s in the inseparable preposition, trans, whenever it is followed by a tonic. A strong analogy requires this, and it is thought to be according to the best usage, although the authorities in orthöepy do not warrant the rule in a universal form. Following the rule, all such words as transaction, transit, transition, transitive, should be pronounced, tranzaction, tranzit, tranzition, tranzitive.

(e.) It is represented by s in the inseparable preposition, dis, when followed by an accented tonic or subtonic, except sometimes u, w. Under the analogy of this rule we have also discern, dissemble, dissolve; pronounced dizzern, etc. In the following words, therefore, and in all their derivatives in which dis is followed by the accent, s has the sound of z in zone.

Disarm, disaster, disband, disbark, disbench, disbind, disburden, disburse, discern, disdain, disdeify, disease, dissemble, disgage, disgarland, disgarnish, disgorge, disgrace, disguise, disgust, dishonor, dishonest (h silent) disintegrate, disin'terest, disjecta, disjection, disjoin, disjoint, disjunct, dislike, dislimn, dislodge, disloyal, dismantle, dismast, dismay, dismember, dismiss, dismount, disnaturalize, disorder, disorganize, disown, disrelish, disrobe, disrupt, dissolve, disvalve, disvalue.

3. *Th as in then.*

Formed of the partially vocalized breath, by placing the end of the tongue between the front, in soft contact with the upper teeth. Neither of the atonics, t, h, which in our imperfect symbolization are taken to represent this sound, forms any part of it. For each of these is formed by an entirely different position of the organs, and they are without vocality, whilst this is partially a vocal sound.

It is represented by th in verbs ending in the, and in some without the e; also, in the plural of some nouns the singular of which have the sound of th in thin, and in other words. It is heard in the following, and in all their derivatives.

Bathe, baths, beneath, bequeath, blithe, breathe, burthen, clothe, clothes, hither, farther, further, lathe, laths, lithe, loathe, mother, mouth (verb) mouths, oaths, other, paths, rather, smooth, smother, scythe, soothe, swathe, swaths, teethe, than, that, the, thee, their, them, then, thence, there, these, they, thine, this thither, those, thou, thus, thy, tithe, underneath, with, wreathe, writhe.

4. *V as in vile—v, f, ph.*

Formed of the breath as in the preceding, by placing the under lips in soft contact with the upper front teeth. This sound is represented by f in one word, the preposition, of; pronounced, uv; by ph in a few words, such as nephew, Stephen; pronounced nevu, Steven; and by v wherever it occurs, as in the following examples.

<small>Avail, brave, cave, dove, eve, five, grave, hive, ivy, Jove, knave, live, move, novice, oven, pave, quaver, rave, strive, trav'erse, valve, velvet, vulviform, wave.</small>

5. *J as in joy—j, g.*

Formed of the partially vocalized breath, and with the organs very nearly in the position of z in azure, except that the tongue is brought a little farther forward, and at first is in harder contact with the roof of the mouth, which contact is relaxed in forming the sound. The two sounds consequently are closely cognate with each other.

(1.) It is commonly represented by g before e, i, y, in words derived from the Latin, and in some derived from the French in which g does not represent z as in azure. It is also represented by g preceded by d in the same syllable, in which case the d is silent; as in budge, fudge, pronounced, buj, fuj.

(2.) A slight sound of 'j enters in transition after d at the end of an accented syllable followed by u in use, as in the words credulous, educate, individual, pendulous; pronounced, credjulous, edjucate, individjual, pendjulous. It is a common error to render this transition sound with too great fullness and strength; also, to introduce it after d before accented syllables, and sometimes even to turn d into j in such cases: thus dupe, during, obdu'rate, are often mispronounced, jupe, juring, objurate.

(3.) It is represented by j wherever j occurs.

A*g*itate, bour*g*eon, ca*j*ole, dud*g*eon, en*j*oin, fled*g*e, *g*erm, *g*yration, hed*g*e, in*j*unction, *j*ust, ked*g*e, led*g*e, ma*j*esty, nud*g*e, obli*g*e, pa*g*e, ra*g*e, sa*g*e, tra*j*ection, ur*g*e, villa*g*e, wa*g*e.

§ 160. **The sub-tonic hard checks, m, n, ng, nk, g, d, b, are all formed of the vocalized breath, with the mouth organs in a state of perfect closure.**

These sounds are formed of the vocalized breath, with the mouth organs as above, so that the outflow of the sound through the mouth is perfectly stopped off. A certain resonance of the voice then takes place in the nasal cavities, which gives these sounds their peculiar character. The proof of this is that no sound can escape from the mouth, and that the vibrations of the sound in the nasal cavities is quite sensible upon close attention. This resonance, however, is very different in the case of the nasals from what it is in the subnasals (§ 111).

§ 161. **The nasals m, n, ng, nk, all except the last, have a very full vocality, and are capable of being indefinitely prolonged.**

In all these sounds, except nk, there is a perfectly free escape of the vocalized breath through the nostrils. Hence their vocality is nearly equal to that of the tonics themselves, and, with the above exception, they are capable of performing all the functions of tonics in the formation of syllables. This capacity is much more fully exhibited in some other languages than it is in English. In that large and interesting family of African tongues, called the Kaffir or Nilotic, which are spoken by almost all the African tribes south of the Mountains of the Moon, these nasals form syllables by themselves quite as frequently as the tonics. Thus in the Bake'le and Mpong'we dialects, mpa'ka, mpa'ga, *gift*—nto'thi, nto'no, *breast*—ngu'ba, ngu'wa, *shield*. This is the case also in some of the islands of the Pacific. In English, however, ng never forms a syllable by itself; m sometimes does, as in yes-m, the colloquial pronunciation of yes ma'am; and n very frequently, as in even, heaven, seven; pronounced, evn, heavn, sevn, (§ 153—2, (2.)) The nasals are properly humming sounds. There is, however, a false or impure sound, which is called "the nasal tang," and which is formed by closing or obstructing the nostrils in front, so that a peculiar resonance takes place immediately behind the obstruction; but this abominable impurity, which sometimes affects all the sounds of speech, is no legitimate nasal. When, moreover, the cavities of the nostrils are closed or obstructed farther back, in consequence of which the resonance of the sound is confined to these cavities at the point where they open into the mouth, the result is that the nasals are reduced to subnasals; that is, m, n, ng, are perfectly identified respectively with b, d, g. A person with such an obstruction, attempting to say, Uncle John made me sing, will say, Ugle Jod bade be sig. This exhibits the close cognate relation between the nasals and subnasals respectively, and points out the precise difference between the two kinds of sound.

Pronunciation. 277

1. *M as in may.*

Formed by closing the lips in hard contact, and allowing the whole volume of sound to pass through the cavities of the nostrils. Hence the strong vocality of this sound.

It is represented by m wherever m occurs, except in the words, compt, accompt, accomptant, comptable, comptroller, comptrollership; pronounced, count, account, accountant, countable, controller, controllership.

Arm, cram, doom, emmet, fame, groom, hum, impart, jam, limit, Mamma', namby-pamby, ombre, pump, ram, sum, timber, umbrella, vim, wampum, yam.

2. *N as in nay.*

Formed by placing the flat surface of the tongue at its tip in hard contact with the roof of the mouth near the upper front gums, the sound passing freely through the nostrils as before. Its vocality is of equal strength to that of the preceding.

(1.) It forms a syllable by itself much more frequently than m, as in most dissyllables ending in en without the accent; also in many in on—e, o, being silent in these cases. Examples of this have been given before (§§ 153—2, (2); 154—1). In the following words, however, it does not form a syllable by itself, the e of the last syllable being fully sounded; aspen, chicken, flower, Hymen, hyphen, kitchen, latten, linen, marten, mitten, mynchen, omen, patten, platen, pollen, siren, sloven, sudden, ticken, woolen, women.

(2.) N is silent when it follows l, m, in the same syllable; as in condemn, contemn, hymn, hymning, kiln, limn, mnemonics; but not in condemning, contemning, nor in such words as government.

<small>A*n*, ca*n*not, du*n*, e*n*unciate, fa*n*, gra*nn*y, hunter, i*n*, ju*n*to, ke*n*, le*n*t, ma*n*, none, o*n*, pi*n*, re*nn*et, sti*n*t, te*n*d, u*n*der, vi*n*e, wi*n*e, yo*n*, we*n*t, we*n*d.</small>

3. *Ng as in sing—ng, n.*

Formed by placing the back part of the tongue in hard contact with the corresponding part of the roof of the mouth, the breath as in the preceding. The sound of n does not enter into it at all, being formed with the organs in a different position. It is represented by n as often perhaps as by its own proper sign of ng, as in the following cases.

(1.) Where ng is followed in the same word by another syllable beginning with a tonic, the n has the sound of ng, and the g retains its own sound; as in the words, England, finger, longer, longest, stronger, strongest; pronounced, Inggland, fingger, longger, strongger. There are several exceptions to this rule, as where the following syllable is any of the verbal endings, est, eth, ing, ed, er of the *nomen agentis;* as in singest, singeth, singing, singer, winged; in all which ng represents its proper sound.

(2.) Where n is followed by k, or c, ch, q, representing the sound of k, n commonly represents the sound, ng; as in ankle, anchor, conquer, uncle; pronounced, angkle, angkur, congker, ungkle. The exceptions to this rule are the very few words in which nk, nc, represent the fourth nasal as given below.

(3.) Where n is followed by x, as in anxious, larynx, lynx, sphinx; pronounced, angshus, laryngx, lyngx, sphingx.

Under these three rules, n represents the sound of ng in the following words, and in all their derivatives.

Anger, angle, anguish, angular, anxiety, bank, banquet, blank, blanket, brink, bungle, cancrine, canker, cinque, clangor, clank, concord, conger, congress, crank, crink, dangle, dank, donkey, drink, drunk, elongation, English, flank, frank, function, fungous, gangrene, gingle, hank, hanker, hunger, ink, jangle, jungle, junk, lank, language, languish, languor, linger, link, mangle, mingle, mink, minx, monger, mongrel, monk, monkey, pink, precinct, prink, quincunx, rancor, rank, rankle, sanction, sanctify, sanctuary, sanguine, shingle, single, singular, sink, sphincter, sunk, spank, sprinkle, spunk, tank, thank, think, tinkle, tingle, unguent, unction, unctuous, vanquish, wink, wrinkle, Yankee, zink.

4. *Nk as in blink—nk, nc.*

Formed by placing the organs in the same position as in the preceding, and then stopping off the sound with the atonic k. There are only a few words in the language in which this sound occurs, among which are blink, kink, shrink, cunctation, cunctator.

§ 162. The sub-nasals, g, d, b, are incapable of being prolonged.

The principal difference between the nasals and subnasals, with respect to their formation, is that in the former, the resonance of the voice takes place throughout the whole length of the nasal cavities, from which, except in the case of nk, it escapes in a sound capable of indefinite prolongation; whilst in the latter, the resonance is restrained to the back cavities, and to the mouth where these cavities open into it, and where the sound is soon stopped off. In the case of the subnasals also there is a peculiar pressure of the breath upon the place of contact of the organs. The nasals and subnasals are cognate with each other, and also with the atonic hard checks, k, t, p, as hereafter exhibited.

1. *G as in gay*—*g, n, x.*

Formed by placing the back part of the tongue against the corresponding part of the roof of the mouth, and pressing the vocalized breath against the place of contact. The sound thus produced seems to be stopped off by the closing of the nasal cavities, where these enter the mouth, by the pressure of the soft palate. This sound is cognate with ng, and with k; the organs in all three cases being very nearly in the same position.

(1.) It is represented by g before a, o, u, as in gave, gone, gun; gaol, pronounced, jale, is the only exception; also, in most words of Anglo-Saxon origin before e, i, y, as in get, give, boggy.

(2.) It is represented in x in the inseparable preposition ex, which follows the analogy of dis (§ 159 —2, (3), (e)); that is, the x of this preposition represents the sound of gz (z as in zone) when followed by an accented tonic; also, in some derivatives from such words, where the following tonic is without the accent; as in exaltation; pronounced, egzaltation. Luxurious, and uxorious, pronounced lugzurious (z as in azure), ugzorious (z as in zone), follow the analogy of this rule. There are a few exceptions to it, mostly in words transferred, with little or no change, from Greek or Latin; such as exæresis, exangia, ex-animo, exan'thema, exan'thesis, exect', exe'dra, ex-e'sion; pronounced, ekse'resis, eksan'gia, eksan'imo, etc.; also, a few words in which u is the accented tonic, such as exude, exudate; pronounced, eksude', eksu'date.

(3.) For the sound of g represented in n, see § 161—3.

(4.) G is silent before n at the beginning and end of words; also before ht, and commonly before h, at the end of words; as in feign, fight, gnaw, high, nigh, right, sigh, sign. It is sometimes improperly suppressed, as in recognize, mispronounced, reco-nize.

In the following words, and in all their derivatives in which x is followed by an accented tonic, it represents the sound of gz (z as in zone).

Exa'cerbate, exa'cinate, exac'ulate, exact', exag'gerate, exag'itate, exalt', exam'en, exam'ine, exam'ple, exan'gulous, exan'guous, exan'imate, exan'imous, exan'them, exant'late, exar'illate, exas'perate, exauc'torate, exau'gurate, exau'thorate, exau'thorize, exec'utive, exec'utor' exec'utory, exec'utrix, exem'plar, exempt', exen'terate, exergue', exert', exes'tuate, exhaust', exher'itation, exhib'it, exhil'arate, exhort', exhume' (h silent) exic'cate, exig'uous, exile' (verb) exist', exi'tial, exolve', exon'erate, exor'bitant, exor'dial, exor'dium, exos'culate, exot'ic, exult', exul'cerate, exun-date.

2. *D as in day.*

Formed by placing the flat surface of the end of

the tongue in hard contact with the front roof of the mouth, and pressing the vocalized breath against the point of contact. The resonance of the voice in the back cavities of the nostrils, and in the mouth where these open into it, is quite sensible while it lasts, but is soon stopped off. This sound is cognate with n, on the one hand, and with t, on the other—the organs hardly varying in position at all.

It is represented by d wherever d occurs, except that this letter is silent in Wednesday, and wherever it is followed by g in the same syllable, as in abridge, edge.

Ad*d*ition, bi*d*, cree*d*, dee*d*, e*d*it, fe*d*, gra*d*e, hea*d*, i*d*iom, ja*d*e, ki*d*, hi*d*, li*d*, ma*d*, no*d*, o*d*e, pai*d*, qui*d*, ru*dd*y, stai*d*, to*dd*le, u*dd*er, vi*d*el'icet, wi*d*ow, yiel*d*, ze*d*.

3. *B as in bay.*

Formed by placing the lips in hard contact with each other, and pressing the vocalized breath against the place of contact. The resonance is as in d. The sound is cognate with m and p.

B is silent before t, and after m, in the same syllable; as in debt, doubt, redoubt, lamb, limb, comb, dumb; pronounced, det, dout, etc.; except in the word, succumb and its derivatives. It is silent also in some other words which do not strictly fall under the rule, as in subtle, pronounced, suttle.

A*b*bey, ca*b*bage, da*bb*le, e*bb*ing, fa*b*le, ga*b*le, ha*b*it, inhi*b*it, jo*b*, li*b*erty, mo*b*, no*b*, o*b*lige, pe*bb*le, qui*bb*le, ra*bb*le, sa*b*le, tu*b*, um*b*rage, we*b*.

§ 163. **The atonics, h, th in thin, sh, s, f, k, t, p, are distinguished from their cognate sub-tonics by their want of vocality, and by a different action of the breath.**

These sounds are simply articulations, which check, or stop off, the whispering breath. For even where they are preceded by a full tonic, and seem to stop off its vocality, as in the word, hot, it will be found, upon close attention, that the vocality is limited to the tonic, o, and does not affect the t. They are further distinguished from their cognate sub-tonics, by a slight variation of the position of the organs in some cases, and in all, by a marked difference in the action of the breath. If this were not so, it would be impossible to distinguish cognates of the two classes, when speaking in a whisper; but any one will readily notice the difference between the whispering sound of b and p. Upon the same principle as that applied to the subtonics, the atonics also are divided into the three corresponding subdivisions of hard, soft and feeble checks.

§ 164. **The atonic feeble check h as in hay.**

This is the only feeble check of this class. It is formed by a simple emission of the whispering breath, through the open mouth—the shape of the opening corresponding to that of the tonic by which h is followed in the syllable. This variation in the position of the organs in forming this element, might be exhibited throughout the whole range of the tonics; as in harsh, high, here, hot, huge, hoist, house.

H is frequently silent, as in the following cases.

1. Often at the beginning of words, as in the following, and all their derivatives—heir, herb, honest, honor, hostler, hospital, humble, humor.

2. After another consonant in the same syllable, and before another consonant, or alone, at the end of a syllable; as in ghost, aghast, light, bright, ah!

3. Before th, as in aphthong, diphthong, triphthong, diphtheria, naphtha, ophthalmia, pronounced, apthong, dipthong, naptha, opthalmia.

4. At the beginning of syllables preceded by dis, ex, when pronounced, diz, egz; as in dishonest, dishonor, exhale, exhalation, exhibit, exhort; pronounced, dizon'est, dizon'or, egzale, egzort.

What is called the cockney dialect in England, is characterized chiefly by sounding the silent h, by suppressing h where it has its proper sound, and by introducing it where the letter does not occur; also, by a similar perversion of the euphonic n of the indefinite article. It is a very curious phenomenon, and well worthy of minute investigation.

H is silent in the following additional examples.

Anthony, burgh, cirrhous, delight, Esther, freight, ghastly, gherkin, height, isthmus, John, knight, light, myrrh, night, nigh, pallah, right, sep'ulchre, sirrah, Thames, Thomas, thyme, wright.

§ 165. **The atonic soft checks, th as in thin, sh, s, f, are formed of the whispering breath by soft contact of the organs.**

The principal difference between these sounds and their corresponding subtonic soft checks, th as in then, z as in azure, z as in zone, and v, is in their want of vocality. The contact and position of the organs is almost the same.

1. *Th as in thin.*

Cognate of the subtonic th in then, and formed by the organs in the same position, except that the tongue is raised a little higher within the mouth, and the end of it placed a little further between the teeth. The sounds represented by t, h, do not enter into it. No certain rule can be given to determine when th represents this sound, and when th as in then; although many nouns have this in the singular, and th as in then, in the plural; and some verbs have the latter, to distinguish them from the nouns with the former, from which they are derived. Thus the first two of the following words have the atonic, and the last two the subtonic: lath, mouth, laths, to mouth. This sound is heard in the following examples.

A*th*let′ic, ba*th*, bir*th*, bo*th*, brea*th*, ca*th*olic, dea*th*, do*th*, e*th*ical, e*th*nology, for*th*, fif*th*, Go*th*, ha*th*, hea*th*, in*th*rall, jacin*th*, ki*th* la*th*, li*th*ot′omy, me*th*od, mir*th*, my*th*, no*th*ing, orni*th*ol′ogy, pa*th*, pa*th*ol′ogy, plin*th*, quo*th*, ra*th*, some*th*ing, *th*ird, *th*orn, *th*rash, *th*rush, tru*th*s, wra*th*, you*th*s.

2. *Sh as in shun—sh, sc, s, ss, c, ch, t, x.*

Cognate of z in azure—organs the same—breath atonic. Neither s nor h forms any part of this sound. For in the formation of h, the organs are perfectly open, whilst in sh, they are in contact; and in s, the contact is considerably further forwards in the mouth than in this sound. Its symbolization is peculiarly complicated and difficult. It is represented as follows.

(1.) By sh wherever both these letters occur together in the same syllable.

(2.) By c, sc, preceded by an accented tonic, and followed by ea, eo, ia, ie, io, as in ocean, cetaceous, facial, nescient, precious; pronounced, o'shan, ceta'shus, fa'sheal, nesh'eënt, presh'us.

(3.) By ch in all words transferred from the French with little or no change of spelling, as in chagrin, chaise, chateau; pronounced, shagreen', shaze, shato'; except in the word chivalry and its derivatives, pronounced, tshivalry; also, by ch preceded by n, t, in the same syllable, as in batch, catch, cranch, ditch; pronounced, batsh, catsh, cransh, ditsh; and it enters, together with t, into the sound of ch in all other circumstances, except where ch represents k (§ 166—1, (3)), as in child, much, such, pronounced, tshild, mutsh, sutsh.

(4.) By s, ss, preceded by an accented tonic and followed by ea, eo, ia, io, iu, u (except where s has the sound of z in azure) as in nauseate, nauseous, cassia, passion, Cassius; pronounced, nausheate, nausheus, cashea, pashun, Casheus; and in a few words which do not fall under this rule, as in sure, sugar, sumach; pronounced, shure, shugar, shumak Following the analogy of these few exceptions, instead of the rule, many speakers erroneously give to s the sound of sh in such words as assume, superb, superstitious, etc. mispronounced, ashume, shuperb, shuperstitious, etc.

(5.) By t preceded by a syllable with either the primary or secondary accent (except when such syllable ends in s) and followed by ia, ie, io, as in expatiate, sentient, vitious, pronounced, expasheate, sensheënt, vishus.

(6.) By x preceded by n at the end of an accented syllable, and followed by io, as in anxious, pronounced angshus; also it enters, together with k, into the sound of x at the end of such a syllable. and followed by io, u, as in noxious, fixure, pronounced, nokshus, fikshure.

(7.) It enters as a transition sound after t preceded by the accent and followed by u, either with or without silent letters; also, when the preceding accented syllable ends in s, and t is followed by ia, io; and before the termination, ure, in all cases in which it is preceded by t; as in righteous, christian, bastion, fixture, creature, garniture, legislature, nature, nurture, mixtion, mixture, virtue; pronounced, rightshus, christshan, bastshun, fixtshure, creatshure, gar'nitshure, legislatshure, natshure, nurtshure, mikstshum, mikstshure, virtshue. This transition sound in all such cases should be very slight. It is a common error to render it with too great fullness; as, also, to insert it after t in other connections not covered by the rule, as in beauteous, calamitous, covetous, duteous, opportunity, perpetuity, Tuesday, tune, etc. mispronounced, beautsheous, calamitshus, covetshus, dutsheous, opportshunity, perpetshuity, Tsheusday, tshune, etc.

It is also a common error to give sh the sound of s in such words as shrewd, shrink, shrine, shroud, mispronounced, srewd, srink srine, sroud.

Under the preceding rules, the italicized letters in the following words have the sound of sh.

Action, branch, cham'ois, champagne', champaign', chevalier', chemise', crucial, diversion, enunciation, expulsion, expatiation, faction, fissure, gracious, Hessian, issue, jaculation, kitchen, Letitia, luscious, militia, negotiate, nescience, osseous, partial, patient, prescience, prescient, pronunciation, propitiation, quassia, rapacious, ratiocination, satiate, sensual, scissure, social, tenacious, tensure, tissue, tonsure, voracious, watch.

3. *S as in see*—*s, c, x.*

Cognate with z in zone, the organs being the same, except perhaps that in this sound a little less of the surface of the tongue is brought into contact with the roof of the mouth. This is a sharp hissing sound, of which also the representation is complicated and difficult.

(1.) It is represented by c before e, i, y, as in certain, acidity, cycle, pronounced, sertin, asidity, sycle; except in a few words, such as discern, suffice, sacrifice, for which see § 159—2, (2).

(2.) It enters, together with k, into the sound of x at the end of monosyllables, and in the derivatives from such monosyllables; as in fix, fixation, lax, laxative, laxation, mix, mixture, wax, waxwork, etc. pronounced, fiks, fiksation, etc. also, in all cases in which x has not the sound sh (§ 165—2, (6)), or of gz (§ 162—1, (2)), or of z in zone (§ 159—2, (1)).

(3.) It is represented by s in the following cases, and in others not reducible to rule.

(*a.*) At the beginning of words, as in safe, see, son; except in a few words in which s represents sh (§ 165—2, (4)).

(*b.*) At the end of words terminating in as, is, us, ss, as in bis, cullis, gas, fas, genius, Marcus, dress, careless, carelessness, fairness; except the plural of words ending in ea, as in seas, pease; pronounced, seaz, peaz; and except the words, as, has, his, was, together with all their derivatives, such as whereas, hisown; pronounced, az, haz, hiz, waz, whereaz, hiz-own.

(c.) In some nouns ending in se, to distinguish them from the verbs or adjectives with which they are etymologically connected (§ 159—2, (3), (a)) as in grease, mouse, rise, use; pronounced, greace, mouce. rice, uce.

(d.) S represents this sound whenever it is preceded or followed by an atonic, as in acrostic, ask, bits, caps, clasp, dust, fast, locks, muffs, sister, whisper.

(e.) In the inseparable preposition dis, followed by an atonic or unaccented tonic or subtonic, as in disavow, discuss, discred'it, discretion, disfavor, dislocate, dishearten, disperse, displace, dissuade, dissever, disthrone; except in some words in which s has the sound of z in zone, following the analogy of § 159—2, (3), (e).

(f.) In the inseparable preposition, trans, this sound should be represented by s whenever it is followed by a subtonic or atonic, as in transfix, transmute, transplant, but the authorities do not warrant this limitation—see § 159—2, (3), (d).

S at the end of words transferred from the French, is commonly silent, as in debris, pronounced, debree'; also in some other cases, as in isle, island, pronounced, ile, iland. It is sometimes mispronounced by being unduly prolonged, and sometimes by giving it the sound of sh.

According to the above rules it is heard in the following words.

Ace, brace, cynic, censure, dice, docility, efface, facility, fracas, fuss, grass, haste, hostage, ice, industry, justice, kiss, lost, laps, lots, maps, mast, must, nips, obstacle, postulate, guest, rats, servile, sorrow, subtle, task, taste, use, vice, whist, yesterday, zest.

4. *F as in fee—f, gh, ph.*

Cognate of v—lips in the same position. This sound is represented by f, ph, wherever these signs occur, except in a few words in which ph has the sound of v (§ 159—4), and by gh at the end of some words, and in their derivatives.

Afraid, baffle, craft, cough, chough, draught, enough, fifth, graft, haft, if, laugh, laughter, muff, off, phantasy, Philip, philanthropy, philosophy, phlegmatic, phrensy, raffle, rough, rougher, soft, staff, thereof, tough, tougher, toughest, trough, waft.

§ 166. **The atonic hard checks, k, t, p, stop off the whispering breath by hard contact of the organs.**

These sounds are the cognates of the subnasals, g, d, b, and of the nasals, ng, n, m ; the position of the organs being nearly or quite identical. These articulations stop off perfectly the whispering breath.

1. *K as in key—k, c, ch, ck, g, gh.*

This sound is the cognate both of g and ng; it is distinguished from them by its want of vocality, and further from ng by a harder contact. The difference in the action of the breath, here, and in the following cases, is also to be observed.

(1.) This sound is represented by k, ck, q, wherever these signs occur, as in beck, like, quill; pronounced, bek, like, kwill.

(2.) By c before a, o, u, l, r, and at the end of syllables, as in car, come, cut, climb, cram, public, lacteal, pronounced kar, kome, kut, klimb, kram, publik, lakteal.

(3.) By ch before l, r, as in chloroform, christian, pronounced kloroform, kristshan; also, in words derived from Latin and Greek, except in chalice, charity, charter. The prefix, arch, is governed in its pronunciation by the character of the word to which it is prefixed; *i. e.* ch in arch has the sound of k in all words derived from the Greek, except in archdeacon, pronounced, artshdeacon, and in a few other cases; whilst in all purely English words, it has the sound of tsh, as in archbishop, pronounced artshbishop

(4.) By gh in the words, hough, lough, shough, and their derivatives; pronounced, hok, lok, shok, etc.

(5.) K enters into the sound of x, together with s, as in § 165—3, (2).

Archangel, archipelago, archiepiscopal, archidiaconal, archives, architect, architype, architrave, back, bequeathe, bequest, chlorosis, crime, dyke, eccentricity, fickle, lake, magna-charta, make, neck, oak, occiput, pickle, poke, quake, quick, racket, ricochet, smoke, ticket, vaccinate, wake, wicket.

2. *T as in tell—t, d, ght, ch.*

Cognate with n and d—organs in the same position—a mere articulation stopping of the atonic breath.

(1.) This sound is represented by t wherever t occurs, except where it has the sound of sh (§ 165

—2, (5)), and where it forms a part of th as in then or thin, and where it is silent.

(2.) It is represented by its subtonic cognate d in all words ending in ed in which e is silent and preceded by an atonic sound; as in asked, basked, frothed, placed, scraped, tossed, whiffed, whipped, pronounced, askt, baskt, plast, scrapt, tost, whift, whipt.

(3.) By ght wherever this sign occurs in the end of a word, as in bright, light, might, plight, sight, pronounced, brite, lite, mite, plite, site.

(4.) It enters, together with sh, into the sound of ch in all words of pure English origin; also in arch prefixed to such words (§ 166—1, (3)); as in archfiend, archrebel, birch, broach, church, larch, lurch, march, micher, niche, rich, which, etc. pronounced, artshfiend, birtsh, tshursh, whitsh, etc.

(5.) T is commonly silent when preceded by f, s, and followed by en, le, as in the following examples and all their derivatives.

<small>Apostle, bristle, bustle, castle, chasten, christen, epistle, fasten glisten, gristle, hasten, hustle, jostle, justle, listen, moisten, nestle, often, pestle, rustle, soften, thistle, throstle, whistle, wrestle.</small>

3. *P as in pay—p, gh.*

Cognate with m, b—all formed with the lips closed. It is seldom represented by any other sign than p. In the word hiccough, pronounced, hikkup, it is represented by gh. It is sometimes confounded with its subtonic cognate b, as in baptize, and its derivatives, mispronounced, babtise. P is silent before s, t, at the beginning of words, as in psalm, psalter, Ptolemy, also in receipt, raspberry; pronounced, sam, salter, Tolemy, reseet, razberry. Examples of its correct sound are given in the following words.

A*p*ple, be*p*aint, ca*p*tain, dee*p*, em*p*loy, fla*p*, gra*pp*le, ho*p*e, irru*p*tion, ju*p*e, kee*p*, li*p*, ma*p*, na*p*, o*p*en, *p*ale, qui*p*, ri*p*, sa*p*, to*p*, u*p*, wi*p*e, yel*p*.

CHAPTER VI.

The Qualities of the Voice.

§ 167. Elocution aims, not to obliterate the personal characteristics of voice, but to correct the bad, and to develop the good qualities.

1. *Every voice has its own characteristic quality.*

This differential character of every voice has no reference to anything which makes one voice better than another. It is a quality like those which distinguish the sounds of different musical instruments from each other. When *e. g.* the same note is sounded upon the flute, violin, and piano-forte, each of the three sounds has its characteristic quality, though all of them may be equally good. In the same way, each person's voice has its characteristic quality, or general character, without reference to anything which makes it either good or bad; whence it is as easy to distinguish different persons by their voices, as it is by their features or countenances.

2. *Elocution does not aim to obliterate these differences.*

It is no part of the aim of this art to tone down these characteristics to a common sameness. For they are founded in nature, as truly as the differences of countenance and expression of the features; and in vocal music, and conversation between several persons, they give a fullness and variety, which is as much an element of beauty and power, as variety of instruments in an orchestra. In oratory it is essential to the greatest power that the speaker's voice should be distinctively characteristic of his own personality, and incapable of being confounded with the voice of any other person.

3. *Elocution aims to correct the bad, and to develop the good qualities of voice.*

In another sense of the word quality, it denotes the good or bad traits which appear in the same, or in different voices; such as purity and impurity, smoothness and roughness, roundness and flatness. And here, Elocution proposes to teach the methods of training and exercise by which the bad qualities may be exterminated or reduced, and the good developod and perfected.

§ 168. A good voice with respect to quality, is one whose tones are pure, full, round, solid, smooth, clear, liquid, sweet, musical.

The qualities of the voice, which, it will be observed, have no reference either to pitch or force, are too numerous, and complicated with each other, to be analyzed. In fact, both the good and bad qualities necessarily overlap, and, to a certain extent, imply each other. Their names are highly metaphorical; and frequently the principal differences between them, is that they are various aspects of the same quality, expressed in different metaphors.

1. *Purity of tone is tone unmixed with noise, and is the most important of all the good qualities.*

There are properly but two kinds or species of sound *i. e.* tones and noises. Tones are produced by regular, periodical, isochronous vibrations in the sounding body; they are such sounds as we hear from tuning forks, violin strings, and organ pipes. Noises are produced by irregular impulses or concussions, such as the slamming of a door, or the fall of a body upon the earth. Of all the good qualities purity of tone in the human voice is every way the most important, and may be taken as inclusive of all the others.

2. *It is produced by regular and unobstructed vibrations of the vocal chords, in the resonant cavities.*

A sound thus produced is unmixed with noise, smooth clear, liquid, sweet, musical. Fullness, roundness and solidity of voice are qualities nearly allied to purity, and partly included in it. They cannot be better described than they are by these names. They are all exemplified in the tones of a superior church organ, which seem to come from each separate stop and pipe in a full, round and solid form. Hence we speak of the organ tones of a fine voice.

§ 169. The physiological causes of the good qualities are free vibration of the vocal chords, healthy condition of the

resonant cavities, and facile control of the breathing and articulating organs.

The physiological causes or conditions of the good qualities of the voice, are exceedingly numerous and complicated; only the most important and obvious are here enumerated.

1. *The free vibration of the vocal chords.*

That those chords should vibrate freely and perfectly, is the most indispensable condition, inasmuch as it is by these vibrations that the breath is converted into tone (§103—2). In order that all the breath that is expelled from the lungs, should thus be converted into pure tone, and none of it be allowed to escape in an unvocalized or whispering form, it is indispensable that these organs should be kept in a healthy condition, well moistened, but not obstructed or clogged by unhealthy or excessive secretions.

2. *Adequate capacity and healthy condition of the resonant cavities.*

The good qualities of the voice depend also upon the size, function and healthy condition of the resonant cavities of the windpipe and mouth. It is necessary that these should be of adequate size or capacity, and that they should present a clean, firm and elastic resonant surface. They must not be too dry, nor yet obstructed by secretions; and the throat and mouth must not be too full of the organs which they contain, viz. palate tonsils, tongue, gums and teeth. The bronchial tubes and trachea must be large enough to allow a full-sized column of air to pass freely through them.

3. *Facile control of the organs of speech.*

This is especially important with respect to the diaphragm, and whole breathing apparatus, in order that the breath may be expelled regularly, and in such quantities that it can all be converted into pure tone, and that the sound thus produced may be full, round and solid. Such control over the articulating organs is indispensable, also, in order that they should perform their functions smoothly and without noise.

§ 170. **The bad qualities of the voice are impurity, roughness, hoarseness. harshness, wheezing, flatness, hollowness, shrillness and the nasal tang.**

The bad qualities of the voice are also extremely numerous, and complicated with each other. They are in general the opposite of the good qualities, and consequently most of them may be regarded as included in impurity. Roughness, hoarseness, harshness, wheezing, and the nasal tang, are obviously different forms of impurity. Flatness of voice is opposed to roundness and fullness; and hollowness to solidity. Both of these are exemplified in the tones of a poor church organ, from which the sound seems to come, as it were, flat, hollow, unsubstantial. Shrillness is a certain sharpness or acuteness of sound, which seems to pierce the ear like a sharp instrument. There is also a trembling of the voice, which, when habitual, should be classed with the bad qualities. As in the case of the good qualities, many of these names are little more than various metaphors presenting different aspects of impurity.

§ 171. The physiological causes of the bad qualities are in general the opposite of those upon which the good qualities depend.

1. *Impurity is due to the causes by which noises are mixed with the tone of the voice.*

These causes are very numerous. When the vocal chords do not vibrate freely, but are obstructed by excessive or unhealthy secretions, or by any other cause, or when the uncontrolled action of the diaphragm and breathing muscles forces too much breath over these chords, a greater or less portion of it escapes in an unvocalized, or whispering, or wheezing form. When the chords are inflamed and swollen from the affection of colds, or sore throat, hoarseness is the result; and, in extreme cases, as we have seen, aphonia, or voicelessness. In all cases of hoarseness and wheezing, there is more or less of unvocalized breath mingled with the tone of the voice. When the resonant cavities and breathing tubes are obstructed, the voice becomes impure from imperfect resonance, and from rattling noises of various kinds therein produced; when the organs of articulation are too large, or under imperfect control, so that they perform their functions clumsily, the tone of the voice is confused and blurred by the noise which they make at their work

When control over these organs is lost from their being overtaxed or strained, the noise which they make, combined with other impurities, is sometimes like that of the bellows, keys, and other machinery of a very poor organ, which nearly drowns its feeble tones. In shouting, screaming, and passionate vociferation, it is almost impossible to prevent a large quantity of breath from escaping in an unvocalized state, and the organs are most liable then to make a noise at their work; so that, in these cases, the voice is commonly loaded with impurities.

2. *Flatness is due to the want of a sufficiently elastic resonance in the vocal cavities.*

This want of a sufficiently elastic resonance itself arises from a variety of causes, such as excess, fatigue, exhaustion, whether physical or mental. The want of elasticity and spring in the physical organism, or mental faculties, in consequence of ill health, overtaxing the powers, or any other cause, seems to reflect and express itself in a flat, or dull, or dead sound of the voice.

3. *Hollowness is due to the feebleness of the breathing organs, and to defects in the resonant cavities.*

In such cases, the breathing apparatus fails to expel a sufficient volume of air to be vocalized by the chordal vibrations into solid sound. Inadequate size, and imperfect construction of the resonant cavities, also, impart this bad quality to the sound of the voice. It is due, further, to the imperfect action and co-operation of the other vocal organs.

4. *Shrillness is caused by too high pitch.*

When the voice is exerted on too high a pitch, its capacity in this respect is strained, and it becomes shrill. In this case, the resonance is thrown almost wholly into the arch of the roof of the mouth.

5. *The trembling quality is due to a want of control over the breathing organs.*

In this quality, the organs fail to expel the breath in that steady stream which gives steadiness to the sound of the voice. The quality may also be voluntarily produced, for purposes of expression, by alternately checking and expelling the breath.

6. *The nasal tang is produced by obstruction of the front nasal cavities.*

Any cause which obstructs in front the free passage of the breath through the nostrils, will render the voice nasal. When this takes place, there is a peculiar resonance of the sound apparently about the middle of these cavities, and the speaker is said to "talk through his nose." It would be more correct, however, to say, he talks in his nose. Very frequently this results from mere carelessness or slovenliness in speaking, when there is no organic obstruction; but the habit once formed, is very difficult to correct.

The above are the principal good and bad qualities of the voice, together with the most important physiological conditions or causes upon which they depend. The knowledge of them all in detail is not essential, but some such exhibition of them as has now been made, can hardly fail to aid in understanding the use and importance of the good qualities, as an element of power in delivery, and in the training and practice which they require.

§ 172. The good qualities of the voice are the most easy, audible and agreeable, and some of the most important elements of expression.

It is chiefly the good qualities of the voice with which we have to do, as an element of power in delivery. Their importance for this purpose, as exhibited in the following particulars, can hardly be overestimated.

1. *They render speaking comparatively easy to the speaker.*

One reason of this is that pure tone is formed with the least possible expenditure of breath and vital force; all the breath expended is utilized; whilst, on the other hand, impure tone commonly implies the escape of a greater or less proportion of the breath in an unvocalized form, consequently a waste of the vital forces. It is truly surprising how little breath is required for speaking when it is all utilized, and the tones consequently are perfectly pure. This may be shown by holding a candle close to the mouth while speaking; when, if the tones are free from all impurity, the breath will hardly stir the flame; but if they are impure from unvocalized breath, the flame will flicker, as from a draught of air through a broken window. One car speak, therefore, in pure tones with comparatively little effort or fatigue; whilst impure tones are very exhausting. Hence the bad qualities tend also to generate disease in the vocal organs.

2. *They render hearing easy to the audience—they are the most audible.*

One reason of this is that pure tone is musical sound; and it is well known that music, under anything like favorable circumstances, can be heard at a vast distance; whilst mere noise, though of much greater force, or loudness, will travel but a very little way. Hence, in the degree in which the tones of the voice are rendered impure by admixture of noise, is its audibility impaired; whilst the good qualities enable the speaker to make himself heard much more effectively, and by a much larger audience, than were otherwise possible. Even in the open air, a pure, full, round and solid voice, though of inferior strength, can be heard by an amazing number of persons.

3. *They are the sounds which are most agreeable to hear.*

A voice of good qualities is sweet and musical; and such qualities excite only pleasurable sensations in the audience. Hence they engage their attention and sympathy, and commend the sentiments thus delivered to their favorable consideration, by the pleasure experienced in listening to the sounds. On the other hand, impure tones, and the other bad qualities, produce only disagreeable sensations. Rough, harsh, shrill, or nasal sounds irritate the audience; and, by placing their minds in an attitude of opposition, predispose them to reject all that is said.

4. *They are some of the most important elements of expression.*

The good qualities of the voice are the natural symbols, and oral body, or expression of all that is true and beautiful and good in thought and feeling. They are required for the expression of all thoughts, whether grave or gay, elevated or common-place,— and no less of all affections and emotions—that are true or right, pure or lovely, serene, gentle, tender, affectionate, faithful, truthful, hopeful, earnest, or in any way praiseworthy or helpful to man. In fact, almost everything that a speaker can legitimately seek to communicate to others, or to excite in them, requires purity of tone, and the other good qualities of the voice. Nothing of this nature can be adequately expressed in any other qualities. Pity or love *e. g.* expressed in impure, rough, harsh, or hissing sounds, is not expressed at all; elevated or sublime sentiments, expressed in a thin, hollow, cracked, or wheezy voice, are simply caricatured, and reduced from the sublime to the ridiculous; sentiments of self-sacrifice or devotion, expressed in a nasal tang, suggest insincerity and hypocrisy. It is impossible to conceive of our Saviour as speaking with any other than the good qualities of voice.

THE QUALITIES OF THE VOICE. 305

§ 173. The bad qualities of the voice are an element of power in expressing the bad passions.

For the elocution of the stage, and perhaps for some other purposes, it may be desirable to have under control the bad qualities of the voice. For they are the natural symbols, and oral body, for the expression of all the vile and hateful states of mind. Impure tone is the natural and appropriate expression of anger, wrath, malice, envy, jealousy— of all evil passions and inordinate affections. For the effective rendering of such evil passions upon the stage, and sometimes in forensic and deliberative oratory, it may be well to have at command the different varieties of impure tone; but the art of Elocution, as here taught, can have little to do with the training of the voice for such expression.

§ 174. The training required for the development of the good qualities of the voice, consists in exercising it daily in these qualities.

The particular rules for these exercises, having for their object the correction of the bad, and the development of the good qualities of the voice, are few and simple, but of great efficacy where they are faithfully applied.

1. *The services of a good teacher should be secured.*

This rule applies to all the exercises which elocution prescribes. Wherever it is possible, the student should have the advice and direction of a good teacher, especially for the purpose of pointing out faults and defects, and to exemplify all the good and bad qualities of voice. For we become so accustomed to our own peculiarities, whether of voice, or in other respects, that we are, for the most part, insensible of them ourselves, however prominent and striking they may be to others; and it is extremely difficult for us to become conscious of them, until they are pointed out and exemplified to us by some other person. Where a teacher cannot be had, a judicious friend should be consulted for this purpose.

2. *The ear must be cultivated to distinguish the qualities.*

If the ear of the student be naturally dull, it is indispensable that it should be trained up by the exercises already prescribed for it (§ 105—4) until it becomes capable of distinguishing the different qualities of voice from each other with facility and precision.

3. *The exercises required are nearly the same as those prescribed for articulation and the ear; the attention being specially directed to the quality of the vocal sound* (§§ 105—4; 114).

Under the guidance of the ear, the student should exercise his voice in forming, with purity of tone, and all the good qualities, the various sounds which constitute speech, both separately, and in their various combinations. The practice should be first upon the vowel sounds taken separately; next upon these sounds in combination each with a single consonant; then upon single words; and finally upon connected oral discourse. In practicing upon the vowels, the student should hold or prolong them to the utmost capacity of his breath, with all the good qualities, but especially aiming to prevent any portion of the breath from escaping in an unvocalized form, and to utter the voice without allowing it to become tremulous. In practicing upon words and sentences, he should aim to work the organs of speech with neatness and facility, so that they may perform their functions without noise. By such exercises, the bad qualities of the voice are gradually corrected, and the good are developed.

4. *Great care is necessary not to strain the voice.*

The liability to this, in these and in all other elocutionary exercises, is very great; and the inevitable result is that the voice is rendered impure, rough and harsh. It is believed that a voice once spoiled in this way, can never be restored to purity and sweetness. Hence in all exercises it must be kept down or subdued; in other words, the vocal organs must never be exerted to their utmost capacity.

5. *These exercises should be performed once or twice a day, for a half or a quarter of an hour at a time.*

A single exercise each day for a half hour, will produce excellent effects in a short time; but for the best possible results, the exercise should be twice a day, for a quarter of an hour.

CHAPTER VII.

THE POWERS OF THE VOICE.

§ 175. The powers of the voice are strength, compass and flexibility.

THESE powers are capable of being sharply distinguished from the qualities of the voice. For as the qualities refer to the character of the sound, regarded chiefly as pure or impure tone, so the powers of the voice refer to its degrees of strength and pitch, and to its capacity of changing from one quality, and one degree of force or pitch, to another. Consequently there are but three such powers, strength, compass and flexibility.

§ 176. Strength of voice is the power to utter loud vocal sounds.

A strong voice is one that is capable of producing with ease loud sounds, in distinction from a weak or feeble voice, which is capable only of weak or feeble sounds. Strength of voice has no reference to quality, nor pitch, nor compass, but solely to loudness. Thus *e. g.* if the same key of a piano be

THE POWERS OF THE VOICE. 309

touched first softly, then more forcibly, it produces two sounds of the same pitch and quality, but differing in their degree of loudness. In this way, the same vocal organism gives forth strong or feeble sounds; and in this power, different organisms are superior or inferior to each other.

§ 177. Strength of voice depends chiefly upon the strength of the organs of respiration, and upon the size and capacity of the resonant cavities.

1. *Strength in the breathing organs is essential to expel the breath with adequate force.*

We have seen that the sound of the voice is generated by the vibrations of the vocal chords; and that, whilst pitch depends upon the number of these vibrations, force or loudness depends upon their amplitude, in other words, upon the width of the space through which the chords are made to vibrate (§ 103—2, 3, 4). Now this amplitude of the vibrations, is due to the degree of force with which the column of breath is driven against the chords, by the contraction of the diaphragm, and other muscles which co-operate with it in respiration. Consequently the stronger the breathing muscles, other things being equal, the greater the strength of voice.

2. *Adequate size and capacity of the resonant cavities contribute to the strength of the voice.*

The reason of this is that vibrations of the same amplitude, will not produce the same degree of loudness in resonant cavities of different sizes and capacities. The same concussion *e. g.* in a bell of large size, and of superior capacities in other respects, gives forth a much louder sound than it does in a small bell of inferior qualities. In like manner, the same force of breath, which causes the vocal chords to vibrate with the same amplitude, produces a much louder sound in resonant vocal cavities of ample size, and otherwise well constructed, than it does in cavities of small size, or otherwise of small capacity. Defects, therefore, in the breathing tubes, or in the larynx, pharynx, or mouth, whether from organic malformation, disease, or want of development, always tend to render the voice feeble.

§ 178. **Strength of voice, as an element of power in delivery, enables the speaker to speak with ease, with the good qualities and natural tones, and it is the natural symbol of power.**

1. *Strength of voice enables the speaker to speak with ease, and without injury to his organs, and to be heard without effort or weariness.*

It is sufficiently obvious that a speaker with a strong voice, can make himself heard with ease, in large assemblies, and in the open air, where one with a feeble voice cannot be heard except with difficulty, or not at all. For the same reason, one can speak for a much greater length of time than the other, without exhaustion or fatigue. For a speaker with a feeble voice soon becomes exhausted, and all his powers of elocution enfeebled. His vocal organs, also, from this cause, are liable to suffer irreparable injury, and his general health to break down. This is a principal cause of the ill health of so many clergymen. Moreover, when the audience hear with difficulty, they soon become wearied and discontented; their appreciation of what they hear is unfavorably affected, and they cease to give their attention. But where the voice is of adequate strength, all these and other causes of feebleness are obviated, and give place to the opposite elements of power.

2. *It is favorable to the good qualities of the voice.*

Purity of tone requires, as we have seen (§ 174 —4), that the voice should not be overstrained, nor taxed to its utmost capacity. But a speaker with a feeble voice can hardly refrain from exerting it to the utmost, in order to make himself heard, especially in large assemblies; and thus it soon becomes loaded with impurities. Hence a speaker with a strong voice can much more easily and effectually guard its purity of tone.

3. *Also, to natural tones, and to variety of tone, in speaking.*

One of the most fruitful causes of feebleness in delivery, is a certain unnaturalness in the tones of the voice, which is as far removed as possible from the tones which prevail in conversation, or common talking. This is due, in great part, to the straining and effort of the speaker to make himself heard and understood. When *e. g.* the voice is feeble, it tends to rise in public speaking above its natural pitch, especially in all animated and impassioned discourse, in order to compensate by shrillness for what it lacks in strength. Also it tends to run along on this high pitch, with little variation. In like manner, when it is overstrained in order to make every word audible, it is incapable of varying the degree of force, for the expression of more or less impassioned sentiments. It can neither rise nor fall in pitch, nor vary in force or quality, according to the ever varying character of the sentiments to be expressed. Hence monotony, and unnatural, impure, and otherwise disagreeable sounds. On the other hand, if the voice be of adequate strength, the speaker can deliver himself, even in the largest assemblies, in his natural, and almost in conversational tones, which are the point of departure for all good speaking. From this point, he naturally rises and falls in pitch as the sentiment requires, with varying force and quality of voice, according to the degree of animation or passion, and to the greater or less importance of what he has to deliver. Strength of voice is thus essential to naturalness, and to that variety of force, pitch and quality of the vocal sounds, which are among the greatest charms and excellences of delivery.

4. *Strength of voice is the natural symbol and expression of power.*

From this consideration, more than all others, we are enabled to appreciate the vast importance of this element of power in delivery. For of all the natural symbols of power, strength of voice is the most striking and expressive. The African hunters

The Powers of the Voice.

tell us that the roar of the lion in his native wilds, produces the most awful impressions that are conceivable, of the vastness of his force; and this impression is not more than adequate, for the lion has the strength of forty men. The voice of the cataract, and of the storm-tossed ocean, produces a similar impression of immeasurable force. The thunder itself, the most sublime of all sounds, is the voice of the Almighty, *i. e.* it is the symbol and expression of infinite power. Accordingly, a speaker with a powerful voice comes before an audience, clothed, as it were, with power. Thereby he is enabled to command their attention, and to impress his sentiments upon them, more powerfully than were otherwise possible. Hence the great orators and tragedians have almost always had great voices. The power of Cicero and Demosthenes in this respect, need not be again alluded to. But it is said that Garrick could speak with ease to ten thousand persons. The vast powers of Spurgeon's voice are certainly one of the greatest elements of his power in delivery. And it was estimated by Dr. Franklin, whilst listening to Whitefield preaching in the open air at the State House in Philadelphia, that he could be heard on that occasion by thirty thousand persons. In fact, the marvelous effects of Whitefield's oratory were due, in great part, to his almost incredible powers of voice—intellectually, he seems to have been a man of only moderate abilities.

§ 179. The exercises for cultivating strength of voice, are the same with those prescribed for the development of the breathing organs, and of the resonant cavities.

By the proper exercises, the human voice is capable of wonderful and rapid development, to almost any degree of strength. It is rare to find a voice whose power would not be more than doubled by two or three months of such exercises. But it is indispensable to the best results that they should be practiced daily and systematically; otherwise a great part of what is gained one day, or one week, is lost the next (§§ 100—4; 101—3; 102—3; 104—4).

1. *In the exercises for strengthening the breathing organs, the sound should be gradually increased in force.*

These exercises are those which have been already prescribed for the diaphragm (§ 100—4), and lungs (§ 101—3). In this case, however, it is especially necessary to hold or prolong the sounds to the full capacity of the breath, and gradually to increase them in force or loudness from day to day, yet without straining the voice so as to render it impure. These exercises should be accompanied also with what is called the explosion of the voice, which consists in uttering the sound as shortly and abruptly as possible, and with as great force as the organs will bear without straining. The danger of injuring them in this way is very great, so that not more than four or five such explosions should be allowed each day, until they have become accustomed to the exercise. To these should be added reading aloud and declamation; and the improvement will be much more rapid and satisfactory if these exercises are performed in the open air, which greatly promotes the health and vigor of the vocal organs. Thus the muscular organs of respiration are increased in size and force; and strength of voice is developed, on precisely the same principle upon which the arm of the blacksmith acquires its great size and force by wielding the hammer, and upon which the muscular organism of the body is developed by gymnastic exercises. Every one knows how rapidly this takes place in the latter case, and the improvement in the voice is not less but rather more rapid.

2. *In the exercises for the development of the resonant cavities, the immediate aim should be to enlarge their capacity.*

These exercises are in part the same with those prescribed for the mouth organs (§ 104—4), and for the good qualities of the voice (§ 174—3). The result here aimed at takes place by the effort to render the sounds, but especially the lower and lowest sounds in pitch of which the voice is capable, with constantly increasing force, purity and solidity. By every such effort, as any one may observe for himself, nature instinctively strives to throw the interior organs of the mouth, throat and windpipe into such a position as to render the cavities as large and capacious as possible. In this way, therefore, their size and capacity of resonance is gradually increased, and strength of voice is correspondingly developed.

§ 180. **The compass of the voice is its range of pitch.**

A good compass of the voice consists in its capacity of sounding, with purity and force, both the high and low notes of the musical scale. The voice is ot small compass when on the high notes it *breaks*, or runs into *falsetto*, becoming shrill or screaming, and when it is incapable of sounding the low notes with fullness, force, roundness, or solidity.

§ 181. **A much greater compass of voice is required for singing than for speaking.**

The highest excellence in singing demands a compass of at least three octaves, whilst in speaking, the range is seldom greater than one. Sometimes, however, especially in the most impassioned oratory, a more extensive range can be employed with good effect.

§ 182. **The compass of the voice depends upon the action of the vocal chords, and upon the capacity of the resonant cavities.**

When the vocal chords are so finely organized that a small number of vibrations will render a perfect sound, and this sound has a good resonance in the trachea and bronchial tubes, then the voice has a good command of the low notes, or chest-tones.

When the chords are capable of a great number of vibrations in a given time, and the upper cavities of the mouth give a good resonance, then it has a good command of the high notes, or head-tones. Where either of these conditions is wanting, the voice is wanting in range, either upwards or downwards.

§ 183. **Adequate compass of voice is an important element of power in delivery.**

A great range of the voice upwards is not of so much importance in speaking, as an ample command of the lower and lowest tones—these, beyond all comparison, are the most effective in oratory. A voice full, rich and mellow on the low notes, is a mighty element of power in delivery. A voice of good compass, however, in both directions is required, in order to that variety of pitch and inflection, which is essential to the adequate expression of the ever-varying movements of thought and feeling; otherwise a dull and stupefying monotony can hardly be avoided. It is indispensable in all animated and impassioned speaking. For deep and strong emotion cannot be fully expressed on the middle or common pitch of the voice, but it requires both the high and the low sounds, often in rapid alternation. In impassioned questioning *e. g.* the voice must rise or fall by inflection through a whole octave. Hence, as an element of power in delivery, adequate compass of voice is only inferior to adequate strength.

§ 184. The exercises for developing the compass of the voice, consist in sounding the high and low notes of the musical scale.

These exercises are very much the same with those prescribed for the ear (§ 105—4). Almost every voice, however, has a range of pitch, adequate for speaking, in one direction or the other, either upwards or downwards. The student should aim, therefore, to develop his voice in the direction in which it most needs it. The exercises for extending the range in either direction, consist in sounding the notes of the musical scale, running up as high as the voice will rise without breaking, or taking the *falsetto* character, and down as low as it can be made to descend. It is not necessary that its lowest notes should be perfectly pure, or very strong, at first; it may be practiced at first on notes so low as to be both feeble and impure; but it should be the aim of the student to bring out these low sounds with ever greater purity and force. This practice should be accompanied with daily reading aloud, and declamation, on a low or high pitch, according to the direction in which the voice may require development.

§ 185. Flexibility of voice is its power of changing its pitch, quality, or force; and it depends chiefly upon facility of control over the organs.

This power consists in the faculty of changing from one pitch, or one quality, or one degree of force, to another. When these changes can be effected with facility and rapidity, the voice is one of great flexibility; when they cannot be effected without difficulty, or otherwise than slowly, it has little flexibility. This power depends upon a neat and smooth and proportionate construction of the vocal organs; but more especially, upon a perfect voluntary control over them, by which only can they be made to assume those rapid and facile changes of position and action, which are the immediate causes of these variations of sound.

§ 186. **Flexibility of voice is an essential element of power in delivery.**

This power of voice is a fundamental element of all animated and forcible delivery; the changes of sound which depend upon it, are the very life and spirit of expression. It is required, moreover, in the utterance of every word and syllable, which do not maintain the same pitch, or degree of force, throughout. In further illustration of its importance, it may be sufficient to refer to those numerous occasions on which almost every speaker is painfully conscious that his voice is not under his control in this respect; that it does not answer to the changes which the expression of the changing sentiment requires; in other words, he does not express what he really means and feels. The cause of this is that the voice is wanting in flexibility.

§ 187. **The exercises for the development of this power, consist in rapid and extreme transitions from one degree of pitch and force, and from one quality, to another.**

The exercises prescribed for obtaining the most perfect control of the vocal organs, are the best for the attainment of flexibility. The references to these need not be again repeated. In addition, the student should practice his voice in the most rapid transitions from one degree of force and pitch, and from one quality of sound, to another. He should select for declamation the most animated and impassioned passages, because they require the greatest variety of pitch, force and quality of sound. But probably the best exercise is that of reading aloud or speaking dialogues, in which the reader represents alternately a number of interlocutors. The animation which is characteristic of this species of discourse, and the frequent and rapid changes of the voice which are requisite to maintain the distinction of persons and characters, afford the most effective aids to the development of this power. Humorous selections also are good for this purpose.

CHAPTER VIII.

PITCH AND INFLECTION.

§ 188. *Pitch is the character of sounds as high or low, grave or acute.*

THE pitch of a sound is something entirely different both from its force and its quality, being determined, as we have seen, by the number of vibrations which take place in a given length of time, in the sounding body (§ 103—4). The keys of a pianoforte exemplify, in the simplest manner, the distinctions of pitch. On the extreme left of the key-board, we have the lowest bass note, the most grave sound; as the hand moves to the right, each succeeding note rises in pitch above the preceding, until we reach the extreme right, which gives us the highest, or most acute sound. The variations in pitch of which the human voice is capable, in the exercise of compass and flexibility, are very great. The extent, rapidity and accuracy, in varying the pitch, which is attained by great vocalists, especially when we consider that the vocal chords, upon which these changes depend, cannot vary in length more than one eighth of an inch, is one of the wonders of our physiological constitution, and a striking example of the control which mind or life is capable of exercising over matter.

§ 189. **Inflection is a function of pitch.**

In the books on Elocution, inflection is commonly treated under a distinct head from that of pitch. But it is properly a function of pitch, that is, it is one way of varying the pitch of sounds. For there are two distinct forms of such variation, which are characterized as *discrete* and *concrete*, each of which has important functions in the expression of thought and sentiment.

1. *Discrete variations are skips from one degree of pitch to another.*

These variations may be exemplified by sounding in succession any two or more of the keys of an instrument. This will give sounds of different pitch, with intervals of silence between them—one sound does not slide into another. Hence such variations are called *skips*, in distinction from slides.

2. *Concrete variations are slides from one pitch to another.*

These may be exemplified by moving the stop-finger up or down one of the strings of a violin, whilst the bow is drawn across it. A continuous or sliding sound, from one degree of pitch to another, will thus be produced. Such variations, called *slides*, in distinction from skips, are properly inflections.

§ 190. In music the discrete variations predominate, in speech the concrete.

Both of these variations are heard in music and in speech, but the predominant form in each is different.

1. *In music the discrete changes predominate.*

This is evident from the structure of the musical staff, which is composed of alternate lines and spaces, on which the notes, one above another, represent sounds of different pitch, with intervals of silence between them. The notation of the slide in music, though it frequently occurs, is *comparatively* rare. That these discrete changes predominate in music, is further evinced by the fact that music can be produced from keyed instruments, which are totally incapable of executing the slide. Yet the judicious introduction of the concrete changes of pitch in music, is one of the most important elements of its expressive power, for the reason that they impart a certain speaking character to the sounds. Hence also the acknowledged superiority of stringed instruments, from their capacity of executing these speaking slides.

2. *In speech the concrete variations predominate.*

This is evident to the ear. For if we give close attention to conversation, especially to the free and animated conversation of ladies, we easily perceive that their voices are continually sliding up and down the musical scale, with amazing rapidity and flexibility; in fact, as we have seen, every syllable ter-minutes in a slide (§ 118). Hence, when we speak of discrete variations in speech, we do not mean that there is no slide at all in these sounds; for they all end in a sliding vocule, or vanish; but only that the slide does not reach from one sound to the other, and that the interval is reckoned from one radical pitch to the other. This predominance of the sliding sounds, or concrete changes of pitch, is, in fact, the differential character of speech as distinguished from song. Hence very much of that vicious speaking which is called sing-song, will be found to arise from the introduction of the discrete, in place of the concrete variations.

§ 191. **Both melody and expression depend upon the variations of pitch.**

This is equally true in music and in speech. In the case of the latter, it is evident from the consideration that, apart from these variations, speech would consist of a succession of articulate sounds on the same line of pitch, in which certainly there could be neither melody nor expression of sentiment. Such, however, is the nature of the vocal organism, that it is perhaps impossible to pronounce the shortest sentence in a perfect monotone. But it is easy and common enough to have so little variation in speaking as to render it powerless. Any one can make this plain to himself by pronouncing the following lines with as little variation of pitch as possible.

> The evil that men do lives after them;
> The good is oft interrèd with their bones.

PITCH AND INFLECTION. 325

But when they are rendered with the proper variations, both their melody and expression are at once brought out.

§ 192. **Melody in speech consists in such discrete variations of pitch in succession as are pleasing to the ear.**

If the following extract be properly read, it will readily be perceived that the several clauses and phrases range on various degrees of radical pitch, and that such variations are essential to its pleasing melody.

It is an impression which we cannot rid ourselves of if we would, when sitting by the body of a friend, that he has still a consciousness of our presence; that, though the common concerns of the world have no more to do with him, he has still a love and care for us. The face which we had so long been familiar with, when it was all life and motion, seems only in a state of rest. We know not how to make it real to ourselves, that the body before us is not a living thing.

Now, in order to attain this melody, the student will do well to avoid all attempts to apply those multiplied and minute rules which the elocutionists have given us, however accurate those rules may be; for it is more than probable that, by such attempts, he will lose more than it is possible to gain. The almost inevitable result will be sing-song, instead of melodious speech. He will best succeed in cultivating this grace of prose speech, by applying his ear, from time to time, to his sentences, that the ear may judge for itself, so to speak, whether it is satisfied or pleased with the successive variations of pitch

When his own ear is thus satisfied, the speaker may hope that the melody of his sentences will be such as to please the ears of his audience.

§ 193. Violations of melody consist in monotony, sing-song, false changes in the body of the sentence, false cadence, and too great variations.

According to the principle just laid down, it would be useless, and perhaps worse, to attempt to specify all the violations of melody, which are constantly occurring, even in the delivery of good speakers. Yet it may be useful to characterize, in some general way, those that are the most common and most damaging.

1. *Monotony, or too little variation of pitch.*

The voice in speaking may run along nearly on the same line of radical pitch, through a whole sentence, or paragraph, or even a discourse. This frequently arises from commencing too high, so that the compass of the voice does not allow of its rising and falling in melodious variations. The result, in this case, is a kind of monotonous rant, which is extremely unpleasant, and even painful to hear. In other cases, the pitch of the voice is too low throughout. This may be due to a want of emotion in the speaker, or to timidity, or to other causes. The result is a monotonous tameness, which is worse perhaps than rant. In both cases; there is no melody in the delivery.

2. *Sing-song, or recurrence of the same or similar variations.*

The too frequent recurrence of the same changes of pitch, is a very common violation of melody. The speaker commences all his sentences nearly or quite on the same pitch; in each sentence, he runs over nearly the same routine of changes; at each change, he delivers a few words as nearly as possible on the same line of radical pitch; and he closes his sentences with about the same cadence. In such cases, moreover, the discrete changes will commonly be found to predominate over the concrete, accompanied with an undue prolongation of the last syllables of the words. The effect of all this is what is called "the college tone," or "college sing-song," which turns speaking into singing, or rather into the dullest kind of chanting, and is extremely difficult to correct when it has once become a habit.

3. *False changes in the body of the sentence.*

Many speakers end almost every clause in their sentences with the full downward skip, allowing the voice to fall as low at the end of clauses as at the end of the sentence. This renders the delivery, with respect to melody, extremely harsh and abrupt. It is always, moreover, a violation of melody to let the voice fall where it ought to rise, and *vice versa*, although the determination of these cases belongs rather to expression than to melody.

4. *False cadences, or false changes at the close of the sentence.*

The character of a sentence, with respect to melody, is most conspicuous at its close. In a sentence ending with the falling inflection, melody, as well as expression, commonly requires that the voice should fall on the last word to the pitch on which it commenced. This fall, moreover, ought not to be a skip, but a slide; *i. e.* the last word should begin quite or nearly on the pitch of the preceding, and the voice should slide down on that word to the initial pitch of the sentence. Instead of which, many speakers drop the voice on the last word by a skip, often of two or three degrees of the scale, the effect of which is always more or less of the sing-song. Others close their sentences on the middle instead of the lowest pitch, the effect of which is like that of ending a tune on a sound not in full accord with the keynote. Others again, and not a few, close every sentence with a little rising inflection on the last syllable, like the upward flourish of a little dog's tail, which renders the gravest discourse ludicrous.

5. *Too frequent and too great changes of pitch.*

When the variations of pitch are too frequent or too great, especially the slides of the voice, the effect in public speaking is to render it too conversational. The measure and proportion of the variations to each other, which are essential to melodious speech, are lost; and the delivery is wanting in dignity, and in respect for the audience.

§ 194. **The principal function of pitch and inflection, is in the expression of sentiment.**

The changes of pitch, both concrete and discrete, upwards and downwards, are one of the principal means of attaining to full and adequate expression, both of thought and feeling. In fact, there are innumerable differences and shades of sentiment which are incapable of being expressed by any other means. Hence it is absolutely necessary for the student to give the subject his attention, bearing in mind, however, that the few principles and rules which follow, do constantly modify and limit each other. For although the writers on Elocution have given us a vast body of rules, some of them as many as fifty, to determine where the upward and downward skips, and where the rising and falling slides, should occur, it is perfectly certain that, except in a few cases, no invariable rules can be laid down.

§ 195. The sentiment determines the changes of pitch and inflection.

This is the most general principle applicable to the subject. It applies to questions equally with all other forms of expression. For although it is often supposed that a question mark (?) indicates the rising inflection, it will be found, upon examination, that questions take either the rising or falling inflection, according to the sentiment which they are intended to express, and the one perhaps as often as the other. This may be evinced by one or two examples.

1. The former part of the following sentence requires a high pitch of the voice, reaching the highest pitch on the words, weak, and unable; whilst the latter part, although a question, because the sentiment gives the principal emphasis to the word, when, closes with the full downward slide on the word, stronger.

<small>They tell us, sir, that we are weak, and unable to cope with so formidable an adversary; but when shall we be stronger?</small>

2. In the following questions, the last words take either inflection, according to the sentiment which the speaker intends to express. If the sentiment require the emphasis on the verb, is, both questions will close with the downward slide; but if the principal emphasis be placed upon the words, servant and slave, each will take a strong rising inflection.

<small>Is Israel a servant? Is he a home-born slave?</small>

We shall find, in all that follows on this subject, that the form of the sentence, whether interrogative or affirmative, has little or nothing to do with determining its changes of pitch and inflection, and that these depend wholly upon the character of the sentiment to be expressed.

Pitch and Inflection.

§ 196. Higher and lower ranges of pitch and inflection express different degrees of emotion and passion.

This is another general principle, and one of the greatest importance. For if we utter the exclamation, ah! expressing a slight degree of surprise, it naturally takes a slight rising inflection, running through the interval of the second or third of the musical scale; a greater degree of surprise will express itself by an upward slide on the word, of a fourth or fifth; and for a very strong expression of this feeling, the rising inflection will traverse a whole octave. In like manner, the word, no, expressing a mild dissent, will commence on the middle pitch of the voice, and take a slight falling inflection; when pronounced so as to express a stronger dissent, it will commence on a higher pitch, and end in a longer downward slide; and when it expresses a very strong or passionate dissent, the downward slide will run through a whole octave. Thus, *no*, NO, NO.

§ 197. Thoughts without emotion express themselves on the middle pitch of the voice, with the least variations.

Plain explanatory passages, requiring little emphasis, being altogether destitute of any peculiar emotion, are thus expressed. Also, where the speaker is supposed to be incapable of human passion, as in the case of a spiritual being, an apparition or ghost, his delivery should be as nearly as possible in monotone, that is, on the same line of pitch. In this way the words of the spectre in the book of Job,* should be pronounced.

> Shall mortal man be more just than God?
> Shall a man be more pure than his Maker?

So also the speech of the ghost in Hamlet.

> Thus was I, sleeping, by a brother's hand,
> Of life, of crown, of queen, at once despatched;
> Cut off even in the blossoms of my sin,
> Unhouseled, disappointed, unannealed;
> No reckoning made, but sent to my account,
> With all my imperfections on my head.

§ 198. **Calm and equable emotions express themselves on the middle pitch, with slight variations.**

In the expression of sentiments in which there is no peculiar strength or vivacity of feeling, the voice ranges on its natural or middle pitch, with little variation, whether of skip or slide, upwards or downwards. The variations, in this case, will seldom pass beyond one tone or degree of the scale. This is the predominant interval in common speech. It has upon the ear a pleasing effect, analogous to that produced upon the eye by the prevailing green of nature. In the words of Dr. Rush, "The ear has its green as well as the eye, and the interval of the second is widely spread to relieve sensation from the fatiguing stimulus of more vivid impression."

---

* Job, ch. iii. v. 17.

Writers of every age have endeavored to show that pleasure is in us, and not in the objects offered for our amusement. If the soul be happily disposed, everything becomes capable of affording entertainment, and distress will almost want a name. Every occurrence passes in review like the figures in a procession; some may be awkward, others ill-dressed, but none, except a fool, is for this enraged with the master of the ceremonies.

§ 199. Strong emotions express themselves in more frequent and greater variations of pitch and inflection.

When the emotions are more animated and excited than in the preceding case, the voice naturally changes its pitch more frequently, and ranges through wider intervals. In this case, the range both of skip and slide, up and down, will be to the extent of a third or fifth of the scale.

Is not this crime enough to turn Mercy herself into an executioner! You convict for murder—here is the hand that murdered innocence. You convict for treason—here is the vilest disloyalty to friendship. You convict for robbery—here is one who plundered Virtue of her most precious jewel.

§ 200. Violent passions express themselves in the greatest variations of pitch and inflection.

In fine, when violent and uncontrollable passions clamor for expression, the voice rises to its highest and sinks to its lowest pitch, traversing, with rapid and extreme variations, often the whole octave. This will be found to be the case in any true expression of the insane remorse and grief of Othello, over the body of the murdered Desdemona, after he had discovered her innocence.

> O cursed slave! Whip me, ye devils,
> From the possession of this heavenly sight!
> Blow me about in winds—roast me in sulphur—
> Wash me in steep-down gulfs of liquid fire!.
> O Desdemona! Desdemona! Dead!
> Dead! O! O! O!

§ 201. **Subdued emotions of grief, sorrow, pity, desire, love, hope, and fear, express themselves in variations of the semitone.**

The subdued and chastened expression of these, and other similar affections and passions, very frequently consists of semitone variations, in which the voice rises and falls, both concretely and discretely, a semitone above and below the middle line of pitch. Of course, this rule does not exclude other variations, but these are the most frequent, and to a certain extent indispensable. Hence they are much heard in the language of complaint, condolence, and of audible prayer. In this last case, if the greater concrete variations of the second, third and fifth, predominate, the result is an irreverent, undevotional, conversational manner, which suggests that he who is praying feels himself to be almost on a footing of equality with the Being addressed, and which consequently is extremely offensive. It has been remarked that children cry in semitones. Hence the pathetic complaint of Desdemona, after being charged by her husband with infidelity, cannot be adequately rendered but by means of these semitone variations of pitch.

PITCH AND INFLECTION.

Iago. Madam, how is it with you?
Desdemona (with sobs and tears).
  Alas! I cannot tell. Those that do teach young babes,
  Do it with gentle means and easy tasks.
  He might have chid me so, for, in good faith,
  I am a child to chiding.

§ 202. Grave and earnest, but not impassioned sentiments, express themselves in variations of the second and third, and mostly in the falling inflections.

In the following example these variations prevail, and every clause ends in a downward slide of the voice.

  Be wise to-day; 'tis madness to defer.
  Next day the fatal precedent will plead.
  Thus on, till wisdom is pushed out of life.
  Procrastination is the thief of time;
  Year after year it steals, till all are fled,
  And to the mercies of a moment, leaves
  The vast concerns of an eternal scene.

§ 203. Sentiments of great animation and vivacity express themselves in variations of the third and fifth, with frequent upward slides.

As the interval of the second is the green of the ear, so " these variations of the third and fifth are the lights and shadows of discourse, and are indispensable to give life and power to the vocal picture." They predominate in the expression of wit and playfulness, and of all sentiments of a highly animated character. Skips of the fifth, indeed, do not often occur in such discourse, but slides of this interval are not at all uncommon. In animated and playful conversation, the range of the voice up and down these intervals, both in skips and slides, is incessant. When they prevail in what is intended to be grave and dignified, and, of course, not highly impassioned discourse, they lower its dignity, and render it conversational in style or manner. The wit and playfulness and ever restless vivacity of Falstaff, afford constant examples of these variations.

> A good sherris sack hath a two-fold operation in it. It ascends me into the brain, and dries me there all the foolish and dull and crudy vapors which environ it; makes it apprehensive, quick, forgetive (inventive) full of nimble, fiery and delectable shapes; which, delivered o'er to the voice, the tongue, which is the birth, becomes excellent wit. The second property of your excellent sherris, is the warming of the blood; which, before cold and settled, left the liver white and pale, which is the badge of pusillanimity and cowardice: but the sherris warms it, and makes it course from the inwards to the parts extreme; it illumineth the face, which as a beacon gives warning to all the rest of this little kingdom, man, to arm; and then the vital commoners, and inland petty spirits, muster me all to their captain, the heart; who, great and puffed up with this retinue, doth any deed of courage—and this valor comes of sherris. .... Hereof comes it that Prince Harry is valiant. For the cold blood he did naturally inherit from his father, he hath, like lean, sterile and bare land, manured, husbanded and tilled, with excellent endeavor of drinking good, and good store of fertile sherris; [so] that he is become very hot and valiant. If I had a thousand sons, the first human principle I would teach them, should be to forswear thin potations, and addict themselves to sack.

§ 204. **Animated expressions of certainty, positiveness, and determination, range through intervals of the third and fifth, mostly with falling inflections.**

The following passage affords an example of such intervals, more of the third, however, than of the fifth, and nearly every clause ends with a downward slide.

Nay, more—I can, and I will say, that as a peer of parliament, as speaker of this right honorable house, as keeper of the great seal, as guardian of his majesty's conscience, as Lord High Chancellor of England—nay even in that character alone, in which the noble duke would think it an affront to be considered, but which charact r none can deny me, as a man—I am at this moment as respectable, I beg leave to add, as much respected, as the proudest peer I now look down upon.

§ 205. **Animated expressions of uncertainty, hesitation, surprise and irony, range through intervals of the third and fifth, mostly with rising inflections.**

The bitter irony of the Prophet Elijah, ridiculing the prophets of Baal, exhibits these changes of pitch and inflection in a very striking manner, although on several of the words, the inflections may be downwards with the best effect. On several of the words, also, the wave, or double inflection (§ 213) is required.

Cry aloud, for he is a god. Either he is talking, or he is pursuing, or he is on a journey, or peradventure he sleepeth, and must be awaked.

So also in the bitter irony of Job's reply to his friends.

No doubt, ye are the people, and wisdom will die with you.

Solemn irony, such as that of our Saviour, addressed to his sleeping disciples, more frequently takes the falling inflection.

Sleep on now, and take your rest; (this is, indeed, a time for you to sleep!) for the Son of Man is betrayed into the hands of sinners·

In the reply of the woman at the well of Samaria to our Lord, we have a fine expression of doubt and surprise, with these strong upward inflections on the words in italics.

Sir, thou hast nothing to draw with, and the well is deep; from whence then hast thou that living water? Art thou greater than our father *Jacob*, who gave us the *well*, and drank thereof *himself*, and his *children*, and his *cattle?*

§ 206. Questions which require answers, if the emphasis be not on the interrogative word, commonly take the rising inflection.

Of such questions there are two classes:

1. *Those expressing a desire for information*, which is to be furnished by the answer; as in the following example, in which the words, looked, and frowningly, both take the rising inflection, but the latter a much longer one than the former.

What! looked he frowningly?

2. *Those intended to draw a mental response from the audience*, but which require no vocal answer. Thus the following questions are intended to call forth the most emphatic mental response; conse-

quently the words, now, and stoop, take the strongest rising inflections.

What! are ye daunted *now?*   *Now* will ye *stoop?*

§ 207. **Questions which express affirmation, except when the emphasis is on the last word, commonly take the falling inflection.**

This rule might have been expressed nearly as well in the form of the converse of the preceding, viz: Questions which require no answer, either vocal or mental, commonly take the falling inflection. For the principal reason why questions require no answer, is that they express affirmation. In applying the rule in either form, it is necessary to scrutinize the question narrowly, to see whether it does not require a mental response. In the following questions, the italicized words all close with the falling slide.

Have I not reason to look *pale* and *dead?*
Is she not with the *dead,* the *quiet dead,* where all is *peace?*

§ 208. **Questions in which the principal emphasis is on a substantive verb, or an auxiliary, commonly take the falling inflection.**

Cases in which the substantive verb or auxiliary is the last word in the sentence, are exceptions to this rule, as in the questions, He is? They have? in which the last words take the rising slide. The following are examples under the rule.

Did he show himself a brother? *Is* he not rightly called a sup planter? *Can* I do otherwise? *Must* I not do it? *Have* I not given him enough?

In these, and all similar cases, the questions close with falling inflections. But if the principal emphasis were on any other words, the questions would all take the rising slides, as follows.

Did he *show* himself a brother? Is he not *rightly* called a *supplanter?* Have I not given him *enough?*

§ 209. Questions in which the interrogative words, such as who, which, what, when, whence, where, why, how, are followed by other words, commonly take the falling inflection.

This rule is nearly or quite universal, and one of great importance. For this class of questions is probably more numerous than all others taken together; and the attempt to render them with the rising inflection, mars the elocution of a great number of speakers. In the following, and all similar cases, the questions end with falling slides.

From whence then hast thou that living water? For why will ye die? O death, where is thy sting? O grave, where is thy victory? Who shall deliver me from the body of this death?

In the case of such double questions as, When, did you say? and in case the interrogative is the last or sole word in the question, it may take either the rising or falling slide. If *e. g.* I say, He is now in Baltimore; and you, not perfectly understanding me, ask, Where? or Where, did you say? the question will always take the rising inflection.

But if I say, He is now lying very ill, and you ask, Where? the question will take the falling slide.

§ 210. Double questions, implying a negative in the former, and an affirmation in the latter, take the rising inflection on the former, and the falling on the latter.

This rule illustrates the importance of this whole subject of inflection in a very striking manner. For such questions as the following,

Was he a poet? or an orator?

are susceptible of a great variety of meanings, which can be expressed in no other way than by different inflections. For if in this question, I would ask whether the person was either a poet or an orator, or neither, both words, poet and orator, take the rising inflection. If I would affirm that he was neither, the emphasis being on the substantive verb, was, then both take the falling slide. But if I mean to deny that he was a poet, and to affirm that he was an orator, or if I would learn which of the two he was, the former question takes the upward, the latter the downward slide; while, to distinguish those two last cases from each other, we have to resort to a different emphasis on the word, orator. Again,

Is a candle brought to put under a bushel, or under a bed?

This question in itself is capable of a similar variety of meanings. But because its object is to call forth a mental response, affirming that a candle is not brought to be put under a bushel, nor under a bed, the emphasis being on bushel, and bed, both words take the rising inflection. But now, if the rising inflection be given to the former clause, and the falling to the latter, the question will express either a desire to learn which of the two is the proper place for a candle, or it will affirm that a candle is not brought to be placed under a bushel, but is emphatically to be put under a bed.

Let any one try these changes, and he cannot fail to satisfy himself of the great significance of the inflections of oral speech.

§ 211. Words and phrases in pairs commonly take, the first a rising, the second a falling inflection.

This variation is a requirement both of melody and of expression. It is exemplified in the following.

For I am persuaded that neither *death* nor *life*, nor angels, nor *principalities* nor *powers*, nor *things present* nor *things to come*, nor *height* nor *depth*, nor any other creature, shall be able to separate us from the love of God, which is Christ Jesus our Lord.

§ 212. The principal inflections always occur on the emphatic words.

This is equally true in questions and all other sentences. It will require more full treatment under the head of emphasis. In asking questions, it is a common error to let the voice rise on an inclined plane, as it were, equably from the beginning to the end of the sentence. It is not possible to give adequate expression to the sentiment in this way. The principal inflection in questions should always be given to the most emphatic word; and in order to do this, the voice must often fall on the preceding words to a low pitch.

Thus, in the following example, the voice rises by inflection on the first, seems, through a fifth or an octave, and the following word, Madam, is pronounced on the high pitch thus attained, or with a slight fall.

Seems, Madam?
Nay, it *is*—I know not *seems.*

Again, in the following, the rising inflection on who, king, father, runs through a fifth or an octave, and in order to this, the voice must fall from king to the next word through a like interval.

Saw *who?*
My Lord, the King, your father.
The *King?* my *father?*

The case is similar in the following example, in which, after a full rise on the word, dog, the voice runs along on the high pitch thus attained to the word, thing, on which occurs another slight rise.

Is thy servant a *dog,* that he should do this great thing?

Once more:

Moneys is your suit.
What should I say to you? Should I not say,
Hath a *dog* money? Is it possible,
That a *cur* should raise three thousand ducats?

Here upon the emphatic words, dog, and cur, the voice should rise in an impassioned slide through a fifth or an octave, and the words that follow in each question, should be pronounced on the high pitch thus attained, with another slight rise on the last words.

§ 213. The wave, or circumflex variation of pitch, is used to express drollery, impassioned irony, sarcasm, and sneer.

This variation of pitch is a combination of the two slides on the same word, and often on the same syllable. Sometimes the upward movement comes first, and sometimes the downward. The elocutionists run into great minuteness in the treatment of this element of expression; what they have given us can hardly be made practical to any but the most thorough students. It is true, however, that these waves of the voice are often extremely effective in the expression of their appropriate sentiments. Those who would see them thoroughly discussed, are referred to Dr. Rush, and Professors Mandeville and Day. Here an example or two must suffice.

Hereof comes it that Prince Harry is *valiant*.

On the word, valiant, the voice runs up and down through a fifth. So on the word, you, in the following.

You Prince of Wales!

Again, in the words, Daniel and now, in the following.

A second Daniel, a *Daniel*, Jew.
Now, Infidel, I have thee on the hip....
A *Daniel*, still I say, a second *Daniel*.
I thank thee, Jew, for teaching me that word.

CHAPTER IX.

TIME AND PAUSE.

§ 214. The time occupied in the delivery of thoughts and sentiments, is an element of their expression.—Pause is a function of time.

WE have seen that increasing the time of syllables is one form of accentuation (§ 126); and we shall hereafter see that it is also an element of emphasis, (§ 235). But here we have to consider the time which is occupied in the delivery of a passage, whether a clause, or sentence, or paragraph, or general division of a discourse, in its relations to the expression of the meaning and sentiment. For the various grammatical and logical relations of thought cannot be fully expressed in speech, otherwise than by corresponding modifications of time and pause. Some thoughts and sentiments require to be slowly delivered, with pauses of considerable length between the words and parts of the discourse; others more rapidly, with shorter pauses. When these requirements are violated, the speaking is either powerless, or its power is greatly diminished. Only the most general principles, however can be here laid down, chiefly for the purpose of drawing the attention of the student to the subject, that he may be led to consider and determine for himself, in each case, what modifications of time and pause may be required by the character of the thoughts and sentiments which he has to express.

§ 215. **Elevated, sublime, solemn and sorrowful sentiments require slow time.**

This is one of the most obvious general rules of expression. Such sentiments naturally prompt to slow movements of every other kind, besides that of speaking. A burial procession moves slowly. A dead-march, or funereal dirge, is performed in slow time. In the same way, elevated, sublime, solemn and sorrowful sentiments require to be slowly delivered. A rapid delivery of such sentiments destroys their effect, and turns them into burlesque. It is as incongruous as the performance of a dead march in quick time, or as the galloping of a funeral procession. Yet, however slow the enunciation may be, it must never fail to maintain a firm and steady movement; and it must be carefully guarded against becoming too slow, which would render it dull and tiresome, or put the audience to sleep. The following passage affords a good example of slow time.

Behold, I show you a mystery; we shall not all sleep, but we shall all be changed—in a moment, in the twinkling of an eye, at the last trump. For the trumpet shall sound, and the dead shall be raised, and we shall be changed. For this corruptible must put on incorruption, and this mortal must put on immortality. So when this corruptible shall have put on incorruption, and this mortal shall have put on immortality, then shall be brought to pass the saying that is written, Death is swallowed up in victory. O death, where is thy sting? O grave, where is thy victory?

§ 216. **Condensed, abstruse, and obscure passages require slow time.**

The reason of this rule is that, where the thought is difficult or obscure from any cause, more time must be allowed to enable the audience to possess themselves of it—they must have more time than otherwise would be required, to elicit the sense or meaning of the discourse;—if it be rapidly delivered, it becomes unintelligible. Here, as before, however, it is very important to guard against too great slowness, and for the same reason (§ 215). In the following example, very slow time, and long pauses are required, because the thought is both condensed and obscure, and at the same time the sentiments are solemn and sublime.

>Thou from primeval nothingness did'st call,
>First chaos, then existence. Lord, on thee
>Eternity had its foundation ; all
>Sprang forth from thee ; of light, joy, harmony
>Sole origin ; all life, all beauty thine.
>Thy Word created all, and doth create ;
>Thy splendor fills all space with rays divine.
>Thou art, and wert, and shalt be, glorious, **great,**
>Life-giving, life-preserving Potentate.

§ 217. **Grave, serious and moderate sentiments require moderate time.**

The delivery of such sentiments should not be very slow, nor yet too rapid—both extremes are to be carefully avoided. For if the movement be too rapid, it will be out of keeping with the sentiments, which, therefore, will fail to affect the minds of the audience in the proper manner ; and if it be too slow, the audience will be constantly running ahead of the speaker, and will soon cease to give their attention. Nothing, in fact, can be more fatal to power in delivery than for the speaker to allow his audience to keep ahead of him. This, however, is partly a rhetorical, as well as an elocutionary fault. A deliberate or moderate movement is required in the following extract.

The firmest works of man are gradually giving way ; the ivy clings to the mouldering tower, the brier hangs out from the shattered window, and the wall-flower springs from the disjointed stones. The founders of these perishable works have shared the same fate long ago. If we look back to the days of our ancestors, to the men as well as to the dwellings of former times, they become immediately associated in our imaginations, and only make the feelings of instability stronger and deeper than before. In the spacious domes which once held our fathers, the serpent hisses, and the wild bird screams.

§ 218. **Sentiments of greater vivacity require a quicker movement.**

The following is an example.

When over the hills like a gladsome bride,
Morning walks forth in her beauty's pride,

> And leading a band of laughing hours,
> Brushes the dew from the nodding flowers,
> Oh! cheerily then my voice is heard,
> Mingling with that of the soaring bird,
> Who flingeth abroad his matins loud,
> As he freshens his wing in the cold gray cloud.

§ 219. Impassioned sentiments commonly require a rapid delivery.

Almost all the passions, except those of grief, sorrow, pity, and the like, when in a high state of excitement, prompt to rapid motions, both of body and mind. A man, when thus highly excited, does not walk nor speak in a slow or stately manner, all his motions naturally correspond to the excited state of his nervous system, and of his mental faculties. The audience, moreover, naturally partake of the speaker's excitement; consequently their minds act with greater rapidity than at other times. This is especially true and significant of the irascible passions. Hence the expression of such impassioned sentiments requires a rapid movement; which, however, must be carefully guarded lest it become so rapid as to mar the articulation, and render the speaking unintelligible. For uncontrolled passion always tends to indistinctness of articulation. The following extract requires a rapid movement.

> Banished from Rome? What's banished but set free
> From daily contact with the things I loathe?
> Tried and convicted traitor! Who says this?
> Who'll prove it at his peril on my head?
> Banished? I thank you for't—it breaks my chain.
> I held some slack allegiance till this hour;
> But now my sword's my own.—Smile on, my lords.

> I scorn to count what feelings, withered hopes,
> Strong provocations, bitter, burning wrongs,
> I have within my heart's hot cells shut up.
> But here I stand and scoff you. Here I fling
> Hatred and full defiance in your face.
> Here I devote your Senate. I've had wrongs
> To stir a fever in the blood of age,
> And make the infant's sinews strong as steel.

§ 255. The commencement of speeches, heads and paragraphs, require slower time than the subsequent parts.

This is a rule of great importance, and one which is often violated with damaging effect. The following are some of the reasons upon which it is founded.

1. *Slow time is necessary to gain the attention of the audience.*

Of course, it is of the utmost importance to fix the attention of the audience at the beginning of the discourse; but this can hardly be done, unless time be given them to master the full meaning of the opening words and sentences.

2. *New matter is presented.*

At the commencement of a speech, the matter presented is altogether new and unfamiliar to the minds of the audience. Hence it is naturally more difficult for them to master it. It cannot be anticipated, nor comprehended in sequence from anything going before. Therefore it requires to be delivered more slowly than the subsequent parts.

3. *More general and abstract terms are commonly employed.*

The speaker properly aims at first to communicate to his audience some conception of his whole subject, and of the object which he aims to accomplish, that they may be able to anticipate, in some degree, the line of argument, and general drift, of the discourse which is to follow. Hence the necessity of abstractions and generalizations. In order to master these, and to form adequate conceptions of what is to follow, the audience must have time given them to weigh every word. If the commencement of the speech be hurriedly delivered, the whole of it will probably be a mass of confusion to the audience.

4. *The mental operations are naturally slower.*

At the commencement of a speech, the feelings of both speaker and audience are yet calm and placid; consequently their minds naturally operate less promptly and rapidly than in the subsequent parts, when their emotions and passions are fully excited, and the whole mind is kindled into a glow by its own activity. Hence the speaker requires more time to express, and the audience to follow the thought. This is more especially the case with the speaker in extempore discourse; and all delivery should be precisely as if the whole thought were originated and elaborated at the moment.

5. *All these reasons apply, but with less force, to the commencement of heads and topics.*

All these reasons apply not only to speeches, but also to the general and subordinate heads, topics and paragraphs, only with diminishing force, in the order in which these divisions are here enumerated

Hence the slowest time of all is required at the commencement of the speech; less slow time, at the commencement of a general head; still less, at that of a subordinate head; and still less, at that of a paragraph; but all these beginnings should be delivered more slowly than the subsequent parts.

§ 221. **Pause in speech is a function of time.**

As inflection is a function of pitch (§ 189), so pause is a function of time. For it is obvious that the time given to the delivery of a discourse, or of any part of it, will be greater or less, and the movement more or less rapid, as the pauses, or intervals of silence, between its parts are longer or shorter. This, moreover, is a very important function. For these pauses are not only very numerous, inasmuch as they occur between all the parts of discourse (§ 148—3), except syllables, and thus occupy a considerable proportion of the time; but, also, very many of them are essential to clearness, and even to intelligibility, in the communication of thought, and to power in the expression of sentiment.

222. **The three functions of pause are the grammatical, the rhythmical, and the rhetorical.**

These are all distinct functions, or, as they may be called, different varieties of pause in speech; and they contribute in different ways to the result of power in delivery. The grammatical pauses are intended to symbolize the syntactical relations of words and clauses in sentences. The rhythmical pauses contribute a principal element of the rhythm of speech. The rhetorical pauses have two functions; first, to symbolize the relations between the rhetorical divisions of the discourse; and, secondly, to aid in giving a more powerful expression to the sentiments.

§ 223. **Grammatical pauses indicate the syntactical relation of words and clauses in sentences, and are of varying length according to the sentiments expressed.**

This rule covers the ground of the period (.) colon (:) semicolon (;) comma (,) and dash (—) in punctuation. But the speaker or reader must be on his guard against attempting to govern his pauses by these marks. The sense of the words, and the character of the sentiments, are his only reliable guides. For the punctuation marks the pauses, and the pauses indicate the syntactical relations, only in a very imperfect and defective manner.

1. *These signs and pauses symbolize only a more or less close relation.*

They indicate nothing of the character of that relation. Thus the period, the longest pause, indicates that a syntactical structure of words, or a sentence, is completed. The colon, the next in length, indicates the most remote separation which can occur between the different parts of a sentence. The semicolon marks a less wide separation, and the comma, the least of all that have signs; whilst the dash properly signifies that the particular syntactical structure with which the sentence began, is broken off, and that the sentence is to be completed with another which is inconsistent with it. It is used, however, for other purposes.

2. *All these pauses vary in length.*

The causes of their variations are the greater or less rapidity of the general movement, and the character of the sentiments expressed. Under the influence of these causes, a colon, or a semicolon, or even a comma, may represent a pause longer than a period; whilst a dash may represent a pause of any length whatsoever.

3. *Pauses are constantly required that are not marked in punctuation.*

In good reading and speaking, these pauses are constantly occurring, where punctuation marks would be wholly out of place.

The foregoing observations may serve to guard the reader or speaker against undue reliance upon punctuation, and to impress upon his mind the principle, that his true guides are the sense of the words, and the character of the sentiments to be expressed.

§ 224. Rhythmical pauses, in connection with accent, produce the rhythm of speech.

Rhythm is an element of beauty, consequently of power, both in poetry and prose. It depends upon the distribution of accented and unaccented syllables, and of brief pauses. It is, of course, most conspicuous in poetry; in which, the pauses upon which it depends, occur most frequently in or near the middle, and at the close of the lines or verses. But a searching analysis of good reading or recitation of poetry, will disclose to the ear a great number of minor prosodial or rhythmical pauses, which are essential to the perfection of the rhythm, but which cannot be subjected to any fixed or certain metrical laws. The rhythm of prose, both with respect to accent and pause, is essentially free, that is, not subject to any invariable rules; it is governed only by the sense and the sentiment to be expressed. The following are examples from our greatest master both of poetical and prose rhythm.

> Haste thee, nymph, and bring with thee
> Jest and youthful jollity,
> Quips and cranks and wanton wiles,
> Nods and becks and wreathed smiles;
> Such as hang on Hebe's cheek,
> And love to live in dimple sleek;
> Sport, that wrinkled care derides,
> And Laughter, holding both his sides.
> Come, and trip it as you go,
> On the light, fantastic toe;
> And in thy right hand lead with thee
> The mountain nymph, sweet Liberty.

For I am about to discourse of matters neither inconsiderable nor common; but how a most potent king, after he had trampled upon the laws of the nation, and given a shock to its religion, and begun to rule at his own will and pleasure, was at last subdued in the field by his own subjects, who had undergone a long slavery under him; how, afterwards, he was cast into prison; and when he gave no ground, either by words or actions, to hope better things of him, he was finally, by the supreme council of the kingdom, condemned to die, and beheaded before the very gates of the royal palace.

§ 225. **Rhetorical pauses indicate the relations between the rhetorical divisions of the discourse, and aid in the expression of the sentiments.**

These two functions, or varieties of the rhetorical pause, are quite distinct, in so far, at least, as the former symbolize relations of thought, and the latter are expressive of emotion and passion. Both, however, are of very great importance, as contributing in different ways to the result of power in delivery.

§ 226. **General heads of discourse require longer pauses between them than subordinate ones; subordinate heads, longer than paragraphs, and paragraphs than sentences.**

All the primary and subordinate divisions of every discourse, require to be delivered with pauses between them; and these pauses vary in length according as the general movement is more or less rapid, and as the parts are more or less closely connected with each other. Their importance arises from the fact that they signify to the audience, according to their different lengths, that one general or subordinate head, or one paragraph, or sentence, is concluded, and another about to be commenced. Thus they impart *discreteness* and clearness to the speaking; and enable the audience to comprehend and follow the drift and progress of the discourse. Hence they constitute an essential element of intelligibility. Where they are neglected, and the several divisions of the discourse are hurriedly run into each other, the speaking fails in clearness and intelligibility, and makes the impression upon the audience of a crude and confused mass, instead of an organized body of thought. The effect is similar to that produced upon the mind of the reader by a discourse written or printed without primary, coördinate, or subordinate parts, and without paragraphs or sentences.

§ 227. The rhetorical pause is expressive of overwhelming emotion.

This pause is in place when either the emotions of the speaker have become uncontrollable, or those of the audience have been worked up to a very high degree of excitement. The attempt to introduce it without either of these conditions, must result in complete failure, and call forth only ridicule. But when rightly timed, it is one of the highest forms of elocutionary art. Accompanied with the appropriate expressions of gesture and countenance, its effects are sometimes prodigious. Whitefield was accustomed to resort to it. The awful silence of the thousands who hung upon his oratory, whose very breathing seemed suspended, produced impressions which could never be forgotten, and which were vividly remembered long after the thoughts of his discourses had faded from the mind. The expressive power of this pause is due, first, to the excited state of the feelings, which only can justify it; secondly, to the fact that it gives full scope to the activity of the imagination, which it stimulates to run far beyond anything that can be expressed in words. In this latter respect, it is analogous to that stroke of high art employed by the ancient painter, who, in order to represent the overwhelming grief and despair of Agamemnon at the sacrifice of his daughter Iphigenia, at Aulis, portrayed him with a veil over his face, that the imagination might be left to conceive of what no art could depict.

Such a pause was intended by Shakspeare after the following words of Anthony; although it may be doubted whether Shakspeare himself has not erred in giving it so formal an announcement.

>My heart is in the coffin there with Cæsar,
>And I must pause till it come back to me.

CHAPTER X.

FORCE.

§ 228. Force in elocution is the application of strength of voice in different degrees, chiefly for purposes of expression.

WE have already treated of strength as one of the powers of the voice (§§ 176-179). We come now to treat of the application of this power in the expression of thought and feeling. The procedure here is analogous to the application of the other powers of the voice, compass and flexibility, which has been made under the head of pitch and inflection (§§ 188-213). We have seen also how force enters as an element of accent (§ 127); and we shall see hereafter how it constitutes an element of emphasis.

With respect to the application of force, there are two general rules to be observed.

§ 229. The first general rule is that in the rhetorical divisions of a speech, force varies as the time.

The parts of a speech which require to be rapidly delivered, commonly require also the greater degrees, and those which require to be more slowly delivered, the less degrees of force. Accordingly the beginnings of speeches, heads and paragraphs should be delivered with less force than the subsequent parts. A distinction is also to be observed between these parts. For the commencement of a speech should be delivered, as nearly as the size of the audience will allow, with no more loudness of voice than that which belongs to ordinary conversation. The speaker should always aim to make the conversational tones his point of departure. A greater degree of force is allowable in commencing the general heads; but it should be sensibly less than that which is given to the delivery of what follows under these heads. And still greater force may be given to the commencement of subordinate divisions and paragraphs, provided the speaker be able to increase it yet further as the sentiment rises. These variations are absolutely essential to the adequate expression of the distinctions and transitions of thought. If they be neglected, the audience will not be duly informed when one thought is ended and another commenced, nor of the relations of the different thoughts to each other.

§ 230. The second general rule is that in the expression of sentiment, force varies as pitch and inflection.

Those sentiments which require the higher ranges of pitch, and the greater inflections, require also for their adequate expression, the greater degrees of force or loudness of sound. Thus strong emotions of anger, grief, scorn, joy, hope, fear, and the like, commonly express themselves in loud sounds. Sometimes, however, the force of the feeling may choke the voice; at other times, the most intense passion, under the control of a strong will, expresses itself in low tones, and with the utmost deliberation and quietness. On the other hand, those sentiments which require the lower ranges of pitch, and less extended inflections, commonly require also less stress of voice. Thus calm or subdued emotions of grief, sorrow, pity, love, hope, joy, and the like, express themselves in soft or subdued tones; whilst animated expressions of certainty, positiveness and determination, range through louder sounds.

The relation of force to the expression of sentiment, is touched by Dr. Rush as follows.

"Secrecy muffles the voice against discovery; and doubt, whilst it leans towards a positive declaration, cunningly prepares the subterfuge of an undertone, that the impression of its possible error may be least exciting and durable. Certainty, on the other hand, in the full desire to be heard distinctly, assumes all the impressiveness of strength. Anger, in like manner, uses force of voice, because its charges and denials are made with a wide appeal, and in the sincerity of passion; and .... the same mode is employed in uttering those feelings which are blended with anger, such as hate, ferocity and revenge. All those sentiments which are unbecoming or disgraceful, smother the voice to its softer degrees, in the desire to conceal even the voluntary utterance of them. Joy is loud in calling for companionship, through the overflowing charity of its satisfaction. Bodily pain, fear and terror are also strong in their expression; with the double intention of summoning relief, and repelling the offending cause, when it is a sentient being. For the sharpness and vehemence of the full-strained cry, are universally painful or appalling to the animal ear."

§ 231. The different kinds of stress of voice express different classes of sentiments and emotions.

There are several varieties of force or stress of voice, which are distinguishable from each other by their falling respectively upon different parts of the sound, and which are expressive of different varieties of sentiments and emotions.

1. *The radical stress falls on the beginning of the sound, and is appropriate to the expression of lively and startling sentiments, and strong passions.*

This mode of stress consists in an abrupt or explosive utterance of the voice on the initial part of the sound, the latter part being allowed gradually to die away. It is exemplified in the pronunciation of the words, go away! as expressive of strong aversion; in which the sounds of o in go, and ay in way, commence with explosive force, and decline in loudness until they cease. It is much used in the expression of unrestrained and lively passions and emotions, in startling thoughts, and in animated, earnest and stirring sentiments; as, also, in confident and earnest argumentative discourse. Too much of it indicates too much self-confidence. The want of it denotes the absence of sharp and vigorous thought. It has been called "the salt and relish of oral communication, inasmuch as it preserves its pungency, or penetrating effect." It is properly heard in almost every word of the following example.

> He woke to hear his sentry shriek,
> To arms! they come! the Greek! the Greek!

>   He woke to die midst flame and smoke,
>   And shout and groan and sabre stroke,
>   And death shots falling thick and fast
>   As lightnings from the mountain cloud;
>   And heard, with voice as thunder loud,
>   Bozzaris cheer his band:
>   "Strike, till the last armed foe expires;
>   "Strike, for your altars and your fires;
>   "God, and your native land."

2. *The median stress swells out on the middle of the sound, and is appropriate to the expression of grave, solemn, sad and elevated sentiments; also, of sublimity, admiration, authority, and the like.*

This mode of stress, as defined above, gives a swell to the middle of the sound, as in the common pronunciation of the word, grave. It has nothing in it of an abrupt or explosive character. It is adapted to the expression of grave, elevated, sublime, sad and solemn sentiments; of admiration, pure and serene joy, and of unquestioned authority and power. It is peculiarly expressive in the melody of such poetry as is not characterized by intense passion; and, also, in the reading of the less impassioned portions of Scripture. The following are examples.

>   Hail, holy light! Offspring of Heaven first-born,
>   Or of the eternal, co-eternal beam,
>   May I express thee unblamed? since God is light;
>   And never but in unapproachèd light
>   Dwelt from eternity; dwelt then in thee,
>   Bright effluence of bright essence increate.

Then said Jesus unto his disciples, If any man will come after me, let him deny himself, and take up his cross, and follow me. For whosoever will save his life, shall lose it; and whosoever will lose his life for my sake, shall find it. For what is a man profited, if he shall gain the whole world, and lose his own soul? Or what shall a man give in exchange for his soul?

3. *The vanishing stress falls on the last part of the sound, and is expressive, for the most part, of violent and evil passions.*

This mode of stress makes the sound loudest at or near its close, as in the expression, I won't, uttered in passion. It is mostly expressive of the evil passions, or those which are evil by excess, such as impatience, contempt, scorn, obstinacy, malignity, anger, wrath, malice, and all uncharitableness. It is not, however, limited to these, but is often required by the utmost violence of other passions. The following is an example.

> Now bind my brows with iron; and approach
> The raggedest hour that time and spite dare bring,
> To frown upon the enraged Northumberland.
> Let heaven kiss earth; now let not nature's hand
> Keep the wild flood confined; let order die;
> And let this world no longer be a stage
> To feed contention in a lingering act;
> But let one spirit of the first-born Cain,
> Reign in all bosoms; that, each heart being set
> On bloody courses, the rude scene may end,
> And darkness be the burier of the dead.

4. *Thorough stress falls upon the whole sound, and is expressive of deep and lofty, and, for the most part, of joyful emotions.*

In this mode of stress, the whole sound is filled out, so to speak, and sustained, as in the word, friend, pronounced with deep emotion. It is appropriate to the expression of great joy, rapture, triumph, exultation, patriotism, and the like. It may be employed also with good effect in the expression of lofty indignation and disdain.

> These are thy glorious works, Parent of good,
> Almighty ; thine this universal frame,
> Thus wondrous fair ; thyself how wondrous then!
> Unspeakable, who sitst above the heavens,
> To us invisible, or dimly seen
> In these thy lowest works ; yet these declare
> Thy goodness beyond thought, and power divine.

§ 232. The most common faults, in respect of force, are too much and too little, and the indiscriminate use of it.

All of these faults are very common, and any one of them is fatal to genuine power in delivery.

1. *In general, the speaking should be only loud enough to be distinctly and easily heard.*

Whenever the speaker goes beyond this, he should be very sure that increased force is necessary to the adequate expression of the sentiment. For speaking too loud throughout the body of the discourse, is often due to "a plentiful lack" of ideas. Speakers who are deficient in this respect, unconsciously try to compensate for their want by an increase of noise, mere "sound and fury, signifying nothing." But rant is a poor substitute for thought. It is, moreover, a vulgar fault, most common with speakers who are destitute of culture and refinement.

2. *Speaking which is not loud enough, fails in expression, and distresses the audience.*

This fault is, of course, frequently due to feebleness of voice, the remedy for which must be sought in vocal culture (§ 179). But this is not the only cause; for it is not at all uncommon in men who have voice enough, but who seem to think it is ill-bred to speak loud, even where the sentiment most requires it. Such "playing proper" is utterly inconsistent with true oratory. For when the speaking is not loud enough to be distinctly and easily heard by the whole audience, much of what is said is lost to a portion of them, and all are distressed by their oral efforts, so that they soon cease to give their attention. The feebleness of sound also expresses feebleness of thought. Consequently, when the thought is good in itself, it is inadequately expressed, and fails of its proper effect, whilst those sentiments which require peculiar energy in the delivery, are simply caricatured.

3. *The indiscriminate employment of force is the opposite of true expression.*

Not unfrequently stress of voice is inappropriately distributed. The speaker seems to feel that some parts of his discourse ought to be delivered in loud, and others in soft tones; but he fails to increase and diminish the sound in the proper places. Sentiments which require the greatest, he delivers with the least force; and words which require only to be heard and understood, he bellows out, as if he were crying, *Fire! Fire!* The delivery thus becomes the opposite of true expression. Frequently also this indiscriminate use of force takes place on corresponding parts of the same sentence; which results in a painful monotony of increasing and diminishing sounds.

CHAPTER XL.

EMPHASIS.

§ 233. Emphasis is the giving of relative vocal prominence to particular words or phrases for purposes of expression.

THE word is pure Greek, derived from the verb *emphaino*, to show, which, in its rhetorical applications, signifies to express in a vivid, or forcible manner. Hence expression is the characteristic function of emphasis, by which in part it is distinguished from accent, which, exceptional cases (§ 130—2) apart, has little to do with expression. It is further distinguished from accent in that it gives prominence to whole words and phrases, whilst accent affects only particular syllables. Yet it is to be borne in mind that emphasis itself falls chiefly, though not exclusively, on the accented syllables, except in the case of monosyllabic words, which commonly take no accent (§ 133).

All emphasis is relative; that is to say, the degree of prominence which is to be given to words or phrases, is to be determined by the connection in which they stand, and by the occasion or circumstances of the delivery. Where the whole passage is of a more or less emphatic character, the em phatic words require greater or less prominence. The highly wrought emphasis of impassioned oratory, would be wholly out of place in a parlor reading of the same speech; and in large audiences, a much stronger emphasis is in place, than in small. Propriety requires this relative character of emphasis to be carefully observed.

§ 234. **The principal elements of emphasis are force and quality of voice, time, pitch and inflection.**

Any two or more, and, indeed, all of these elements may be combined in the emphasis of a single word; in fact, the requisite prominence and significance can seldom be given to an emphatic word by any one of them. When used in combination, however, it will commonly be found that some one of them predominates over the others, and gives a distinctive character to the emphasis. It is of great importance to recognize and master all these elements of this mode of expression, because many speakers seem to think that there is no other way of emphasizing a word than by increased stress of voice. They simply pronounce every emphatic word louder than the others, with little or no other variation; the result of which is a tame and heavy thump, thump, in their delivery, which soon ceases to have any of the effect of emphasis, or expression, and becomes insufferably monotonous and wearisome to the audience.

§ 235. The emphasis of stress gives prominence to the word or phrase by increasing the loudness of the sound.

This is the most obvious and easy way of emphasizing, and therefore the most common, even whe e it is altogether inappropriate. Hence it is necessary to guard against the too frequent use of it. The increase of force, in this kind of emphasis, may be any one of the various modes of radical, median, vanishing, or thorough stress; the different sentiments appropriate to each of which have been given in § 231. When judiciously employed, especially with due reference to these several modes, this form of emphasis is very significant and expressive.

§ 236. The emphasis of quality distinguishes the word or phrase by some peculiar quality of voice.

The qualities of voice, their importance in expression, and the means of acquiring the command of them, have been treated of in §§ 167–174. There are several of these qualities, however, which are specially available for expression by emphasis, and which admit of being used separately, or in combination with each other; such as the following.

1. *The guttural emphasis is mostly expressive of the evil passions, repressed for the moment by a strong effort of will.*

This quality of voice depends essentially upon pitch, inasmuch as it is produced by the fewest vibrations of the vocal chords, and the resonance takes place deep in the guttur or windpipe, whilst this organ is contracted so as to interrupt the even flow of the sound, and render it impure. It is exemplified in the angry growl or snarl of a dog. It is expressive of pent-up or smothered rage, contempt, loathing, and similar feelings; but, especially, of a deep, vindictive determination to wreak the malignant feeling upon its object at some future time, since the present does not afford the desired opportunity. "The deep, laboring, guttural enunciation seems to suggest a smothered, pent-up, but heaving emotion, just ready to burst out, without restraint or control;" as in the following example.

Desdemona. Alas! what ignorant sin have I committed?
Othello. Was this fair paper, this most goodly book,
Made to write *whore* upon? *What committed?*
Committed! O thou *public commoner!*
I should make very forges of thy cheeks,
That would to cinders burn up modesty,
Did I but *speak* thy deeds. *What committed!*
Heaven stops the *nose* at it, and the moon **winks**.
The *bawdy* wind that *kisses all* it meets,
Is hushed within the hollow mine of earth,
And will not *hear* it. *What committed!*
Impudent strumpet!

2. *The aspirated emphasis is expressive of fear, terror, horror, amazement, and of intense earnestness.*

This quality of voice is produced by the violent expulsion of a greater quantity of breath than can be vocalized, seeming to overpower and confuse the delicate vocalizing organs. Hence it requires a strong action of the organs which expel the breath. The whisper, without emphasis, is expressive of secrecy or concealment; but the emphatic use of the aspirated quality of voice, expresses great violence of the passions. It is also significant of intense earnestness, from the fact that it intensifies the action of the articulating organs, in order to compensate for the want of the oral qualities of pure tone. This form of emphasis is frequent in the following example.

> *Have mercy, Jesu!*—Soft, I did but dream.
> O *coward conscience,* how dost thou afflict me!
> The *lights burn blue*—It is now *dead midnight.*
> *Cold, fearful drops* stand on my *trembling flesh....*
> My *conscience* hath a *thousand several tongues;*
> And *every* tongue brings in a *several tale;*
> And *every tale condemns* me for a *villain.*
> *Perjury, perjury,* in the *high'st* degree,
> *Murder,* stern *murder,* in the *dir'st* degree,
> *Throng* to the *bar,* crying all, *Guilty! guilty!....*
> Methought the *souls* of *all* that I had *murdered,*
> Came to my tent ; and every one did threat
> To-morrow's vengeance on the head of Richard.

3. *The emphasis of tremor expresses pity, grief, sorrow, desire, hope, joy, and kindred emotions.*

This quality is produced by alternately, in rapid succession, withholding and expelling the sound. It is easily acquired, and sometimes becomes habitual, so that almost every emphasis is given with a tremor; which is a great fault, being significant of a want of force, and command over the organs. It is often heard in prayer. When properly introduced, which should be sparingly, this mode of emphasis is very expressive. It may be employed with good effect on the italicized words in the following passage.

> *Farewell*, a *long* farewell to *all* my greatness.
> *This* is the state of man : to-day he puts forth
> The *tender leaves* of *hope ;* to-morrow blossoms,
> And bears his blushing honors thick upon him ;
> The third day comes a *frost*, a *killing* frost :
> And when he thinks, good easy man, full surely
> His greatness is a ripening, *nips* his *root ;*
> And then he *falls* as I do.

§ 237. **The temporal emphasis distinguishes the word or phrase either by prolonging the sound, or by a pause before or after it.**

There are thus two modes of this emphasis, the former of which may be characterized as the temporal emphasis proper, and the latter, as the emphatic pause. These require to be treated separately, for this reason among others, that the latter is appropriate to a much wider class of sentiments than the former.

1. *The temporal emphasis proper, dwells on the sound, and is appropriate to those sentiments which require slow or moderate time* (§§ 215—217).

This mode of emphasis is, as it were, the ground or condition of several others; for the emphasis of stress, quality and inflection, all require an increase of time in order to their full effect. This increase falls, of course, on those elements of the sound which are capable of indefinite prolongation; that is, upon the tonics and subtonics, except, in this latter class, the subnasals (§ 111). The fullest form of this mode of emphasis, is appropriate to the expression of elevated, sublime, solemn and sorrowful sentiments; in a less full form, to such as are of a grave, serious and moderate character. It is a very common and a very damaging fault, to load the delivery with this mode of emphasis, which renders it drawling and heavy, and awakens disgust in the audience. The increase of time on some of the emphatic words of the following sonnet, will readily be perceived.

>When I consider how my *light* is spent
>Ere *half* my *days*, in this *dark* world and *wide*;
>And that one talent, which is *death* to hide,
>Lodg'd in me *useless,* though my soul *more bent*
>To *serve* therewith my *Maker*, and present
>My *true* account, lest he returning *chide*—
>Doth *God expect* day-labor, *light denied?*
>I fondly ask : but *Patience*, to prevent
>That murmur, soon replies, God doth not need
>Either *man's work,* or *his own gifts;* who *best*
>*Bear* his *mild yoke, they serve* him *best* ; his *state*
>Is *kingly ; thousands* at his bidding *speed,*
>And post o'er *land* and *ocean* without rest ;
>*They* also *serve* who only *stand* and *wait.*

2. *The emphatic pause is appropriate to almost all kinds of sentiments, and may be introduced either before or after the emphatic word or phrase.*

This form of emphasis differs from the rhetorical pause (§ 227), inasmuch as that is expressive of overwhelming emotion, and has reference to the sentiment of the whole passage ; whilst this is intended to give effect to some particular word or phrase, and is appropriate to all kinds and degrees of feeling. It frequently occurs where both syntax and prosody would seem to forbid it. In fact, it overrules the connections of syntax (and equally the rules of prosody) to such a degree that it is often required between words in the closest regimen; as between the verb and its subject and object, the noun and its adjective, the adverb and that which it qualifies. In the following examples, the emphatic pause is marked with a dash.

>Ye know too well
>The story of our thraldom; we are—*slaves*.
>The bright sun rises to his course, and lights—
>A *race* of *slaves*; he sets, and his last beam
>Falls—on a *slave*.

>He said, then full before their sight
>Produced the beast, and lo !—— twas *white*.

Henceforth I call you not servants, for the servant knoweth not what his lord doeth; but I have called you——*friends;* for all things that I have heard of my father, I have made known unto you.

>"*Traitor!*" —I go—but I *return.* *This trial*—
>Here I *devote*—your senate....

>Look to your hearths, my lords;
>For there henceforth shall sit, for household gods,
>*Shapes*—hot from Tartarus.

§ 238. The emphasis of pitch distinguishes the word or phrase either by a discrete or a concrete change of pitch.

Here again are two very different modes of emphasis, yet both depending upon changes of pitch. These are properly characterized by Prof. Day, according as the change of pitch is either a skip or a slide (§ 189), as discrete and concrete emphasis. In both, it is to be observed, only the greater changes can be made available for effective emphasis; and the strength of the emphasis varies as these changes are greater or less; that is, the fifth is stronger than the third, and the octave than the fifth.

1. *The discrete emphasis, according as the skip is upwards or downwards, is appropriate to the sentiments which require a high, or a low pitch.*

The emphasis of the upward skip is mostly appropriate to light, gay, ironical and scornful sentiments; also, to doubt, uncertainty, hesitation and surprise; and often it is expressive of violent passion, and intense anguish. That of the downward skip is more appropriate to grave, solemn and indignant sentiments; also, to fixedness of purpose, or settled determination; and sometimes to violent, but restrained passion. Both of these modes, however, not unfrequently occur in the same sentence, especially where one branch is opposed to, or contrasted with the other. In the following example, some of the upward skips are marked in italics, the downward, in small capitals; but their different degrees are not marked.

Brutus. If there be any in this assembly—any dear friend of Cesar's—to *him* I say, that Brutus' love to *Cesar* was no less than HIS. If then that friend demand, why Brutus rose *against Cesar*, THIS IS my answer: Not that I loved Cesar *less*, but that I loved Rome MORE. Had you rather Cesar were living, and die all *slaves;* or that Cesar were dead, and live all FREEMEN? As Cesar loved me, I weep for him; as he was *fortunate*, I rejoice at it; as he was valiant, I honor him; but as he was ambitious, I SLEW HIM. There is tears for his love, joy for his fortune, honor for his valor, and DEATH for his AMBITION. Who is here so base that would be a bondman? If *any*, SPEAK; for HIM have I OFFENDED. Who is here so rude that would not be a Roman? If *any*, SPEAK; for him have I offended. Who is here so vile that would not love his country? If *any*, SPEAK; for him have I offended. I pause for a reply. . . .

Citizen. None, Brutus, none.

Brutus. Then NONE have I offended. I have done no more to Cesar than you shall do to Brutus. . . . With this I depart; that as I slew my best lover for the good of Rome, I have the same dagger for myself, when it shall please my country to need my death.

2. *The concrete emphasis is expressive of various sentiments, as determined in §§ 201—211.*

The various powers of expression which belong to the upward and downward inflections, have been sufficiently explained in the sections referred to above; in which, we have seen also that the principal of these inflections always fall on the emphatic words. Here then a single example must suffice; as before, the upward slides being marked in italics, and the downward, in small capitals.

Brutus. Let me tell you, Cassius, you *yourself*
Are much condemned to have an ITCHING PALM,
To sell and mart your offices for GOLD
To undeservers.

Cassius.   *I* an itching palm?
You know that you are Brutus that speak this,
Or, by the GODS, this speech were else you LAST.

Brutus. The name of Cassius honors this corruption,
And chastisement doth therefore hide his head.

Cassius. Chastisement?

Brutus. Remember MARCH, the IDES of MARCH remember.
Did not great *Julius* bleed for justice sake?
What villain touched his body, that did stab,
And not for JUSTICE? *What!* shall one of *us*,
That struck the foremost man of all this world,
But for supporting robbers—shall *we now*
Contaminate our fingers with base *bribes*,
And sell the mighty space of our large honors
For so much trash as may be grasped *thus?*

>   I had rather be a DOG, and BAY THE MOON,
>   Than such a Roman. . . .
> *Cassius.* Urge me no more; I shall forget myself.
>   Have mind upon your health; tempt me no further.
> *Brutus.* AWAY! slight man!
> *Cassius.* Is't POSSIBLE?
> *Brutus.*   Hear me, for I WILL speak.
>   Must *I* give way and room to your rash *choler?*
>   Shall *I* be frightened when a madman *stares?*
> *Cassius.* O ye gods! ye gods! must I endure all this?
> *Brutus.* All *this?* Ay, MORE. Fret till your proud heart BREAK.
>   Go show your SLAVES how choleric you are,
>   And make your BONDMEN tremble. Must *I* budge?
>   Must *I* observe you? Must *I* stand and crouch
>   Under your testy humor? By the GODS,
>   You shall digest the venom of your spleen,
>   Though it do split you.

§ 239. The distribution of the emphasis is governed by the meaning to be expressed, whether emotion or thought.

The right distribution of the emphasis is essential, both to render the thought intelligible, and to express the emotion or passion which the thought is intended or adapted to excite. Emphasis, in fact, is a substantive element of language itself, since by varying it the meaning of any combination of words may be wholly changed; whilst a wrong emphasis, not only fails of expression, but also caricatures or travesties the sense. The following, with a strong emphasis on the word, him, is an example of such travesty.

> And he said to his sons, Saddle me the ass; so they saddled *him.*

Here the emphasis places the saddle upon the prophet, instead of upon the ass.

Again: let the following question be repeated often enough to place the emphasis on every word successively, and in each case, it expresses a different sense.

Do you ride to town to-day?
Do *you* ride to town to-day?
Do you *ride* to town to-day?
Do you ride *to town* to-day?
Do you ride to town *to-day?*

The regimen of the emphasis varies somewhat according as it is expressive of emotion, or of the relations of thought, but only the most general rules are available here; and these rules constantly affect and modify each other. The only way a speaker can be sure of his emphasis, is the perfect mastery of the thought in its grammatical and rhetorical relations, and by the feeling of the emotions to be expressed.

§ 240. **The emphasis of emotion falls on the word or phrase which is the most significant of emotion.**

Under this rule, interjections, exclamations, abrupt and excited interrogations, and the like, require the emphasis. But the rule implies, of course, a careful study of the words to determine which of them are the most significant of emotion or passion.

King Richard. Is thy name *Tyrrel?*
Tyrrel. James Tyrrel, and your most obedient subject.
K. R. Art thou *indeed?*
Tyr. *Prove* me, my gracious lord.
K. R. Dar'st thou resolve to *kill* a *friend* of mine?
Tyr. Please you, but I had rather kill *two enemies.*

K. R. Why, then, thou hast it—*two deep enemies;*
Foes to my *rest*, and my sweet sleep's *disturbers*,
Are they that I would have thee *deal upon.*

1. *The significant words are often a whole clause; but every word in such a clause is not commonly to be emphasized.*

Failure to observe this fact often occasions difficulty and mistakes in adjusting the emphasis. "Boswell tells us that Garrick and Johnson once disputed about the emphasis in the Ninth Commandment, Thou shalt not bear false witness against thy neighbor; the one maintaining that it should fall upon *shalt*, the other, upon *not*. Yet both of these great men were clearly wrong in this case; for the true emphasis is certainly upon the whole clause, *bear false witness against thy neighbor.*"

Through the *whole line* of their march, they did not see *one man*, not *one woman*, not *one child*, not *one four-footed beast*, of any description whatever.

2. *When an emphatic word or phrase is repeated for the purpose of giving it increased significance, it takes a repeated emphasis; otherwise, not.*

This is an important rule, often violated with damaging effect. The following is an example of the former case.

O Jerusalem, Jerusalem, thou that killest the prophets, and stonest them that are sent unto thee, how often would I have gathered thy children together, as a hen doth gather her brood under her wings, and ye would not!

Again :
Leaves have their time to fall,
And *flowers*, to *wither* at the north wind's breath,

> And *stars*, to *set;* but *all*—
> Thou hast *all seasons* for thine own, *O death.*

The following is an example of the latter case.

> Jesus therefore.... said unto them, *Whom seek ye?* They answered him, *Jesus of Nazareth*.... Then asked he them again, Whom seek ye? And they said, Jesus of Nazareth.

3. *Great care is required to guard against too frequent emphasis.*

When there are many words in a passage strongly significant of emotion or passion, a temptation arises to load the delivery with emphasis. In such cases, it must be borne in mind that too frequent emphasis destroys its whole effect, because emphasis consists essentially in distinguishing the most significant words and phrases from the others with which they stand immediately connected. This temptation is sure to be felt in such passionate words as the following.

> *No, by* the *holy rood,* thou know'st it well:
> Thou cams't on earth to make my earth *a hell.*
> A *grievous burden* was thy *birth* to me;
> Techy and wayward was thy infancy;
> Thy school days, *frightful,* desperate, wild and *furious;*
> Thy prime of manhood, daring, bold and venturous;
> Thy age, confirmed proud, subtle, sly and *bloody,*
> More mild, but yet more *harmful,* kind in *hatred.*

§ 241. **The emphasis of thought falls on the words and phrases that are most significant, either in themselves, or from some peculiar relation.**

The significance of words and phrases depends on an almost infinite number and variety of circumstances; so that those which are most significant, in any particular case, can be determined only by careful study of the passage. The following general principles, however, are to be observed.

1. *Words are to be emphasized which suggest more than they express.*

This rule includes the principal words in passages of irony; as in Elijah's mockery of the prophets of Baal, already referred to.

<blockquote>
And it came to pass at noon, that Elijah mocked them, and said, *Cry aloud,* for he *is* a god: either he is *talking,* or he is *pursuing,* or he is *in a journey,* or, peradventure, he *sleepeth,* and must be *awaked.*
</blockquote>

An admirable example of words that suggest more than they express, and thereby become emphatic, is found in the word, committed, which is so often repeated in Othello's charges against Desdemona, in § 236—1. The following is another.

<blockquote>
Casca. Indeed, they say, the senators to-morrow
Mean to establish Cesar as a king;
And he shall wear his crown by sea and land,
In every place, save here in Italy.
Cassius. *I* know where I will wear this *dagger* then;
Cassius from bondage will deliver Cassius.
</blockquote>

2. *Words in contrast or antithesis require to be emphasized.*

These cases are very numerous and complicated, requiring close attention to determine them.

<blockquote>
Man never *is,* but always *to be* blest.

He raised a *mortal* to the skies;
She drew an *angel* down.
</blockquote>

The *young* are slaves to *novelty;* the *old,* to *custom;* the *middle-aged,* to *both;* the *dead* only, to *neither.* The *pleasures* of the im-

agination are not so *gross* as *those* of *sense*, nor so *refined* as *those* of the *understanding*.

3. *Words in close grammatical regimen, with important clauses intervening, require to be emphasized.*

This rule is one of considerable importance, in order to bring out, or make evident the true sense, or grammatical structure of sentences.

> *Go, preach* to the *coward*, thou death-telling seer;
> *Or*, if gory Culloden so dreadful appear,
> *Draw*, dotard, around thy old wavering sight,
> *This mantle*, to cover the phantoms of fright.

4. *Articles, connecting particles, auxiliaries, and the like, take the emphasis only when they have some special significance.*

He made not only *a* speech, but *the* speech of the occasion.
I did not say man *or* woman, but man *and* woman.
Not *this* man, but *that* man.
He was going not *to*, but *from* his home.

CHAPTER XII.

GESTURE.

§ 242. Gesture includes all significant motions and actions of the human body.

UNDER this comprehensive definition, we have all significant motions and actions of the trunk itself, and of all its members—the head and countenance, the hands and arms, and the feet. Motions which have no relation to significance, are not properly gestures; but there are very few if any motions, which a speaker can make, which are not significant of something, or which do not aid or hinder him in the expression of his sentiments. In fact, it would be difficult to overestimate the expressive power of which gesture is capable; and, consequently, the folly of those who despise or neglect this final and crowning element of power in delivery, cannot be too strongly condemned.

§ 243. The language of symbols is more expressive than that of words.

The following considerations may serve to illustrate and confirm this statement.

1. *The expressiveness of figurative language depends upon its symbolical character.*

Just in the degree in which articulate language is enabled to draw upon the expressive power of symbols, that is, in the degree in which it becomes figurative or symbolical, does it become picturesque, vivid and expressive. This is a well-known principle of style. Hence the wonderful power of our Lord's parables, of the imagery employed by the Hebrew prophets, and of all appropriate figurative representations. This power is due to the fact that articulate language is thus capable of laying hold upon, and of appropriating to itself, some small portion of the expressive power of the language of symbols.

2. *Religious ideas express themselves in symbols.*

All the great historical religions of mankind—that of the ancient Egyptians, Brachmanism, Buddhism, fire-worship, the paganism of the Greeks and Romans, Druidism, the worship of Odin and Thor, Judaism, Mohammedism and Christianity, all alike, have striven to set forth the profoundest mysteries of their faith and life, by means of symbolical representations. None of them have ever been satisfied with mere words. The only rational account which can be given of this remarkable fact, is that the language of words is universally felt to be inadequate to the expression of those vast and profound ideas, and of those impassioned sentiments, which belong to the religious life of man.

3. *All profound ideas, and all impassioned sentiments, require symbolical expression.*

This is the fundamental principle from which originate all the symbols of art, which embody the ideas and sentiments of the beautiful in the minds of their authors, and of the people among whom they are produced. But this principle is not limited to religion and art. All profound ideas, and all impassioned sentiments, but most of all, those which prevail extensively, and generally affect whole communities, can never rest satisfied until they find expression in symbolical representation. This might be shown by innumerable examples, such as the following.

(1.) The life and spirit of the ancient Romans was their unrivalled genius for war and conquest. The ideas which universally prevailed among these iron republicans, were that Rome was invincible; that but one result was ever to be anticipated in all wars in which she might become involved; that in these conflicts, other nations must expect to be conquered. In order to express these ideas in the most striking and vivid manner possible, it was their custom to give audience to foreign ambassadors in the temple of Victory.

(2.) Again: in order to express these same ideas, in the still stronger form, that other nations were to the Romans as brute beasts, made to be subjugated, they sometimes erected upon the field of victory an immense wooden frame, in the form of a yoke for beasts of burden, under which they marched the remains of the conquered army, and then dismissed them to their homes. This was called passing under the yoke. What words, what bulletins of exultation, could have expressed these ideas with the life and power of this tremendous symbol.

§ 244. Gesture is a principal element of the symbolical language of nature, and of the passions, which is universally understood.

1. *This language is wonderfully copious and significant.*

The immense copiousness and wonderful significance of this language of nature and of the passions, has been already alluded to in the treatment of feeling as one of the sources of power in delivery; and this must have become still more evident from the preceding discussion of the several elements of this language, consisting of all the variations of quality and stress of voice, articulation, pitch, inflection, time, pause and emphasis.

2. *Gesture is a principal element of this symbolical language, and more expressive than words.*

Strong passion, or profound emotion, is never satisfied with any expression of itself that is possible in mere words; it feels itself to be still pent up, until it finds an outlet by embodying itself in some appropriate act or motion of the body. Nay, even slight and transient feelings require action, in order to their full and adequate expression. Not only does the tempest raise up the great ocean waves; the zephyr also ripples the smooth surface of the mountain lake. Hence nature has provided that certain actions or motions shall correspond to certain feelings; and that these feelings shall instinctively prompt to those actions. Such actions or motions are, in a peculiar sense, the language of nature for the expression of such feelings. Here we have the whole theory of gesture, and the explanation of its wonderful power of expression. Hence it is that anger frowns, fear turns pale, shame blushes, pleasure smiles, love sparkles in the eyes, humility bows the head, and despair grins, gnashes the teeth, and tears the hair. No words can equal the expressive power of such symbolical acts—actions, here as everywhere, speak louder than words. To the same effect, Quintilian teaches us that "gesture is commonly more expressive than the voice. For not only the hand, but even a nod is expressive of our sentiments. A common salute, before the person speaks a single word, gives us an intimation of his disposition; and we discern by the face and the walk the workings of the mind. Nay, even the brutes, devoid of speech, express anger, pleasure and love, in their eyes, and by certain movements of their bodies. .... Painting itself, though motionless as well as silent, sometimes affects us more powerfully than words."

3. *This language is universally understood.*

Articulate speech has very much in it that is purely conventional. Some would even persuade us that it is wholly such; but this surely cannot be admitted. Yet speech requires to be learned before it can be understood; and our knowledge of the sense in which others use the words we hear, is never perfect. It is even maintained, and not with mere show of argument, that we never understand one another precisely in the sense in which we speak.

But in this language of nature, as we have seen (§ 31), especially in this element of it which consists of gestures, there is something which no art can, or ought ever to undertake to teach, apart from the feelings by which it is prompted and inspired; and all that art can do is to aid nature, when these feelings are in full activity, to express them with greater simplicity, fullness, freedom and power, than were otherwise possible. Here therefore nothing requires to be learned before it can be understood. Every symbol has its own natural significance, which all understand instinctively at the same moment. Not a single person in the largest audience, ever fails to understand the natural significance, or to feel the force of appropriate gesture. Who ever misunderstood a blush, or a frown, or the clenched fist, or the eyes and hands raised towards heaven? And when a whole audience is thus affected in the same way, at one and the same moment, the effect is wonderfully intensified by all the mysterious workings of their sympathy with the speaker, and with each other (§§ 55—58).

§ 245. By gesture the orator is enabled to express his sentiments to the eye, at the same time that by his words he expresses them to the ear.

The eye and the ear, beyond comparison, are the noblest of all the senses; upon which, therefore, all the arts of expression depend. No attempt has ever been made to found such an art upon any of the senses of feeling, taste, or smell. But all these arts, except that of oratory, address themselves exclusively to one, or the other, of these two art-senses; poetry and music, exclusively to the ear; painting, sculpture, architecture, landscape gardening, dancing, and the art of ornamentation, to the eye alone. Hence all the effects which any of these arts can produce, must be wrought through a single sense. But oratory—with which the dramatic, or more properly the histrionic art is so closely identified, that for elocutionary purposes they can hardly be distinguished from each other—oratory alone addresses itself equally, and at the same moment, both to the ear and the eye. Consequently its power of expression is incomparably greater than that of any other art. Hence in the words of an able, but anonymous author, "there is no earthly object capable of making such various, and such forcible impressions upon the human mind, as a consummate speaker." For as the concurrent testimony of two witnesses has not merely double, but many times greater force than that of one, so when a sentiment is addressed to both of these senses at the same time, it produces immeasurably greater effects upon the soul, than when it depends upon either of them alone.

§ 246. **The great significance of gesture is exemplified in the art of pantomime, and in the language of deaf mutes.**

We see from the preceding discussion, not only how much gesture aids in the expression of sentiment, but also that it has a significance of its own, which is entirely independent of words. So great is its power of expression that it can be made to stand in the place, and perform the functions of articulate speech. The following are examples of this.

1. *The art of pantomime is capable of exciting a powerful interest.*

In this species of dramatic entertainment, the whole story and action of the drama is represented in dumb show, that is, by gesture alone. These representations excited among the ancient Romans a deep and passionate interest; such, indeed, that they have carefully handed down to us the names of their most accomplished and celebrated performers; and such that serious riots sometimes occurred among the people, from the violence of their partisanship of rival actors. Now the bare fact that the spectators could be kept together for hours at a time, whilst not a word was spoken—much more, that these exhibitions were so popular, and excited such a deep interest, is abundant evidence that the art of expressing thought and sentiment by gesture alone, had been carried to a very high degree of perfection; and that the performers were able, in this way, to tell the whole story, and to represent the whole action of their dramas, in a perfectly intelligible and very affecting manner.

2. *Deaf mutes are able to communicate by signs alone.*

The great significance and power of expression of which gesture is capable, cannot perhaps be better illustrated than by the amazing facility and freedom with which the deaf and dumb communicate their ideas and sentiments. A very little familiarity with their signs, will enable any one to understand and to converse with them, on all ordinary topics and occasions. One of the most entertaining and instructive companions the author ever had, was a deaf and dumb youth, of high literary culture, and the author of an original work on Greek and Roman mythology,* with whom he was formerly accustomed to ramble, for many hours at a time, through the woods, and over the hills of the Schuylkill. The principal means of communication on these occasions, was this natural language of dumb signs. He well remembers also to have heard, or rather seen, the whole story of the monkey that snatched an infant from the arms of its mother, and ran with it up to the mast-head of a ship, together with the anguish of the mother, and the stratagem by which she regained possession of her child unhurt, told by a mute little girl twelve or thirteen years old, not only in a perfectly intelligible, but even in an extremely affecting manner. In fact, a better school of gesture for public speakers, could not possibly be found, than an asylum for deaf mutes, and familiar intercourse with its inmates.

§ 247. Gesture is expressive of passion and emotion rather than of thought.

This is a general principle, and one of great importance in determining the character, place and frequency of the gestures which are required in public speaking. It teaches us to distinguish between the

---

* A Catechism of Mythology. By Wm. Darlington.

orator, and the mimic or pantomime actor. For in oratory, we ought not to gesticulate as if we were limited to dumb signs; we must remember that we have also words to express our thoughts; and, thereby, guard ourselves against the temptation to redundant and inappropriate gesture. The orator should endeavor to express by his gestures his emotions rather than his thoughts or intellectual states. With due discretion, indeed, he may employ gesture for imitative purposes, and for the expression of his thoughts. He may point to the sun, or to a mountain, or river, when speaking of any of these objects, or he may touch his own forehead, or lay his finger on his lips, to express meditation or silence; but he should avoid the frequent use of such imitative gestures, and too great particularity in them; otherwise he will assuredly enfeeble his delivery.

This principle, with the above, and still other practical consequences, rests upon the following reasons.

1. *Emotion rather than thought is the immediate cause of gesture.*

Mere thought is naturally quiet and undemonstrative; it does not of itself prompt to action of any kind; and the more profound the thought, that is, the more a man becomes absorbed in purely intellectual operations, the more still and motionless does the body become. The incongruity of delivering a demonstration in Euclid with abundant or violent gesture, would be apparent to every one. On the other hand, passion, or emotion, is essentially active and demonstrative; it always prompts to action; and the stronger it is, the more abundant and striking does the gesture become. It is not the mere thought or conception of a shameful, or of a sorrowful object, but it is the feeling of shame, or of sorrow, which causes the cheeks to blush, or the eyes to overflow with tears. Hence, also, the equal incongruity of the delivery of impassioned sentiments with little or no corresponding gesture.

2. *Gesture corresponds to the nature of emotion, rather than to that of thought.*

There is ever a likeness to the cause in its effects; hence there is a resemblance or correspondence between gesture, and the emotion from which it springs. Such resemblance might be pointed out in many particulars; but that one to which it seems most necessary to direct attention here, is the indefiniteness of both gesture and emotion. For there is a definiteness or precision in the meaning of words, in which they correspond to the precision of thought, and of which gesture is altogether incapable. The dictionary will give us the definition of a word; but it cannot give us the emotion which corresponds to it, and which it is intended to express, in any particular connection. The emotions, especially in their ever-varying degrees of strength, are essentially incapable of such definition. They do not reflect themselves in distinct outlines upon the intellect, they are the acts of the sensibilities of the soul. They also overlap, involve, or imply each other, in a very different manner from the intellectual operations of the mind. The attempt to define precisely, in character or degree, any particular emotion, whilst we are under its influence, would paralyze it. There is obviously a corresponding indefiniteness in gesture, which renders it better adapted to the expression of emotion and passion, than it is to the expression of thought. Thus tears commonly express sorrow, but they do not tell us, as words would do, whether that sorrow be for the death of a friend, or for the commission of a sin; and the hand raised to heaven expresses recognition of the being and providence of God, but it does not tell us, whether in reverence and submission, or in distrust and fear.

§ 218. **Too much gesture, though significant and appropriate, enfeebles its power of expression; otherwise, too much is better than too little.**

1. *The speaker should be continent of significant gesture.*

When the gesture is highly significant and expressive, a very little of it will go a great way; and too much of it enfeebles its expressive power, and is to be carefully avoided. It has an effect similar to that of too much emphasis (§§ 240—3). It comes so frequently that it does not allow time sufficient for the audience to feel its force. From its redundancy, it ceases to attract attention. A single gesture in a paragraph, provided it be one of striking significance, will often produce a far greater effect than a dozen, in themselves equally expressive. Continence of significant gesture, like continence of words, and of emphasis, is a great element of power in delivery.

2. *Too much of gesture, not specially significant, is better than too little.*

On the other hand, a speaker with little or no skill in the adaptation of gesture to the expression of particular emotions, need not be afraid of too much action. In young speakers, especially during the training period, it ought to be rather redundant than deficient; for it is much easier to prune it down than it is to call it forth, after the habit of speaking with too little has been formed. And, besides, motion as such, even when it has no particular significance, is expressive; for it shows that the speaker is not without feeling of some sort. The want of it makes the impression that he is impassive and unmoved; it is necessarily the want of animation or vivacity (§§ 82—3). He may do something, it is true, to neutralize this impression by means of the vocal elements of the language of feeling; but it is impossible to compensate by these for the want of gesture; and all the elements of this language are so vitally connected with each other that they are well-nigh inseparable. Hence it is nearly impossible to speak with animation, whilst every part of the body is motionless except the vocal organs; and nothing can be more incongruous than a motionless delivery of impassioned sentiments.

§ 249. **The normal position of the body in speaking should be erect, facing the audience, the chest expanded, the head evenly balanced, the arms and hands hanging naturally at the sides, and the feet near together.**

This is the normal position of the body which is best for speaking, and to which it should naturally return after whatever deviations from it the gesture may require. The erect position is necessary to the full expansion of the chest; and this, to the free play and full force and control of the diaphragm, breathing muscles, lungs and voice. The body should not lean back, which seems to say to the audience, I don't much care for you; its weight should rest rather upon the front part of the feet than upon the heels, just a little, perhaps, inclined forwards; which expresses desire to gain the favorable attention of the audience. There should be no leaning or lolling down upon anything for support, as if the speaker were too feeble, or too lazy, to support himself; which also expresses disrespect for the audience. The front of the body should not be turned aside or averted from the audience, otherwise than temporarily, in some gesture which may require such a movement. The head should not be thrown back, which expresses pride or contempt; neither should it be held on one side or the other, which expresses conceited knowingness, or waggishness; nor yet should it be allowed to hang down on the breast, which expresses sorrow, or distress, or shame;—but it should stand evenly balanced upon the shoulders, ready to be moved in any way according to the varying sentiments. The hands should not be thrust into the pockets, nor under the coat-tails, nor clasped behind the back, nor held in front, with the fingers joined together at the extremities, nor with the fists doubled; but they should hang open, though not expanded, at the sides, and not in front of the body. The feet should be kept near, but not too near together, so as to avoid everything like straddling. In this position, which, however, may be varied from time to time, the whole body, and all its members, will be found ready and apt for whatever gestures or movements the expression of the sentiments may require.

§ 250. The countenance has the greatest power of expression; it should correspond to the sentiments embodied in the words.

1. *The countenance speaks.*

The expressive power of the human countenance renders it capable of becoming one of the most important elements of power in delivery. It is such, in fact, that we can say, a speaking countenance, almost as properly as, a speaking tongue. In the words of Quintilian, "this is the dominant power in expression. With this we supplicate; with this we threaten; with this we soothe; with this we mourn; with this we rejoice; with this we triumph; with this we make our submissions: upon this the audience hang; upon this they keep their eyes fixed; this they examine and study, even before a word is spoken; this it is which excites in them favorable or unfavorable emotions; from this they understand almost everything; often it becomes more significant than any words."

2. *It should correspond to the sentiments expressed by the words.*

This general and obvious rule is better than any attempts to describe the particular expressions, or conformations of the features, which are appropriate to all the passions and emotions, in all their different degrees, and innumerable modifications. This, indeed, would not only be an endless task, but also it would leave nothing to the teaching of nature, in this department of her own language. The attempt to govern the expression of the countenance by special and minute rules, telling us where to blush, where to grow pale, where to frown, where to smile, and where to weep—there can be no greater absurdity than this. The feelings themselves, nothing else, can enable us to express them in the countenance; and these, whenever they are in full and free activity at the moment, will express themselves.

This general rule, however, may serve to remind the student, that the countenance ought to correspond to the sentiments of the words, as they are spoken. For by these two modes of expression, brought to bear upon the audience at the same moment, the power of the delivery is greatly increased. It should put him on his guard against indiscriminate smiling and frowning. For not unfrequently the strenuous effort of speaking, is allowed to contract the features in a permanent frown; and some speakers, even in their most pathetic passages, continue to smile, showing their teeth on all occasions, which is extremely unpleasant. The rule also should call the attention to the incongruity of delivering grave, solemn, sublime, sorrowful, or compassionate sentiments, with a scornful, smiling, or indifferent countenance; and to that of delivering playful, witty, joyful, or animated passages, with a sober, sad, or mournful countenance. The rule, however, requires to be qualified in the expression of what is called, dry humor, or grotesque sentiments; in which, the utmost soberness of face will often, by its very incongruity, greatly intensify the effect.

§ 251. The eye is the most expressive of all the features; it should be directed to the faces of the audience.

1. *The eye governs the expression of the other features.*

The expressive power of the human eye is so great that it determines, in a manner, the expression of the whole countenance. It is almost impossible to disguise it. It is said that gamblers rely more upon the study of the eye, to discover the state of their opponents' game, than upon any other means. Even animals are susceptible of its power. The dog watches the eyes of his master, and discovers from them, before a word is spoken, whether he is to expect a caress, or apprehend chastisement. It is said that the lion cannot attack a man, so long as the man looks him steadily in the eyes. Joy and grief, anger, pride, scorn, hatred, love, jealousy, pity—in a word, all the passions and emotions of the human heart, in all their degrees and interworkings with each other, express themselves, with the utmost fullness and power, in the eyes. Through them the soul makes its most clear and vivid manifestations of itself.

2. *It should be kept upon the faces of the audience.*

In order that the speaker may avail himself of this great and mysterious power of expression, he must not allow his eyes to become fixed upon his manuscript; nor to assume a vacant expression, under the influence of the intellectual operations of invention, or remembering; nor to wander around the walls of the audience room, or up to the ceiling, nor to follow the motions of the hands, as if the speaker were looking at them. He must look at the audience, and scan their faces individually, in order to open a personal communication between himself and every one of them, so far as this is possible. He should not allow his eye to wander from the audience, except when this is required by some gesture. Thus he will be enabled to command their attention, and awaken their sympathy; and his eye will naturally express and convey to them all the passions and emotions of his own heart (§§ 51—2; 52—2).

§ 252. **The gestures of the hands are capable of great expression; they are almost infinite in number and variety, and should be adapted to the words.**

1. *The expression of the hands is inferior only to that of the countenance.*

Quintilian seems to regard the hands as nearly equal in power of expression to the countenance itself. "Without the hands," he says, "delivery would be maimed and feeble; for in copiousness of expression, they almost equal words. Other parts of the body aid the speaker; but, if I may so express myself, the hands themselves speak. For with them do we not ask, promise, call, dismiss, threaten, supplicate, detest, fear, interrogate, deny? With them do we not express joy, sorrow, doubt, confession, penitence, moderation, abundance, number, time? Do they not excite, beseech, forbid, prove, admire, and express shame? In pointing out places and persons, do they not perform the functions of adverbs and pronouns? And amidst the so great diversity of tongues, in all races and nations, is not this language common to all men?"

2. *The number and variety of manual gestures is almost infinite; they should accompany and increase the significance of the words.*

"Suit the action to the word, and word to the action." This is the direction of our great master, which covers the ground of all gesture. But to do this—*hic labor, hoc opus*. Here again almost everything must be left to nature, for the reasons given in § 31. "Let your discretion be your tutor." Yet there are certain points upon which more special directions may be of service.

(1.) The hand should express variety or animation. For this purpose its normal position in gesturing should be open, the fingers slightly curved, and touching each other, the thumb somewhat raised in front of the fingers, pointing in the same direction with them. When the thumb is too much raised, so as to point backwards in a different direction, or stands at right angles to the fingers, it wants ease and grace ; and when it is expanded in the same plane with the fingers, the hand seems to be dead, or without expression. In gesture, the fingers should move at their joints, so as to partake of the motion of the arm. When the gesture is made with the arm, whilst the hand and fingers remain motionless, it is necessarily without expression. The hand must show that the speaker is all alive, even to his finger nails.

(2.) The whole arm should move with the hand. The gesture should not be made from the shoulder, nor from the elbow, alone ; but the wrist joint and the fingers should partake of the motion.

(3.) The right hand should be most used. Gestures with the left hand alone, should be much less frequent than with the right. When too frequent, they seem to indicate that the speaker is left-handed. They are useful, however, to aid in giving variety of motion, and to relieve the right hand, that its motions may not be too frequently repeated.

(4.) The double gesture should not be too frequent. The raising of both hands, with the arms expanded or curved, so as to correspond with each other; should seldom be employed, except when largeness, wholeness, or universality, is to be expressed. This gesture, when too frequent, or without special significance, expresses dullness or stupidity. Whenever it is introduced, both hands should be raised and lowered at the same moment ; one should never be brought up to the other, nor let fall while the other is held up.

(5.) The index finger demonstrates. This gesture is very effective when some person or thing is to be pointed out, in sharp distinction from everything else; also, in exhibiting some precise point in argument. Otherwise it should be seldom used. When too frequent, it becomes extremely insignificant and pointless.

(6.) The clenched fist expresses the violent irascible passions. The hand should never be allowed to take this position, without special significance of the passions to which it is appropriate.

(7.) Gesture should begin and end with the words. The sentiment in the words should so prompt the gesture that it shall begin and end with them. When it precedes the words, or continues after they are finished, the effect is incongruous, and very displeasing.

(8.) Gesture should be more or less frequent and rapid according to the sentiment. In general, a due medium is to be observed between too great rapidity and frequency of gesture, and too little.

(9.) After every gesture, the arm and hand should return to their normal position. Having made a gesture, the speaker should be satisfied with it, and end it. The hand should not keep repeating the same motion again and again, as if conscious of its feebleness, and impotently striving to give it some sort of expression.

(10.) Errors in gesture, from Quintilian. "Some speakers raise the hand so high as to expose the whole side; others seem to want the power to draw it out of the bosom; another thrusts it out to its full length; another stretches it above his head; another lays about him, so that it is unsafe to stand within his reach; another describes a large sweep with his left hand. Some manage the hands with indolence or tremor; others seem to saw the air; others use their hands as if they had claws, pawing with them; others thrust out the arm almost on a line with the ear, expanding the hand, and inverting the thumb; and this they call, speaking in a commanding posture. Others again twirl their fingers whenever they think they have said something smart; another hems and coughs, as if something stuck in his throat; another blows and wipes his nose without necessity."

§ 253. Gestures with the feet should be seldom used.

It is lawful sometimes to emphasize a sentiment by stamping with the foot; but such gestures must not be frequently repeated. Some speakers keep up a regular stroke of the foot upon the floor, every minute or two; but this is a mere mannerism, which means nothing, and is offensive to good taste. It is lawful also to change the position on the feet while speaking, and even to walk backwards and forwards, in front of the audience; but the speaker should not keep doing this all the time; otherwise he may remind them of a wild beast in a cage. Occasionally he may rise on tiptoe, and lean forwards; but this must not be done regularly or frequently. In general, all gestures which are made with, or which depend upon the feet, should be few and far between, for the feet are the least honorable, and least expressive, of all the members of the body.

§254. **All mannerisms are to be carefully avoided.**

A mannerism in gesture is a motion which is either without significance, or which is frequently repeated without reference to its significance. Such mannerisms are the frequent stamping of the foot, running the fingers through the hair, adjusting the clothes, using the handkerchief without absolute necessity, hemming, coughing, spitting, placing the thumbs in the armholes of the vest, shrugging the shoulders, and the like. These, and all similar mannerisms, whether of voice or gesture, can never fai to mar and enfeeble the delivery.

THE END.

Printed in the United Kingdom
Lightning Source UK Ltd.
3UK00001B/42/A